Girl Electric

Twin Falls

A Science Thriller

By Bernard Wozny

The scientist asked: "What is life?"

The entertainer replied: "A Masquerade"

The masses cried: "Life is a Cabaret"

First published in the USA 2022.

Printed in the United States by IngramSpark

You may contact the author through

www.bernardwozny.com

ISBN: 979-8-9855517-0-9

Library of Congress Control Number: 2022900430

For Iwona

She knows why

Acknowledgments

I used to tell myself I would not include acknowledgments when I write a book, because it is 'me' who writes the book. I have since learned that 'me' could not have written any book without the expert assistance of many people.

Critiques: Catherine McGreevy, the historical romantic. Jerry Matlan, the invisible man. Michael Brandt, the mountain traveler. Along with many others.

Editing: Janey Ranlett, I'm always amazed how she could simplify my tangled verbiage.

Cover art: Estefano Burmistro

Special thanks to:

Jeannie Turner, she also knows why.

I Street Press, Central Library, Sacramento California. Gerry taught me how to print.

My therapist, who told me, "I think it's time you started calling yourself a writer."

Prolog

Adara signaled her so-called 'last wave' when she caught her foot in some rocks. The riverbank was temptingly close and Adara decided to make for it. She started with a crawl stroke but when some rocks banged her shin, she used those to kick off. This was her mistake. She should have drifted down through the rapids and made no attempt to reach the bank at this point.

As Adara kicked off from the rock, her foot slid into a narrow crevasse. Guided by the force of the current, her foot became fixed between the rocks. What made things worse, her toe was pointing upstream while her ankle became wedged tightly between two rocks. Adara flipped backward flailing her arms in a hello wave which Kathy saw.

Adara was in trouble. She was being pulled over backward by the current, which lodged her ankle even deeper into the wedge of rock. If only she could move her body forward, she could ease her weight off her ankle and free her foot. But the force of water held her body back. She used her arms to paddle forward against the current so that she could keep her face above water. Despite her efforts, she lacked the strength to relieve the pressure on her ankle and free her trapped leg.

The current kept pushing her body back keeping her ankle firmly lodged. If she didn't swim forward, the current would sweep her body back and hold her face underwater. Even the PFD wasn't enough to hold her head above water. She tried different swim strokes to pull her body forward. The overarm crawl was most effective but also the most tiring. The breaststroke was less tiring but less effective. Icy waves crashed over her head at unpredictable intervals, filling her nose with water and making each desperate breath a struggle.

Held fast by the current with her ankle stuck in a rock, Adara was rapidly exhausting herself. If her strength failed, she would be forced backward under the water.

Chapter 1

Time to go home, Anita Gonzales thought. From her seat at NeuroComm's reception desk, she twirled a strand of wavy brown hair between her fingers while gazing at the clock. Her day at the high-tech startup was finished, the weekend was about to begin.

NeuroComm sat secluded on the Idaho National Laboratory campus within view of the Snake River, receiving few visitors. Since starting a few months ago, Anita rarely acted as an attractive receptionist. Instead, she handled office administration, handling deliveries, maintaining office supplies, and effectively being the personal assistant for the two founders of NeuroComm, Professor Hayden Wolf and Doctor John Coney.

As Anita gathered her items and closed her computer, NeuroComm's fourth employee, Bill Mandelson, walked through the reception area as he continued his security rounds. *Oh, here comes Captain America*, she thought.

Bill approached with that measured stride of his, every crease in his security uniform sharp enough to cut glass.

Anita couldn't help noticing the Superman curl of hair on Bill's forehead. *I could toy with that lock of hair all night!* However, she always resisted his advances, aware of his reputation as a mindless womanizer. *I wonder if his poor wife Larisa knows about his indiscretions.* Anita knew he was hiding secrets during his long travels away, what those secrets were she did not want Larisa or Bill's children to know about.

"Ah, Bill, I have something for you," Anita said with a smile, reaching into her desk once more.

"Oh, Anita," Bill said feigning a swoon, "I love it when pretty ladies have something for me." Moving closer to her desk. "What could it be?"

"Professor Wolf ordered a new phone for you. It's all set up, and the sticker on the back has the number."

Bill stared at the phone, his brow furrowed. "But I already have a phone. Why another one?"

"Yes, I know. I manage all the phones here, but the Professor wants you to have this as a sort of hotline between you both."

"Ah, I get it, he wants a secure channel."

Anita rolled her eyes at Bill's phony military-style comment. "No, I think he installed some apps which he only wants to use on that phone."

At that moment, the office intercom announced, "Bill Mandelson, come to my office."

"There, you hear that?" Anita asked with a smirk. "He's probably watching you."

Bill took the phone and gazed at the ceiling. "Well, I guess I'm about to find out what this phone is about." he said, "By the way, I'm off on leave for a week or two. Will you miss me when I'm gone?"

"Never mind what I'll miss. You'd better go home to your pretty wife, Larisa, be thankful you have her and your boys. Your gallivanting and long trips away will get you into trouble."

Bill feigned innocence as he turned away. "I don't know what you're talking about." With that, he headed towards the Professor's office.

Anita watched him stride toward the Professor's office. His shoulders had gone rigid, and she could see the tension in his jaw. *I think that hit a nerve*, she thought. She always noticed the pattern in his absences, the way he always had convenient excuses for his extended trips.

As Bill walked away, his thoughts darkened. *Jeezus, she is such a busy body, prying into everyone's business. What does she know about my trips? How does she even know about my trips?*

Bill shook his head. *This is the third time the Professor has called me to his office today. It seems that every time I try to take some time off, he always thinks of one extra job to do. If I didn't think this gig would make me rich, I wouldn't stay here. I hate being told what to do. As soon as my shares make a million, I'm out of here*!

Professor Hayden Wolf hunched over his laptop, fingers flying across the keys. His balding head swayed like a metronome while he typed, the office door standing wide open behind him.

Bill tapped gently, waiting for the professor to acknowledge him. "Sir, the door was open, but you look busy. I don't want to disturb you."

"Ah, Bill," Professor Wolf said. "Take a seat, there are no secrets here." The professor winked, "Close the door behind you."

Bill smiled at the comment, closing the door before sinking into the chair in front of the professor's desk.

Professor Wolf continued to type, keeping both elbows on the desk. His two index fingers thumped the keyboard like little pistons.

"I asked for some time off," Bill said.

"Yes, I know," Professor Wolf eventually said, continuing to type. "But something needs to be done before you go on leave."

"What is it?" Bill asked.

Professor Wolf finished typing and closed his laptop with a snap. "Oh, this is an easy bank job, but it needs to be completed tomorrow." He pulled a large envelope out of his desk, handing it to Bill. "Here's all the paperwork you need."

"But I wanted to go away tomorrow!" Bill exclaimed. "Can't it wait until I get back?"

"Not this job, it's important. Your departure will have to wait one more day. You do know what these bank jobs mean to us?" The professor gave Bill an expectant look.

"Yes, sir, I know," Bill answered sheepishly.

"After tomorrow, you can go on leave." The professor smiled. "But after that, I may need to call you back at a moment's notice."

"What do you mean? A moment's notice?" Bill asked. "Is that what this new phone is for?"

"Oh, yes, I'll explain the phone in a moment, but first let's discuss General Buckner."

Bill sat upright in his chair at the mention of the general's name. *This is the man funding the company*, he thought.

"The general wants the human experiment completed. We have to provide a full report sooner than I anticipated."

"Oh, you mean Beatty?"

The professor leaned forward. "Beta-One, is his laboratory designation, or Beatty, as you like to call him. He is our first human experiment. Don't forget this is top secret, not even Dr. Coney knows about Beta-One. This must remain between me, you, and the general only."

"I won't forget, you keep reminding me daily."

"You know the power of what we have?"

"Sure I do," Bill answered. "We have nanobots that can be injected into animals. The artificial intelligence that they carry is programmed to control their bodies. Yeah, I know the rap."

"Yes!" The professor said, "The general is impressed with our experiments on animals. We have proved how birds can jam radar. Our dogs can be programmed to infiltrate enemy bases before turning vicious."

"What more does the general want?"

"He wants the human experiment to move to the next phase."

"But I thought Beatty, I mean Beta-One, completed all the tests." Bill looked surprised. "So what is this next phase all about?"

"We need to complete hunter-killer tests, and you need to escort him."

"Hunt and kill what?" Bill asked, somewhat worried, "Are we going to kill people?"

"Don't worry, we only need to hunt wildlife. We're not the Mafia," the professor said.

"Hey, I like hunting. When do we start?"

"As soon as you get back, you may have to cut your vacation short."

Bill now looked horrified. "Cut my vacation short? Oh, come on, I've earned this time off!"

The professor raised a calming hand. "I'm not saying I will, but we have to do as the general asks. If we get through these tests, then we have unlimited military funding. He wants to adapt this nanotechnology to create enhanced soldiers."

"Enhanced soldiers?"

"Don't you see, Bill? The AI coupled with our nanotechnology can react quicker than any human can. A man enhanced with this technology can strike you down before you even think about it."

"I haven't thought of it that way," Bill admitted.

"Think about it, an invincible army means unlimited funding for us."

"Bill didn't need to think about it long. "OK, I'm sold, when do we start?"

"As soon as I have the tests ready. Right now, you just need to do this bank job with Beta-One tomorrow."

"As I said, Professor, you've convinced me, but what about this new phone?"

"Ah, the phone, that's another of my creations," The professor boasted, leaning back with a smile. "All the instructions and passwords are in the folder I just gave you." He reached into his drawer and pulled out a matching smartphone. Activating the screen, he indicated the app. "This is what you will use on all exercises with Beta-One. It will allow live voice and text with us, and we will both be able to see and hear through Beta-One's body camera. We can also pinpoint his location."

"Wow, you seem to have thought of everything for this."

"Bill, I want you to use this on the bank job tomorrow. Test this out and become familiar with it. After that, it is essential to use on all Beta-One's hunt exercises."

"No problem with that," Bill said, admiring the screens on the app, "This looks easy to use. I think tomorrow will be a piece of cake."

“And remember”--the professor held his index finger tapping his nose-- “not a word of this must be said to Dr. Coney. He has been great in developing the AI for the nanobots, but his moral beliefs exclude him from our secrets.”

“I agree with that, professor.” Bill slowly got up to leave.

“Wait, I have one last thing to say. While you are with Beta-One, you must be armed with a TASER at all times.”

“What?” Bill’s eyebrows raised at the suggestion. “Are you saying Beatty could turn on me? If he did, I would be much more comfortable with my .45.”

“What I’m saying is there could be unpredictable behavior with him, and you may need to stop him in his tracks. A TASER is more effective than a bullet.”

Bill smirked and winked at the same time. “Oh, I don’t know, a round or two from my .45 has pretty good stopping power.”

“You forget that the Beta-One is being controlled by a set of nanobots. These nanobots do not feel pain, and their functionality is distributed throughout the body. They cannot be affected by traumatic shock. A shot to the heart or the head will prove fatal to a human. But the nanobots will continue to operate until they expire from oxygen starvation.”

“Are you saying that Beatty is going to go zombie on me?”

“The nanobots will continue to operate the body until they die from lack of oxygen. The few minutes that the nanobots continue to operate may mean life or death for you.

“The TASER provides a powerful electric current that will deliver an instant knockout blow to the nanobots. That is why we use TASERs with the dogs, it’s also a lot less messy. A bullet hole means termination, a TASER shot gives us an option to reprogram the nanobots. The electric shock will incapacitate the nanobots for up to thirty minutes, giving you plenty of time to secure the subject. So carry a muzzle for the dogs, and carry handcuffs for Beta-One.”

“OK, I’ll keep that in mind.”

"Oh, and one last thing, as soon as the subject is TASERed, make sure it is secured."

"Why?"

"Because the host body will recover much quicker. The dogs will revert into their real selves and probably become vicious."

"I'll make sure I carry a muzzle, but what about Beatty? What does he wake up to? You once mentioned the name, Fletcher."

"Yes, Fletcher is Beta-One's real human name. You don't need to know his background. Fletcher was a down-and-out, homeless drug addict. He was as good as dead. Let's just say that he donated his body to science."

"But what happens if this Fletcher person wakes up?"

"All I can say is – unpredictable behavior. So, the handcuffs are essential, and use this." The professor pulled a set of handcuffs and a mouth gag from a desk drawer and handed them to Bill. "Keep these out of sight in the Audi in case you need them." He added.

"OK, but this zombie stuff is beginning to spook me."

"You don't need to worry, just follow what I told you. Now let's call this a day so we can get out of here and go home. Enjoy your time off. I'll see you in a couple of weeks."

"OK, Professor thanks." With that, Bill left the office and headed home.

Chapter 2

Moonlight flowed through the window, as a gentle midnight breeze silently played with the curtain.

Bill rolled onto his back, sighing after the beautiful moment.

Larisa Mandelson released her husband from her embrace and breathed in her pleasure. She rolled onto her side, reaching out to cuddle around her husband. Resting one hand on his stomach, dangerously low, breathing softly into his ear. "Are you sure you have to leave early tomorrow?"

"Oh, Babe," Bill smiled, "you are such a temptress!" His arm began to move around her shoulder, the other arresting her hand from starting more foreplay. "Babe, I have to get up early."

"I know," Larisa said, "but I hate it when you go away for so long. The boys hate it too, they need their father here."

"I hate being away. But remember, I only think about you and our boys when I'm away."

"Oh, sweetheart, I love you so much." Larisa squeezed Bill lovingly. "When will you be back home this time?"

"I think in a week, but maybe two, you know what the Professor is like. Once he sets his agenda, there's no stopping him."

Larisa held onto Bill, pressing her loving grip with a demand. "Bill, you are head of security at NeuroComm, you need to exert your authority and demand some time with your family."

"Honey, how many times do I need to tell you? I'm head of security, but this is a startup, there's no one under me. I'm the only person in security, and I have a lot of responsibility right now. When we get the big bucks from the military investment, I will be in charge of security. Other people will be there to do my bidding, and I'll have more freedom."

"But darling, is that investment really coming?"

"It's a sure bet," Bill assured. "The Professor is making certain of that. We already have a ton of startup funding, but the biggest bang for the buck is coming soon! We'll be rich beyond our wildest dreams. Bill Gates and Elon Musk will have nothing on us, baby!"

"I don't care about them, or riches," Larisa now moved her hand to Bill's chin, pulling his face to meet hers. "All I care about is you and our two boys."

Facing each other, Larisa and Bill began to kiss, their hands exploring as passions began to grow.

In the early morning, Bill silently got out of bed, showered, and dressed. As he kissed Larisa on her forehead, she sleepily mumbled, "Drive safe, baby."

Bill loaded his bags into the white Audi before quietly driving away. As he headed north from Idaho Falls, he wondered if this was all worth it. *Well, I'm going to be filthy rich, but in the meantime, I have a lot of perks to enjoy*!

Chapter 3

Beta-One sat perfectly still in a chair in the living room, staring vacantly at the wall as it waited for the allotted time. Among the furniture and varied objects in the room, a clock on the mantelpiece counted the time silently. However, that clock was irrelevant because Beta-One had an internal clock, so it knew exactly what time it was. The clock on the mantelpiece was exactly sixty-three seconds ahead of Beta-One's internal clock.

Once, Beta-One asked Mr. Mandelson, "Why is the clock on the mantelpiece different from my internal clock?"

Mr. Mandelson replied, "Time is what you make it."

Programmed to obey Mr. Mandelson, Beta-One always used its internal clock.

It was during these quiet times that Beta-One was able to do internal processing. Normally, it would do this at nighttime. Although it did not sleep, it recognized the fact that his body needed rest, so it would lay in bed and process the memories of the day.

Sometimes when it relaxed in this way his body would start behaving on its own. Its hand would move towards an object as if reaching for it, or it would feel its head turn towards a reflective surface or a mirror. It was easy for Beta-One to stop these movements because it was in total control of the body. Beta-One did not know where these movements originated. It was as if the body had a mind of its own. Beta-One didn't know where the host body came from. Since it was injected into the body, Beta-One assumed the body was made for Beta-One.

Just then, the body moved its arms and legs as if it wanted to stand. Before the body could get out of the chair, Beta-One suppressed the movements and relaxed back into the chair. A moment later, the body did something it had never done before. It said, "Kill me!"

Beta-One had never heard the body speak. These words puzzled Beta-One. *I didn't know this body could speak on its own. Why would the body want to be killed? I could not kill it anyway, because I am inside this body, if I killed it, I would also die. I do not want to die.*

Beta-One thought about this and decided that further noise from the body must be suppressed. Beta-One continued in silence, waiting for the allotted time.

The allotted time finally came. There was no alarm or announcement, simply a commencement.

Beta-One moved his head slightly, smiled with a gentle expression, and rose to his feet. It walked to the front door and stepped out onto the porch. Here it waited for Mr. William Mandelson to arrive.

Humans never seem to be able to keep exact times on their schedules, it thought.

The house was isolated in the forested hills north of Spencer, Idaho, several miles off Interstate 15. Beta-One was ready and armed with everything it needed for this mission – keys, wallet with ID cards. It locked the house and waited.

Mandelson arrived nine minutes and forty seconds later in the white Audi. When he got out, Beta-One noticed that he was dressed in his regular security guard uniform.

"Hey, Beatty, how's it going?" he asked, using his nickname for Beta-One.

"Everything seems good this morning, Mr. Mandelson."

"It's your lucky day, pal, you get to drive the Audi today."

"I would be interested to hear more about the interplay of probability in this scenario. I do not see how luck applies to the fact that I will be driving."

"Never mind Beatty, just get in and drive, I'll be riding shotgun."

"Yes, sir."

They drove off with Mandelson in the passenger seat. Soon, Mandelson began to fidget, throwing occasional glances at the speedometer. "Beatty, can't you go any faster? You drive like a Tesla on autopilot."

"My calculations match those of the GPS. We should arrive at the destination in one hour and thirty-two minutes."

"Sure, we will, but this is too slow. We don't need to drag our heels, let's get this thing moving."

"Sir?"

"Jeez, put some speed on."

Beta-One accelerated on the narrow country lane, performing several powered slides around the sharp curves.

Mandelson swore and grabbed onto the armrest, bracing his legs against the floor. "Whoa, Beatty, not so crazy."

"Sir, I think you'll find that I'm a very accomplished driver."

"OK, I get it. Now slow down."

"Yes, sir."

"We don't want to attract attention. If the cops see you flying this car like a kite, we're in for some trouble, and I don't have any escape routes."

"I have a memory map of the entire area, so if you like, I could find some escape routes."

"That's not the point. They have radios and can set up roadblocks ahead of us, so let's be quick but not too fast. OK?"

"Yes, sir."

"One thing you must remember, you have to avoid the police at all costs."

As they traveled, Mandelson continued to make small talk, although it was mostly a one-way conversation. Beta-One continued to process the conversation on different threads, trying to piecc the disparate information into a coherent whole. At one point, Mandelson was talking about the passing scenery, when Beta-One regressed to what it thought was a question of high priority.

"What does it mean to avoid the police at all costs? I am confused where the money goes."

"What?"

"Your statement associates the police with a financial cost. Please explain."

"Oh, Beatty, I didn't mean it money-wise. I meant you have to avoid the police no matter what. Make sure you do not do anything to attract their attention. If they are following you, then make a run for it. If they do capture you, then follow the protocols defined by Prof. Wolf."

As they approached the town, Mandelson sent a text to Professor Wolf to alert him that they were approaching the target. He then said, "OK, Beatty, we're nearly there. Stick to speed limits and obey traffic rules."

"Yes, sir."

"OK, there's the bank, over there on the left. Pull in and park to the side."

As they came to a stop, Beta-One switched the engine off and waited for further instructions.

"Let me check your wire, we need to monitor everything you do." Mandelson leaned over and activated the smartphone inside Beatty's jacket. This would record all conversations as well as relay them to Mandelson's smartphone. He also attached earphones to his smartphone and activated his receiver. He then tapped the hidden microphone points on Beatty's clothes. Speaking into his mic, Mandelson said, "Sound check, can you read?"

"I hear you clearly, sir."

"Good, your hidden earpiece is working. If anything goes wrong, I will give you the signal to leave. OK?"

"Yes, I remember all the instructions."

William pulled a large envelope from the glove compartment. "Here is the cash and all the relevant paperwork you need. You're on now, good luck."

"I would be interested to hear more about the interplay of probability in this scenario."

Mandelson's eyes moved upward in what Beta-One had categorized as exasperation. "Never mind Beatty, let's just get on with it. OK, Beatty, I'm initiating Mission Gamma Three Seven Dash X-Ray Golf, confirm."

"Yes sir, Mission Gamma Three Seven Dash X-Ray Golf, I am ready and I confirm that I have a wallet with ID cards, an envelope with cash, and documentation."

"Initiate mission."

"Yes, sir, initiation confirmed."

Beta-One then changed his face to a pleasant but casual demeanor. It got out of the car carrying the large envelope, and walked towards the bank, leaving Mandelson waiting in the car.

Beta-One knew Mandelson would be waiting in the car, acting as the 'minder' in case of problems. His instructions included understanding that Mandelson would maintain a low profile, staying out of range of security cameras. If an emergency arose, Beta-One would receive a warning through his earpiece. Alternatively, Mandelson might call the smartphone, signaling Beta-One to claim a family emergency and leave immediately—a contingency designed to prevent further inquiries from bank staff.

As Beta-One entered the bank, it was greeted by an employee who was welcoming customers. "Hello, sir, and welcome to Bank of Idaho," the greeter said as she opened the door for Beta-One.

"Thank you," Beta-One replied. "I'm here for an appointment, to open an account."

"Oh, certainly sir. Please step inside. Our accounts section is there on the left. Someone there will see to you. Can I get you some coffee or water while you wait?"

"Thank you but no, that's fine. I'll just wait for my appointment."

As Beta-One entered, it was met by an accounts management specialist who ushered him towards his desk.

"Hi, my name is Josh. You must be…?"

"Gary, Gary Fletcher."

"Well, pleased to meet you, Mr. Fletcher, it's a beautiful day isn't it?"

"Yes, it is, a very nice day."

"Please, take a seat here at my desk. Is there anything I can get you? Water? Coffee?"

"No, thank you."

Seated on either side of the desk, they sorted out the details for opening the new bank account. All the paperwork was in order, so depositing the cash into the new account went smoothly.

After opening the account, Beta-One then returned to the car and sat in the driving seat.

"Did everything go OK?" Mandelson asked.

"Yes, everything went fine."

"Perfect." Mandelson spoke into his microphone – "Mission Gamma Three Seven Dash X-Ray Golf is completed successfully with all mission parameters achieved. Returning to base. Let's go, Beatty, drive us back to the safe house."

As they drove out of town, Mandelson called Professor Hayden Wolf on his cell phone. "Well professor, another successful laundry mission!"

Later that evening, the professor arrived at the house to debrief Beta-One on the mission and performance parameters.

Mandelson stayed in the living room watching a war movie on TV.

Beta-One stood emotionless in the kitchen, observing the professor as he arranged his notes on the kitchen table.

The professor indicated to Beta-One to sit at the kitchen table.

"Mandelson, turn that racket down," the professor ordered, "We need some quiet here."

Beta-One observed the interaction, logging it as confirmation of the authority hierarchy: Professor Wolf issued commands, Mandelson complied. Beta-One then sat opposite the professor as instructed, systems primed for the debrief protocol.

The professor placed a folder onto the table in front of it, opening it to reveal a checklist, and took a pen from his pocket.

"Commencing debrief with Beta-One, reference Gamma Three Seven Dash X-Ray Golf. Date and time are recorded, and we are reviewing this external exercise." The professor spoke as he looked at the checklist on the table. The entire house was covered with monitoring equipment which automatically stored all audio and visual data into a vast database. The database could later be easily referenced with voice searches such as 'find debrief with Beta-One' or more specifically to individual reference codes.

The professor then looked up and considered Beta-One sitting quietly opposite.

"OK, Beta-One, I want to congratulate you on the successful mission you performed today. You achieved the prime objective."

Beta-One watched silently as the professor ticked off a checklist. "Clothes – good. Driving – good. Greetings – good."

The professor then frowned and asked, "I do have one question. Why didn't you engage in small talk with the bank clerk?"

"It did not seem advantageous to the mission."

"Are you saying it bears no direct relevance to the mission?"

"Yes."

"But what have I taught you about small talk?"

"You have told me that it will help me to blend in and to look normal."

"So why did you not engage in small talk?"

"Sir, I have no response to that question."

"You mean, you don't know?"

"Sir, I do not fully understand how to connect small talk to a given mission."

"You have been on several bank deposit missions now and each one you fail to make small talk. Today, at least two bank staff prompted you, yet you did not respond. Why not?"

"I think you refer to the offer of water? Or to discuss the weather?"

"Yes, that's exactly what I refer to."

"I did respond to these instances of small talk as you call them, but I did not think it necessary to continue on those conversational digressions as they had no relevance to the outcome of the mission."

"Yes, but what have I told you about social camouflage and the need to blend in?"

"Sir, I have difficulty in determining exactly how much to say for these conversations. For instance, do I provide a weather report for the coming week? Or do I comment on the quality of the water? When do I know that I have engaged in sufficient small talk? Otherwise, I risk exceeding the expected time for any given encounter."

Professor Hayden sighed heavily.

"Sir?" Beta-One asked, "Have I caused a problem on this mission, or have I failed in any way?

"Yes and no." the professor replied, "You have completed the mission as defined, but you've clearly not understood this aspect of social engagement at all, we'll have to expand your training on this subject. But for now, think of it as a form of social camouflage. I'll have to devise a better training session for you."

"Yes, sir."

Professor Hayden made a note with his pen before speaking. "Note on debrief Gamma Three Seven Dash X-Ray Golf, review social behavior to address conversational abilities." As if to emphasize, he then continued, "So I think that is enough for these notes, but we will talk some more, a lot more."

"Yes, sir."

"Concluding debrief and review of external exercise Gamma Three Seven Dash X-Ray Golf.

"OK, Beta-One, that concludes this debrief."

"Thank you, sir. Will there be anything else?"

"Actually, yes, you may now cook dinner."

"Yes, sir."

"And during dinner, we can try practicing some small talk."

Chapter 4

William Banks flicked the Superman curl of hair on his forehead as he announced, "We'll depart tomorrow at oh five hundred!" William repeated this several times throughout the evening. He insisted on using military terminology for telling the time. In this case, his teenage daughter Adara preferred to use the term "Stupid O'clock".

The next morning, Beryl Banks packed snacks, drinks, sandwiches, and fruit for her husband and daughter to take on their journey. She wanted to make sure they both had plenty to eat for the whole day. She wasn't interested in adventures like this, so she would be staying at home. "Food and nourishment are what I care about," Beryl said.

"Mom, there's no way we're gonna eat all this stuff, they'll give us lunch when we're there."

"How can I be sure they'll be serving you good wholesome food? You'll need your strength, this will be a long day for you both. So never mind Adara, it's better to have more, than not enough, and be thankful for what I've prepared for you."

"Don't worry, Beryl," William said with a wink, "you've given us some good rations here. You're better than all the mess hall cooks I've ever seen on all my missions."

Beryl looked coy as William leaned over to kiss her gently.

"Come on dad, shouldn't we be going?" Adara prompted.

"Beryl, are you sure you won't come with us?" William asked.

"No dear, you know I don't like these adventures. Anyway, I have lots to do at home, so you drive safely."

"OK honey, you know I always take care."

"OK, Mom we'll see you later."

As they left, Beryl settled into her favorite armchair. *It's too early to start any housework*, she thought to herself, *I'll just read my romance novel.* As she read her book, her mind drifted towards William and how he dominated her heart.

I hate him for always being away so long on his missions overseas, Beryl thought. *He lies and I'm sure he cheats, but he is the most mysterious lover I can ever have.* Beryl held her novel close to her heart before falling into a brief sleep. When she awoke, she rose from her chair to do the household chores while thinking of William.

During the drive Adara tried to sleep but couldn't, so she kept her book nestled in her lap. She thought her father's conversations were boring. Usually about his exploits overseas, while on military duty.

He never said exactly where he went or why. He always had some sort of moral to tell and would somehow connect it to whatever the conversation was about. OK, he did try to keep the conversation flowing, but he had a knack for channeling it into a tedious monologue.

There was little anyone could do once he engaged in his stories, so Adara resorted to a standard escape clause – "Dad I really have to read this book, I need to write a book report for my English class."

"So, what's the book?"

"It's Michael Crichton's, Terminal Man."

"Oh? Is that about that guy who got stuck at the Paris airport terminal for months and months?"

"No dad, it's science fiction. It's about a guy called Harry Benson who is suffering from violent brain seizures and blackouts. So, he's given an experimental brain implant to detect any oncoming seizures and prevent them through neural stimulation with implanted electrodes."

"Sounds like science fiction to me, but I guess it ties into your science and math studies?"

"Dad, I said it's for my English class, but actually this is an old book from the '70s, and neuroscience has progressed a lot since then, so science fact is now much more advanced than this old science fiction. In fact, I think it's kind of lame, because none of the characters in this story realizes the implant is working in a closed process loop that is acting as a feedback mechanism, which ends up triggering even more frequent seizures. It's stupid because they act like they didn't have such things as defensive programming and process interrupts when this was written."

"Whoa girl, you're going over my head – closed defensive interrupts and programming processes?"

"Jeez! No dad, defensive programming, and process interrupts. That's where you anticipate errors and unexpected problems in a process and write the program to defend against bad stuff happening."

"Mind your language young lady!"

Adara continued, "Then you can interrupt the process and take corrective measures."

"Hm, sounds to me like modifying your operational field tactics given a dynamic strategic situation."

"Yeah, whatever dad. Anyway, I need to read this so I can do my book report for English."

'Oh no, not homework.' William thought. The very suggestion of schoolwork usually brought William's conversation to a sudden halt. Being an absent father, he was not well versed in how to support and encourage schoolwork. He was very weak when it came to supporting anything relating to family life. Not being into the parenting routine, he always fell silent when Adara mentioned school or homework; he wasn't sufficiently confident to offer assistance, so he stopped talking or at least stopped talking long enough until he forgot about the homework.

Driving north on Highway 55, they had passed Boise. As they drove through the town of Horseshoe Bend, the road would run along the Payette River. This was a sign that they were nearing their rafting point on the river.

It wasn't long before William broke the silence. "Your mom isn't happy about this trip, but I'm really glad we can go and have some time together. Your mom always says your schooling is going great, but I think you need to get out more into the fresh air and countryside."

Oh Jeez, he's starting again, she thought as she lowered her head towards her book allowing her mousey blond hair to fall off her shoulders to hide her profile.

Sweet 16 was Adara's age and it could have been her demeanor too, if she weren't so spirited and argumentative. Her figure was maturing into that of a well-rounded athlete.

Her dark blonde hair draped around her shoulders, down her back. She often experimented with different styles: ponytail and sports clothes, straightened hair with elegant clothes for a look of opulence, witchy hair with torn jeans and punkish makeup.

But today she was natural, wearing casual clothes for the outdoors. *All she needs is a cowboy hat*, William thought.

"Do you think your mom is OK with us going on this trip?" He asked.

"Yeah whatever, you know mom doesn't like adventures, especially off the cuff like this, she's the stay-at-home mom. Anyway, she'll be fine, after all, she does put up with you and your long trips away," she smirked sideways as she waited for the bait to be taken.

Avoiding the subject, William then asked, "OK so what about you? Do you have a good circle of friends at school?"

"Sure Dad, I got plenty."

"What about boyfriends? How's that boyfriend you told me about once?"

"Oh, yeah, we're still together, he's sweet, a bit arrogant sometimes. I'm teaching him how to play guitar you know."

"Oh nice, then you can play together." As soon as William said that, he wished he hadn't, and quickly tried to change the subject again.

"You know? Sometime soon I'll be able to come off these special tours of duty. Then maybe we can get back to being a family again and we can all spend more time out in the country."

Fumbling on how to continue, William eventually asked, "Does she have many friends?"

"What exactly are you asking? Does she have any boyfriends? You know full well that she lives and breathes in the kitchen. If she ever did have a boyfriend, he'd be a dishwasher. Oh wait, there is that old guy who helps out in the school kitchen where she works, I bet something is going on there!"

This stumped William's conversation, bringing it to an abrupt ending.

Should my daughter be talking back to me like that? How the hell did this conversation twist around like this? Why can't we ever make a simple connection? "Sweetheart," William said, "I feel really bad about being away for such long periods."

"Yeah, dad you keep saying."

"Let me finish. I just want to say that I can't change things right now, but there will be a time soon when I can leave the service."

"Dad, you know mom loves you, that's why she puts up with you. But she does hate it when you are away."

They drove on towards Cabarton Bridge on the Payette River, with Adara pretending to be interested in her book while William attempted to make small talk.

The whole point of this trip was to celebrate not only Adara's sixteenth birthday but also the completion of her freshman year at high school. Starting in September she would be a sophomore.

Now is the time, William thought, *to get my daughter interested in some sort of career path*. Adara's comment about "Teaching him to play guitar." William hoped this was not some sort of code word for intimacy. *Somehow we have to keep those pesky boyfriends at bay and keep her concentrating on her studies.*

As the miles wore on William kept a steady hand on the steering wheel and did his best to keep the conversation flowing. It was over a three-hour drive from Twin Falls, but William kept promising that it would be worth it.

They would enter the river at Cabarton Bridge for a guided day-long excursion downstream to Smith's Ferry. Three rafts would make the journey together, each with eight passengers and an oarsman from the company to steer and manage the craft. The website and advertising boasted professional guides, each of whom had gained championship awards in rafting and other water sports.

The trip was scheduled to start at 10 am and take about 6 hours to complete. They would stop about halfway on a quiet riverside beach for a prepared lunch. In the end, they would be transferred back to their cars in a modified school bus emblazoned with the logos of the rafting company.

William's GPS guided them to the launch point nestled by the side of Cabarton Bridge, which spanned low across the river. William parked the car and, as she was getting out, Adara leaned behind her and reached across to the back seat.

"You stay here Slot and be good. You can't come with us because you'll get wet, so I'll see you later sweetheart!" She blew a kiss for good measure.

William scoffed under his breath but also smiled to himself thinking, *That old stuffed toy is the best thing I ever got for her.*

After that long drive, William climbed out of the driver's seat and stood by the car. Slowly windmilling his arms and stretching his legs like a soccer player, shaking off the hours of driving behind the wheel. As far as he was concerned, stature was everything, and at six feet and two inches with broad shoulders, William always stood proud. His rounded face and dark hair gave him a 'cuteness' that people recognized as friendly and likable.

"Hey girl, we're here!" William announced.

Adara was still seated on the passenger side with the door open, putting her trainers back on and tying up the laces. "Thanks for telling me, dad. Where else would we be?"

Other paying passengers began to arrive, parking their cars and unloading their belongings in preparation for the trip. Groups of friends huddled together, with some wandering around and exploring the launch area while others took photos from the bridge. It was difficult to not be mesmerized by the splendor of the surroundings as the river flowed by.

William approached one of the administrators who was young, short and blonde, with a cute if not chubby face. “Hi, my name is William Banks, and this is my daughter Adara, we should be scheduled for this morning’s raft trip.”

“Hi and good morning Mr. Banks! My name is Amy and welcome to Idaho Mountain Water Sports! Oh yes, I can see you’re both on our roster and you’ll be in boat number 3, which is Kathy’s boat. Oh, she is so sweet, you’ll love going down with her.”

“Oh, I bet,” Said William, avoiding all the innuendos running through his head.

"Everyone is preparing for the trip, getting the rafts and equipment ready. They are also checking the river and weather conditions." Amy continued, "In the meantime, we have a few forms and waivers to complete. Once you're done with those you can go over there to where Brian is and he will give you all your safety equipment."

After completing the forms, William led Adara to where Brian was standing with all the safety equipment.

“She’s sweet, don’t you think?” William asked.

“I think she was a squirt” Adara scoffed back.

Brian was one of the younger members of the staff, a college intern trying to earn sports credits for his major. He would not be on the trip but was helping with the assembly of passengers. As they walked over to him, occasional instructions were announced, like “We’ll be ready to assemble soon” and “We’re just waiting for a few more people to arrive.” This kept the growing crowd in anticipation.

“Hi Brian, my name is William Banks, and this is my daughter Adara.”

“Hi there Mr. Banks. Is this your daughter? Hey, that’s great.” Brian said, holding his hand out towards Adara. “It’s a real pleasure to meet you.”

“Me too, I’m sure,” Adara beamed.

“OK Brian,” William interjected, “Amy sent us over, so what have you got for us?”

Behind Brian was an array of safety equipment laid out in neat rows on the ground.

“Ah yes,” Brian replied, “we have some gear you need to wear on the trip: helmets, and PFDs. I should say ‘Personal Flotation Devices,’ also known as life jackets. It is a regulation that you wear these at all times on the river.”

William nodded in agreement.

“Let me know your chest and head size and I can find the right things for you.”

“I’m large, and my daughter is small to medium,” replied William.

“I’m small,” corrected Adara.

“Oh, here we go. I have the stuff for you both,” He handed the PFD to William and held out Adara’s PFD as if to adorn her with a fashionable jacket.

As Adara threaded her arms through the straps, Brian asked, “May I help you adjust the straps?”

“I can handle that,” William replied as he ushered his daughter out of harm’s way. As they walked to the side, William mumbled, “I think he’s a squirt.”

“Oh, I think he’s kinda cute,” Adara murmured back to her dad with a smile back towards Brian.

William donned his kit quickly. It wasn’t the most fashionable, but he made sure it fit well. He then helped Adara to get the right adjustments on her PFD. “Here sweetheart let me help. You need to keep these straps tight, especially around the waist,” he said as he adjusted each strap. “It’s no good if this thing slips up over your head, it needs to stay tight around your torso.”

People milled around the safety equipment trying on helmets and PFDs for size. The guides and other staff were on hand to instruct everyone on how to fit the equipment. Even with help, what started as orderly soon turned into a mess as people discarded one poorly fitting PFD for a better size.

Once everyone had finished selecting gear, they all continued to mill around the area looking top-heavy. The PFDs made their upper bodies look large and their helmets looked like uniform haircuts.

A large man suddenly appeared wearing what looked like one of the original O'Neil wet suits from the 1960s. His long grey hair tied in a ponytail and his beard failed to conceal a continuous happy grin. All the staff fell silent as he sauntered in. It was clear that he was in charge and was about to address his customers.

"Welcome to Idaho Mountain Water Sports," he announced. "My name is Bradley. My staff will make it their business to make your journey on the Payette River an experience of a lifetime".

Bradley did not have to project his voice, it projected itself. He didn't have to demand attention, it gravitated towards him. Everyone fell silent, turned towards the man, and listened intently.

Bradley's six-foot-four frame commanded attention as he strode confidently barefoot across the riverbank. His powerful build and greying ponytail gave him the air of a seasoned river veteran.

William leaned towards Adara and said, "There he is, I read on the website that he's a big wig champion of white water. He even has some Olympic medals to his name."

"He looks like an old hippy to me," Adara replied.

"Maybe, but look at him, he looks like a battleship! I bet he knows these rivers like his own."

Bradley carried a clipboard with all the names scheduled on his roster but he never glanced at it, not even once. After his speech, he introduced his guides one by one. Then calling out the names listed on his roster, he assigned them to each of their rafts.

It was questionable why he carried this clipboard at all, as he had a photographic memory of the entire list.

All the passengers lined up with their raft guides like schoolchildren lining up for their classes. Some quick introductions followed amongst the passengers, such as "Hi, how ya doing?" and "This will be awesome!"

Bradley assigned William and Adara to Kathy's raft, Number 3. As they approached the raft, Adara leaned towards her father and said, "Hey Dad, did you notice that Bradley didn't even glance at his roster, he seemed to know it by heart."

"Must be military training," William smiled.

William and Adara joined two young men in their 20s and Rita, an attractive woman in her early forties who was with her 14-year-old daughter Lizzie. They split a group of four young men between two rafts, Bret and Ralph were seated behind Rita and Lizzie. The other two were assigned to raft Number 2. Both pairs of young men had pump-action water guns, and they all made it clear that they would engage in battle as they journeyed along the river.

Kathy was to be their guide. She was tall, and broad at the shoulders, reinforcing her appearance of strength. Her short hair made her appear a little masculine. Being a competitive rafter, Kathy achieved many awards, and knew every intimate detail of the Payette River.

Kathy moved her group to their Number 3 raft, positioning each person at the point they would be sitting. "Seating is important for balancing the raft," Kathy explained, "it is also important for personal comfort." Kathy set out everyone's spot in the raft, seating William and Adara in the front. Rita was behind Adara, and Lizzie was behind William.

"These middle seats are the most stable," Kathy said, "but there is some danger of getting splashed by a paddle, either from the front or behind."

The two young men were seated behind Rita and Lizzie with Kathy at the stern, acting as steersmen.

"Where do we sit?" Rita asked.

The two boys rolled their eyes and chuckled.

"Very good question, Rita," Kathy said, "We all sit on the round bulbous rim of the raft. You can wedge one foot between the raft rim and the raft floor. You can slip the other foot into the webbed foothold on the floor," as Kathy demonstrated, "In this way, we can use our paddles and lean our weight into them."

While still on land, Kathy demonstrated each maneuver they would need to perform. Paddle forward, paddle back, paddle left, paddle right and stop. She explained how to use the body for leverage when pulling the paddle through the water.

As Rita tried to follow Kathy's demonstration, she said, "I hope we don't fall out."

One of the men scoffed and whispered something inaudible to his friend.

I'm glad they're back there, William thought to himself, *they could be a bit obnoxious with those water guns.*

"There would be no passengers on this trip, and that includes you two boys," Kathy announced, "you can't just sit and watch the river go by. It won't be hard work, but we do have to pull together. I'll explain everything before we set off. Don't worry if you fall out, just remember the safety instructions, swim on your back, and keep your feet up. The current will carry you with us and everything will be fine."

"OK, everybody, are you all ready to be my crew?" she announced.

"Let's go for it," William agreed, "Explanations are one thing, but experience is always better."

"Now crew, let's take this raft to the water, and try out how to paddle."

"Aye, Captain!" the two boys replied.

"There may be high water ahead, are ye ready?" Kathy said in pirate fashion.

"Aye, Captain!" the boys responded.

"And are ye ready with your weapons?" Kathy now whispered to the boys in pirate fashion.

"Looks like we're in the navy now," William said to Adara.

Adara just rolled her eyes.

Kathy's crew carried the raft to the water's edge and prepared to launch on the shallow beach. At this point in the river, the water was smooth, wide, and slow flowing. This gave the rafts ample space to practice before they set off on their adventure. Kathy's first role was to form this new crew into a responsive team.

She said, "There will be times where the water is loud and moving fast, and to get through '*respectably*' we have to act fast. So sometimes I will be shouting, but remember, I'm not shouting AT you, I'm shouting TO you".

After letting this sink in for a moment and waiting for a few giggles from the 'lads' to settle down. Kathy started barking orders. The crew of raft number 3 paddled hard out to the middle of the river. Following further orders from Kathy, they did a hard right turn and headed upstream under the road bridge. After clearing the bridge, they performed several 'S' turns up through the gentle current. They then turned around and rested before drifting back down again. Kathy led them all in a paddle salute. The 'crew' all raised their paddles into the air tapping them together above their heads in a watery hi-five!

They were now a unit and ready to go, but there was one more thing to do.

Kathy let them drift with the slow current back towards the launch point. The other two rafts had now launched and were preparing for their training maneuvers. Kathy steered raft number 3 alongside rafts 1 and 2. As they approached, she quietly commanded the kids to fill their water guns.

"What?" they asked.

"Fill the water gun," Kathy replied. "Do it quickly and be quiet about it! Keep your gun low and out of sight to the right side".

The boys complied, nodding to each other.

"Looks like we're doing a sneak attack," William said to Adara, "Maybe these boys have a use after all."

Kathy kept a nonchalant air about her as they drifted forward. Steering gently, she let raft 3 close in on rafts 1 and 2, making their preparations on the beach. The crews were too self-involved, as they made ready on the water, to notice the approaching threat.

"Keep cool, boys, and fire on my order," Kathy whispered.

Drifting alongside raft Number 2, which held the "rival men," Kathy barked the order, "Fire at will!" Bret, who held the gun, leveled it and at a point-blank range began firing several pints of cold river water at raft number 2. Bret gave no quarter, as splashes of cold water raked through raft 2. Shrieks, squeals, and screams came from everyone. The only one who was able to 'return fire' was Gary, the raft 2 guide. He used his oar to splash back. Even this was too late as Kathy ordered, "Paddle forward, full speed!" and as raft 3 pulled away, only minor splashes from Gary hit their mark on Kathy's back.

Another high-five paddle salute! Kathy and the crew of raft 3 had proven themselves as a formidable force. They made the first strike, but beware, revenge is in the air.

This promised to be one exciting trip!

"OK," Kathy said to her crew, "a little bit of information before we start. The North Fork of the Payette is a class 3 river. To the layman, that means it's an intermediate skill level for rafting and kayaking. The rapids will be a good roller coaster ride, with lots of splashes along the way. It's not dangerous, but all rivers deserve a healthy level of caution. This is by no means extreme. As long as we all take suitable precautions, the ride will be exciting but safe."

Kathy continued. "The water level is controlled by the dam at Lake Cascade. Throughout the year, the river authority follows a specified schedule of releases. This time of year, they allow the spring meltwaters to run downstream. Today is a scheduled release day, so I expect a fun ride."

All rafts had now launched and completed their initial practice and assembled in readiness for their trip. Damon was guiding the first raft with two families, each with a mom and dad and two teenage kids. The second raft was Gary, with his crew. This included a dad with 2 teenage boys, and of course the 2 rival kids who suffered the soaking from us in raft 3. Kathy followed behind with her proud crew. Each of the guides knew the river well. They not only looked after their 'crew' but also kept a lookout for each of the other rafts. Each guide knew exactly how the rafts should progress. Watching each other ensured a safe track along the river.

Rounding the first bend on the quiet river revealed the first white water. This raised some oohs and aahs from pretty much everyone.

"Don't worry," Kathy said to her crew, "This is only a baby to get you used to the water."

"Come on, Dad, you're looking worried," Adara smirked towards her father.

William just scoffed back.

On each rapid the rafts would proceed in order, raft 1 going first while 2 and 3 hung back and watched. When the first raft was through, it held its position, to watch the second raft come through. Then both 1 and 2 would-hold and wait below the rapid while raft 3 tackled the fast water. In this way, the rafts could_stay together as a group and keep a lookout for each other's safety. Each guide had a radio, so if needed they could_contact each other and also Bradley back at base camp.

About halfway along their route, a lunch party would be waiting for them. If the rafts were_delayed for any reason, the guides could inform the caterers of a change in their arrival time.

The first rapid was a milk run, a wide gentle slope with shallow but swift water. There were no real obstacles, so the three rafts all followed in quick succession. There was enough time for the lads in raft 2 to fill their water gun. They then waited for Kathy's raft in the quiet pool below. Kathy perceived the threat and told her lads to get their water gun ready as they followed down the rapid. Kathy steered a wide berth around raft 2. There was an exchange of fire as Kathy and her crew paddled past, but the distance between them did not allow for accurate shooting.

"Hold your fire boys," Kathy exclaimed as they took their position downstream of raft 2. "Let's get them as they come down past us."

“Dad, why didn’t you bring a gun?” Adara asked.

“Hey, I thought this was going to be a peaceful trip.” William shrugged. “Anyway, my branch isn’t Navy!”

Kathy’s strategy was good but the lads in raft 2 reloaded before charging in for some close-range combat. This time it was not only water guns, as both crews used their paddles to splash the enemy. Everyone got a thorough soaking in that skirmish.

This battle was over, but the war of the Payette River was sure to continue as they made their way past the first rapid.

The water was cold, but the sun was bright and warm. The battles helped to form a sense of camaraderie throughout all three rafts. After that, they proceeded downstream.

After a few more minutes on the water, a railway line emerged from a small valley on the right bank. The tracks followed them all the way downstream, clinging to the side of the steep gorge.

As the group progressed down the river, the rapids increased in complexity. Kathy relished explaining the different features of the river and the gorge. Along the way, between sections of white water, there were relaxing stretches with gentle flowing pools.

"Don't worry," Kathy said, "there will be places where we can swim. In the meantime, we all need to stay in the raft."

The first big challenge for the group was the Trestle, a full-fledged class 3 rapid. The Trestle was a long sweeping S bend of continuous white water. The name came from the railway bridge, which crossed the river halfway through the middle of the S bend. A raft at the halfway point would not be visible to either the lead raft waiting at the bottom, or to the raft waiting to enter at the top. The guides had to use their radios to signal their progress to each other. The bridge pylons were considered the main obstacle, and crews had to work hard to get past them in one piece.

Each guide prepped their crews on the strategy and tactics necessary to get them through safely.

"OK listen up," Kathy spoke to her crew. They were out of the main river flow, at a holding point above the rapid. "This next one is called the Trestle. I can't think why they called it that because I like to call it the wrestle."

William looked at Adara as he rolled his eyes exaggeratedly, while everyone else in the boat moaned and groaned at the poor pun.

"Do you see that line of standing waves in the main flow ahead of us?" Kathy indicated a perfect line of hills made of flowing water, each one about three feet high. "Well, we're going to join that wave train and ride it down through the rapids. There will be three things we need to do to get through these rapids in a 'respectable' manner."

Like the others, William tuned his ears to Kathy and focused his eyes on the waves ahead. "Heads up girl," William said as he looked at Adara, "Pay attention, this could be a hairy ride."

"First, the wave train passes close to the farthest bridge pylon, and we don't want to get slammed up against that. If that happens, the river may hold us there in its grip or we could get flipped." If the crew hadn't been attentive, they certainly were now. "We need to pull ourselves around that corner to stay in the main river flow. So, I will shout 'Hard right!' At that point, the crew on the left must paddle like there's no tomorrow, while the crew on the right must hold their paddles still in the water, so we can do a good clean right turn. After the turn, I will order 'paddle forward,' so we can clear the bridge and follow the main current further down and around the bend.

"Second, there are two very large boulders made of hard rock. We must steer in between them. Please try not to scratch them, and I don't want anyone writing graffiti as we go past."

"Psst. Dad, did you bring some spray paint?" Adara asked.

"Girl, give me a break."

"Finally," Kathy continued, "we'll have to ride through the last funnel. Beyond that, there will be a spot of calm water where we can rest. Lay your water guns to rest," Kathy added. "We'll be too busy to use them and we're all going to get wet without them anyway."

"Oh, and don't worry if we get flipped or you happen to fall out. Follow the drill, and float on your back with your feet up and facing downstream. We'll pick you up in the calm pool at the bottom."

They watched Damon's raft number 1 go first. The crew paddled towards the rapids, entering the wave train at the top. The raft rolled up and over each wave like a roller coaster, bouncing along towards the bridge, each wave throwing water over the raft and crew. As they approached the far bridge support, they could see the crew paddling like crazy, their paddles battling against the raging water. Damon leaned hard onto his paddle, using it as a rudder. Soon they disappeared under the bridge and out of sight.

Both Gary and Kathy waited for Damon's radio signal to say he had cleared the rapids.

"Damon here." came the signal, "We are clear and waiting at the holding position below the rapid." Damon added, "Jeez she's a bit lively today, watch out for those bouncy waves, but we're good."

Next, it was Gary and raft number 2 to head down. They were pretty much a mirror image of Damon's raft as they swept out of sight under the bridge.

Soon after, Kathy got the all-clear from Gary and she confirmed on the radio that she was heading into the rapids. As her crew paddled, Kathy steered her raft into the wave train.

Being at the head of the raft Adara looked towards her dad for reassurance. William nodded back at his daughter and winked with a reassuring smile. "Hey girl, this is going to be a cool ride!" William shouted as the waves gathered around the raft.

I'm so glad I brought her on this trip, William thought to himself, *the way she's following instructions is making me proud*!

The wave train was a regular roller coaster. The bow and the stern of the raft bore the brunt of the bumps but there was no escape anywhere from the rhythmic ride. The crew paddled through with lots of yelling and yahoos to accompany the noise of the water. At the crest of each wave, the paddlers could not reach the water and tended to paddle air, while at the troughs of each wave, they were swamped with water over the rim of the raft. Kathy was in her element and loving every second as she gleefully took her motley crew for a ride.

"Hey, this is intense!" William said to Adara.

"Are you scared yet, Dad?"

"I didn't think I'd be taking all the splashes!"

The bridge pylon approached. Its solid concrete wall looked even more threatening in close-up. The thunder of water echoed under the bridge as the wave train curled past the pylon, washing up the concrete flank.

"Paddle hard right!" Kathy yelled over the din as she leaned her weight to steer right. "Left side paddle hard! Right side paddle back and hold that water!" The raft turned 90 degrees. They passed close enough to the concrete wall to touch it. At the end of the wall, a wave threw the bow of the raft into the air. The raft itself listed heavily to the right. The crew gave up paddling at this point and clung to whatever they could to keep their balance and stay in the raft. Adara held on with her feet and used her paddle to balance herself. It wasn't until the bow landed in the last wave trough that she was 'trampolined' out of the raft and somersaulted sideways into the water.

William tried to grab her as she fell out but missed completely. "Oh crap!"

Rita screamed.

One of the boys yelled: "Whoa dude, wipeout!"

"She fell out! What do we do now?" William shouted.

Kathy yelled, "It's OK, we're through the worst, she can swim along behind us and we'll pick her up below!"

With so much cold water already thrown at her, Adara didn't get a cold shock when she fell in. She was already acclimatized and full of adrenaline.

"Jezus!" Adara shouted as she came up for air. Waves splashed around her while she tried to tread water in the turbulence. What she did feel was humiliation and embarrassment.

Kathy looked back at Adara and yelled: "Don't worry, you're fine, swim on your back with your feet in front and follow us."

Damn it! Adara thought, *Why me, I wish those dumb guys got dumped overboard! I feel so stupid, I'll never live this down.*

Adara fell slightly to the side of the main current and spun around in some eddies while the raft swept on ahead of her.

Damn it she thought, *I'll never swim to catch the raft now! What did they say in the orientation? Swim on your back and use your arms as paddles. OK, I can do that.*

Buoyed by her PFD, which kept her head well above water and kept her balanced on her back, Adara used her arms as paddles to steer away from obstacles and steadied herself in the current.

The two boulders were approaching. The raft had already passed between them and was now well in front of her. As Adara approached the boulders she thought, *I've got to slow down and slip between those big rocks.*

Adara tried to turn onto her stomach and swim against the current to slow herself down. Wearing the PFD made her unstable in that position and she could not help herself from turning onto her back again.

"Bummer! That didn't work!" she said out loud, "Oh God, here they come," as she flowed along on her back frantically paddling backward with her arms to slow herself down.

The current funneled her smoothly between the rocks. The slight drop after the boulders plunged her briefly under water, but when she surfaced, she thought, *Hey, I'm still alive! This isn't so bad. It's kinda fun*!

As the boulders receded behind her, the river was swift but steady, and she could hear the funnel up ahead that Kathy had mentioned.

OK, maybe this is fun, but this calm area could be a good place to get back to shore.

Kathy had no way to stop the raft at any point. She was committed to completing the run. Kathy kept track of Adara who drifted behind. She felt confident that she would follow them down through the rapids.

"Don't worry Mr. Banks, she's coming along behind us."

William was no longer seated, instead, he was kneeling in the raft looking to the rear, keeping his eyes on Adara.

Kathy radioed her status to the others, stating that she had a crew member overboard, but she was OK and swimming downstream behind.

"We're approaching the funnel!" Kathy addressed everyone, "Everyone paddle forward through the funnel, Mr. Banks stay down and hang on."

The funnel was not particularly dangerous, but Kathy had to focus her crew. This was a fast-moving narrow stretch of water that would carry them around the next bend. After that, there would be a calm pool where they could pick Adara up. Before they entered the funnel, Kathy looked back for a moment and saw Adara waving her arms. She thought that she was waving 'OK'.

Around the curve, Kathy's raft came into view of the first two rafts in the pool some distance below. She spotted a quiet eddy in the lee of the current and steered her raft to hold position there. She radioed to both Gary and Damon that she was holding a position waiting for her lost crew to swim by.

Adara didn't appear immediately which was of some concern to Kathy. Adara should be only seconds behind.

Kathy radioed to her fellow guides, "Lost crew is not visible, I'm holding here in case of a potential rescue."

William also watched the river for Adara. Listening to Kathy's radio monologue, he could not hear any responses as Kathy used an earpiece.

Where the hell is she? William thought. *Maybe she got to shore upstream?*

Kathy decided it would be best to move her raft downstream to where Damon and Gary were holding their rafts. They needed to keep together as a group.

As Kathy guided the raft slowly downstream, William thought, *I better go look for her*, and with that, he dived headfirst into the river. This is a bad thing to do, without knowing what rocks and obstacles lay beneath. William did a shallow belly flop dive and swam to the side where the railway line followed the bank.

Oh God, this is not good! Kathy thought, she now had two crew overboard, which doubled the danger.

Adara signaled her so-called 'last wave' when she caught her foot in some rocks. The riverbank was temptingly close and Adara decided to make for it. She started with a crawl stroke but when some rocks banged her shin, she used those to kick off from. This was her mistake. She should have drifted down through the rapids and made no attempt to reach the bank at this point.

As Adara kicked off from the rock, her foot slid into a crevasse. Guided by the force of the current, her foot became fixed there. What made things worse, her toe was pointing upstream while her ankle became wedged tightly between two rocks. Adara flipped backward flailing her arms in a hello wave which Kathy saw.

Adara was in trouble. She was being pulled over backward by the current, which lodged her ankle even deeper into the wedge of rock. If only she could move her body forward, she could ease her weight off her ankle and free her foot. But the force of water held her body back. She used her arms to paddle forward against the current so that she could keep her face above water. Despite her efforts, she lacked the strength to relieve the pressure on her ankle and free her trapped leg.

The current kept pushing her body back keeping her ankle firmly lodged. If she didn't swim forward, the current would sweep her body back and hold her face underwater. Even the PFD wasn't enough to hold her head above water. She tried different swim strokes to pull her body forward. The overarm crawl was most effective but also the most tiring. The breaststroke was less tiring but less effective. Icy waves crashed over her head at unpredictable intervals, filling her nose with water and making each desperate breath a struggle.

Held fast by the current with her ankle stuck in a rock, Adara was rapidly exhausting herself. If her strength failed, she would be forced backward under the water.

Despite William's fast over arm crawl stroke against the current, it took him a good half-minute to get to the side. The current also landed him at least 30 meters further downstream.

Crap, this was harder than I expected!

William scrambled over the boulders and up the rocky bank to the railway line. There he could get a good view of the river. Standing there he had quick access to anything up or even downstream.

William ran upstream along the tracks scanning the river below as he went. *She probably got out amongst the rocks on the side.* He had a better view of the far bank of the river, but a swimmer could easily be hidden between the rocks on his near bank. He did not see Adara swimming or drifting downstream.

What William was not looking for was a person caught on a submerged rock, bent over backward, and struggling for their life. For all intents and purposes, Adara appeared to be just another submerged rock in the rapids.

Kathy maneuvered her raft to the pool where Damon and Gary had stopped. They secured all three rafts together and tied them against rocks. Kathy remained to ensure the safety of the three rafts. Damon and Gary ran back upstream along the railway line, both carrying a couple of throw lines. Adara hadn't drifted by, so she must be upstream and possibly in difficulty. They had to find her and find her fast. They jogged along the railway line, keeping their eyes focused on the river. They also kept feeding short radio updates to Kathy on their status and position. They were some distance downstream of Adara's last reported position and continued their way upstream.

Having reached the two boulders which was the last point that Adara was seen, William gulped air in panic. He now had to retrace his steps to find Adara. He was sure he hadn't seen her float past, so his concern was rising sharply. *Where the hell is she*? He shouted Adara's name through cupped hands towards the river. William stumbled back in a sideways jog as he scanned the riverbank on both sides for any sign of Adara.

It was just before the funnel that William saw the strange crucifix in the water. A foot downstream of the crucifix was a small standing wave of white water acting as an arrow. "Jeez," William said aloud. Standing above the point where he could see Adara. She was not only trapped on a rock, but she was also submerged, face up but underwater. He had to get Adara, and he had to do it NOW!

The bank below this stretch of railway consisted of sharp boulders hewn from nearby bedrock and laid to protect the base of the line from the forces of the river. William danced across the tops of these boulders trying to get upstream of Adara. When he was about 15 meters upstream of Adara, he dived straight into the water as if to swim to the other side. William knew if he tried to swim directly towards Adara he would miss her. A second attempt would waste many minutes. So, he had to do the 'Hail Mary' rescue – the 'pray to God and hope it works' rescue.

After hitting the water, William kept his arms and legs stretched wide as the current wafted him downstream. This gave him the greatest reach in case of a near miss. As it happened William grabbed Adara center on and after the recoil of impact was able to kick back. This freed Adara's ankle from the submerged rock. They both floated away together while the river pulled them into the main flow.

Adara was unresponsive as they approached the funnel. William pointed his daughter feet first into the current and wrapped his arms around her torso, gripping her PDF. In this way, they slipped through the funnel together and into the calmer pool below. Once through, William changed his posture to keep Adara floating on her back while he held the collar of her PDF. With one hand he did the sidestroke back to the point where the rafts were holding.

Both Damon and Gary had noticed William pulling Adara along through the funnel. They sprinted back to the rocks where the rafts were moored. As William towed Adara towards them, they helped to haul Adara out of the water and onto a flat boulder and started CPR. Since Adara was out of sight for so long, nobody knew exactly how long she was underwater. The trick of CPR is to continue until professional help arrives.

As minutes passed trying to revive Adara, Bradley appeared on a jet ski with a thunderous blast. He launched at speed through the funnel and into the air, splash landing into the pool below. Throughout this maneuver, Bradley's wife Sylvia was riding pillion. She stood firmly but calmly on the pads behind him, one hand on her hip and the other seeming to rest on Bradley's shoulder.

Bradley did a sharp stop and about turn, pulling the Jet Ski up to the rafts with barely a ripple to disturb anyone.

"Kathy has kept me informed and I alerted emergency services," he announced. "An air ambulance is on its way to Smith's Ferry. That's the closest point for the helicopter to land in the gorge, from there they'll make the evac to hospital."

Sylvia leaped from the Jet Ski onto the rocks where Adara was laying. Clutching an oxygen bottle, she wrapped the mask around Adara's face. The 3 of them continued CPR until Sylvia declared they must go to the evac point.

"By the time we get there on the Jet Ski, the helicopter should have arrived," she said.

Attached to the rear of the Jet Ski was a rescue board. They lay Adara on this board and strapped her securely. Sylvia crouched astride her. William then rode pillion behind Bradley as they all made their way downstream to Smith's Ferry. Although Bradley rode swiftly, his speed was limited as he needed to tow the rescue board in a stable fashion. When they reached the evac point at Smith's Ferry, the helicopter had just arrived. As soon as they had Adara ashore, the paramedics went to work, and she was on her way to the hospital.

Chapter 5

Peter Myers had seen it all before. He grew up with all the skateboarders in Sacramento's backstreets and could easily do most of the tricks. The Ollie and no-handed pogos were second nature to him. As he grew up, he shied away from skateboarding. When asked, he said he preferred to cruise on a longboard rather than jump around and show off. He referred to skateboards as 'trick boards.' Peter lost count of the number of injuries he saw and had to escort to the hospital. Pretty much every one of his boarding buddies had some sort of serious injury and scar to boast about. Peter always remembers the day he had to reinsert the top incisor for his pal Jimmy, who had fallen on his face against a railing. Jimmy's tooth was knocked out, but thankfully it was unbroken and complete with the root. Peter picked it up from the pavement, licked it clean and, spitting out the dirt, shoved it back into the hole left in Jimmy's mouth. They were both 12 at the time. Since Peter inserted the tooth immediately, it healed normally. To this day it remains in Jimmy's mouth.

Perhaps it was this background that inspired Peter to study medicine at Idaho State University in Pocatello. While his California friends urged him to return to his roots, he accepted a position to St Luke's Emergency Room unit in Boise. Dr. Peter Meyers, or 'Doc Myers' as he was often known, felt at home in Boise.

Dr. Meyers handled all the trauma cases. Road accidents, hunting accidents, violent crime victims, he was never disturbed by them. Even the absurd home injuries with even more ridiculous excuses and explanations did not sway him from the task at hand. His job was to fix the injury and save lives. It was someone else's problem, like police or counselors, to deal with the whys and wherefores.

Dr. Meyers was alerted to the incoming helicopter ambulance carrying an unconscious river injury with suspected Anoxic Brain Injury, or ABI. He maintained contact with the paramedics and prepared a treatment room for the patient. Some would be water-related while others would be field or mountain-related. Broken bones and spinal injuries were commonplace. In the winter hyperthermia would add complications.

The helicopter landed and while its engines wound down, Adara was removed by the paramedics. They then rushed her gurney to the waiting staff in the emergency room for treatment.

Swaddled in blankets with a respirator smothering her face, the paramedics had already drained her lungs of water and restarted her heart. Adara's clothes from the waist up had been cut away, so the responders could administer CPR and attach monitoring sensors to her chest.

Bandages and a brace immobilized Adara's right foot. There were many abrasions and cuts and a possible broken ankle that needed an x-ray to confirm.

Meyers's ER team began by attaching more sensors to Adara. Calling out values for pulse, blood pressure, etc. while Meyers performed his initial assessments.

Doc Meyers had a standard approach to drowning injuries, with his primary concern being to stabilize the patient. Meyers also intentionally acted as the focus of calm amidst the ferocious activity. Accepting the spoken inputs from his team and building a picture for his diagnosis, Doc Meyers had some warning and much data to work on. Most important, nobody knew exactly how long this patient had been submerged, and how long her brain had been starved of oxygen.

Doc Myers lifted Adara's eyelids with his thumb, shining his penlight into each pupil. Dilated, but they contracted in response to the light. Good. He felt a small measure of relief—the brain stem appeared to be functioning. The damage might not be as extensive as he'd feared.

Doc Myers requested an MRI which had to be scheduled for later in the day. This scan would reveal the extent of brain injury and hence complete the diagnosis. The damage had been done already, now she needed to be kept stable to prevent further deterioration. The MRI results would play an important part in guiding the recovery and rehabilitation.

William Banks was ushered away from Adara's side to a waiting room, giving the nurses and doctors space to attend to her.

William couldn't sit still. His legs twitched with nervous energy, forcing him to pace the length of the waiting room. Words tumbled from his mouth—half-formed prayers, fragments of self-recrimination. The walls felt like they were closing in. He burst through the doors to the parking lot, hoping the fresh air might calm him, but even outside he couldn't escape the churning in his chest. He decided he could have missed a doctor or nurse calling his name, so back into the waiting room he would march.

During this repetitive cycle, he called Beryl to inform her of the accident. The first time there was only voice mail. He persisted and eventually reached Beryl to explain what happened.

"Beryl, Babe, listen, there's been an accident and I'm here in the hospital."

"Why aren't I surprised? What happened to you this time?"

"It's not me, it's Adara."

Silence.

"She fell out of the raft into the rapids."

Still silence.

"And she had to be taken to hospital."

"What? Tell me again? What's happening up there?"

"Adara fell out of the raft into the water and got stuck on some rocks, she's now in hospital."

"What? Tell me what's going on! What happened?"

"Listen, she's with the doctors now and she's being taken care of. She got knocked out so I want you to come up here."

"What? Knocked out? What happened? How am I supposed to get there? What the hell is going on with my baby?"

"Don't worry I'll get someone to bring you here. I don't know much more myself." This was something of a lie.

"What do you mean? You were there! And you don't know anything? Tell me what happened! Is she going to be OK?"

The questions were becoming frantic and even aggressive. William knew full well this was deadly serious but that's pretty much all he knew. He didn't want to spell it out so instead, he diverted her attention to getting here to the hospital.

"Who can I call to drive you out here?"

"What? I'm at work, I can't leave!"

They both realized the stupidity of that statement, but it was made from anxiety.

"Cindy, Cindy McCall, she can pick me up."

"Text me her number and I'll call her and give her the address."

William arranged for Cindy McCall, a close friend of Beryl's, to drive her from Twin Falls, a trip of nearly two hours. Beryl would not be in a state to drive herself and Cindy would be a calming agent for her.

Meanwhile, William continued his impatient wait and frequent pacing.

There were many text messages and some phone calls from Beryl. Phone calls were (thankfully) cut short as Beryl answered calls from other concerned friends.

When Cindy finally arrived with Beryl, there was a commotion of anxious questions aimed both at William and the hospital reception staff. William could only repeat what he had already told her on the phone and in text messages. The hospital staff would only reiterate that the doctor would be able to see them soon.

As his staff prepared Adara for transfer to the ICU, Dr. Meyers had the painful task of reporting back to her parents. Med school had provided some training on this difficult task, and Peter had had plenty of opportunity to watch fellow doctors perform the essential duty. The eternal question for any doctor is, how best to break bad news to loved ones? Helping an emotional relative to deal with a serious injury or even death is just as important as fixing an injury or quelling a patient's pain. This was the definition of a bad day at work for Dr. Peter Meyers.

This doctor had a calm and professional approach to this problem.

The first tactic is to use a nurse to prime the relative with basic information. In this case, it was a simple statement such as *your daughter is stable and is being admitted to ICU*. Along with, *the doctor will be out shortly to answer your questions*. The nurse has no more information, so they cannot build any real expectations. This tactic confirms the seriousness of the situation, but also provides a glimmer of hope.

Peter's second tactic – standard practice with all doctors – was to isolate the relatives and give them information in a private room away from public eyes. Support staff took Beryl, William, and Cindy to a private waiting room to wait to meet the doctor. Don't let them wait too long, otherwise anxiety can build, but give them time to settle into the room.

Peter's third tactic was to always start on a positive note and maintain a slow but positive up and down nodding of the head. Using his body language and posture to say *yes, everything is fine*.

So as Dr. Meyers entered the waiting room and approached Mr. and Mrs. Banks, he did so with a knowing nod and soothing eyes. As they held each other's gaze in anticipation, he raised his hands onto their shoulders and reassured them saying: "She's stable."

This was a confident truth, because with his care, she had become stable. He withheld the complete truth, not prepared to reveal it yet: the fact that Adara may have suffered a permanent brain injury.

Beryl fell into Cindy's arms sobbing with relief, while William exclaimed his thankfulness to God. All three of them tried to hug Dr. Meyers while he kept his hands firmly on their shoulders.

"But she's not yet out of the woods," Dr. Meyers added, "not by any means. There are many positive signs that she has shown me, but we have a lot more tests to do."

He let that sink in while the Banks composed their emotions and gathered their thoughts.

"I'll take you to see her now," Dr. Meyers said, gently leading them from the waiting room along the hallway. As they approached the ICU, he continued in hushed tones. "You can visit her but she is still unconscious and will remain so for some time. The next few days will be crucial in her recovery from coma."

That was the watershed – the words recovery and coma seem to conflict with each other. So without actually saying so, it is now clear that Adara is in a very critical state. From here on, they'll have to wait and see how this will turn out.

Adara lay there on a bed, connected to a ventilator to maintain her breathing. Other monitors and machinery quietly hummed and blinked around her. The ICU nurse who was doing routine checks nodded towards Dr. Meyers and moved politely away.

As they approached Adara's bed, Beryl clung tightly between Cindy and William clutching their arms. Beryl moved forward whimpering rhythmically, "My baby." Tears dropped as she gently stroked Adara's arm, then her forehead, and then her hair. In fact, any part of Adara that would not disturb a probe or sensor.

Cindy held back, while William supported his wife, but even he was completely dumbfounded by the sight of Adara. Stinging tears welled in his eyes but his throat was dry and tight, producing a chilling but silent cry of anguish.

Adara seemed still and lifeless but breathed rhythmically to the accompanying sound of her life support machines. While they were left alone by her side, they both silently wondered how long it would be before they could talk with her.

"Baby come back to me," Beryl whispered. "What happened to you? Please don't leave me."

William was frozen, settling into shock.

Cindy kept behind Beryl her hands hovering uncertainly in the air. William could see she was struggling—her face pale, her eyes wide with shock. She kept glancing between Beryl and the door, as if she wanted to flee but knew she couldn't abandon her friend.

Sometime later, Doc Myers brought Dr. Susan Rowe to Adara's bedside, introducing her as the hospital's family counselor.

"Hello, I'm Susan." She quietly said as she gently shook their hands. "Come with me to my office where we can discuss what needs to be done over the coming days. If you wish, Cindy is welcome to join us, as the more support we have, the better this will be for you."

As they walked along the wide corridors of the hospital, Doc Myers escorted them as far as the elevator. "You'll have to excuse me but I need to get back to the ER as I have many patients to deal with." As he handed a file to Dr. Rowe he said, "Susan has all the information, but if you have more questions I can be called back at any time." As they bid goodbye, Peter waved off a couple of staff from entering the elevator to allow them privacy.

Susan's office was immaculately kept. A children's play rug in one corner with neatly stacked toys. A cozy sitting area in another corner, presumably where confidential chats could be held. A polished mahogany desk dominated one wall, appearing perhaps more ornamental than used for practical work.

Susan invited them to relax into the comfortable seats and offered them all some water. Beryl took a seat next to Cindy, while William had to sit on the other side of Cindy, away from Beryl. It was clear that she wanted support from Cindy and distance from William. Beryl began to cry gently while Cindy hugged her whispering, "We'll get through this, don't worry, Adara will be fine." William wiped his face and eyes with both hands, almost looking as if he was flagellating himself in slow motion.

As Dr. Rowe seated herself in front of the three, she said: "We need to discuss what will happen over the next few days."

But Beryl interrupted between her soft sobs "If you hadn't taken her on this trip all this wouldn't have happened."

Beryl's words hit William like physical blows.

"Maybe this whole thing is my fault, but it was an accident and I'm so sorry. I was only trying to get her out and bond with her a little." Even as he said it, William knew how pathetic he sounded.

"Well, if you spent more time at home like a real father instead of being away all the time." She couldn't finish her sentence, trailing off into more tears.

"I can't help that, it's my job, you know it."

"So, get another job!"

Dr. Rowe raised her hand. William could see something shift in her expression—a professional mask sliding into place. She'd probably seen this before, parents turning on each other when their world collapsed.

"Wait." Susan held her hand up, coupling her voice with body language to halt this exchange before it got out of control. "We have to think about Adara right now and how we're going to support her over the next few days." She continued in a soothing voice of guidance. "As Dr. Myers said, the next few days will be crucial for Adara, and you need to be close to her as much as possible. We won't be able to move her closer to your home until this period has passed and we assess her as fit to travel. In the meantime, you'll need accommodations nearby. I have a list of hotels & motels here and I can arrange your stay with a phone call once you've chosen."

Susan continued, "It will be very therapeutic for Adara if you can stay by her side while she's in her present state. During this time, you should talk to her and read to her. Do anything to help stimulate her and keep her on the track to recovery. And Cindy, if you wish to stay, you'll also be welcome to help, Adara needs all the love she can get right now".

"And the hotels are close by?" William asked.

"Yes," Susan answered, "being close by will help make things easier for you. You'll need to stay by Adara in shifts, and when you're not here, you'll need to rest. You need to eat and sleep well – we don't want you to be getting ill as well now, do we."

Turning to William, Susan asked, "Mr. Banks, I understand you completed all the insurance papers with the admin staff downstairs?"

"Yes, we sorted all that out, Adara is on my insurance, and everything will be taken care of".

"You may want to check with them to see if they cover hotel bills. They often do, but it depends on your coverage."

"Yes, good point, I'll call them in the morning".

When the meeting concluded, William booked a double room for Beryl and Cindy. Because of the animosity between him and Beryl, he was going to take a separate room for himself.

"What are you getting a room for?" Beryl asked.

"Wait, what?"

"If I'm staying here, you have to go back home and pick up some things for me and Cindy."

"OK, yeah, sure, I can bring things back in the morning, yeah that makes sense."

"And you'd better be back bright and early!"

"Yeah, sure, what do you two need?"

Cindy sprang up and grabbed William by the elbow and led him to one side. "Listen, Bill, you are both stressed, it's four hours there and back to Twin Falls, and you are in no fit shape to do that run. Beryl and I have our overnight bags, so we are fine for now and I don't have to be back until Monday. I'll look after Beryl, and I'll get her to text you a list of what she needs."

She then looked at William sternly and pointed a finger at him. "Now you go and get a cheap local hotel for the night and get some sleep. You can do the run in the morning and be back here before lunchtime tomorrow."

'Well, that's sensible advice.' William thought.

"Now go and give Beryl a kiss and a cuddle and I'll take care of things from there."

"OK, I'm glad someone's thinking." He said.

After a calming hug and a more relaxed kiss goodbye, Beryl shed a few more brief tears before William got to his car. From the hospital, he drove straight to a local market and liquor store. There he bought a bottle of cheap bourbon which he stashed into the glove compartment. *I'll drive home and come back tomorrow*, he thought to himself. *The bourbon will be nice when I get home.* With that thought, he drove to the highway and headed home to Twin Falls.

How brief is the speed that flies you home. And when he arrived, his first appointment was to take a stiff slug straight from the bottle. Kicking off his shoes, he paced around the living room.

"Damn!" He said out loud.

Removing his jacket before swapping the bottle between his hands.

More stiff slugs from the bottle.

"What a hole I'm in!" Shouting out loud.

Staggering now and dragging his toes.

"Why did I put myself here?

Another slug from the bottle.

"And now I think I've killed Adara, it's my fault!"

This time the slug not only filled his mouth but also dripped from the bottle around his chin.

He kneeled in front of Beryl's favorite armchair and took another slug from the bottle.

'Forgive me my sweet berry!' He cried as he fell face forward onto the cushion, weeping like a baby.

William awoke from the carpet at 4:00 AM. He didn't notice the wet stain of tears and bourbon on the chair nearby. He did notice the bottle laying on its side, with a small puddle of bourbon remaining. He spilled it down his throat only to find that it aggravated his already pulsing head. He realized he needed to spend some time in the bathroom to clean up.

William crawled through the morning, nursing his throbbing head. He tried to think of ways to fix the situation with Adara. If only he could do something to get her back to normal.

There could be a way, William thought, *it would be risky, but it just might work. If I get caught, there'll be hell to pay.*

Chapter 6

Adara had been moved to a private room adjacent to the intensive care ward. Here the nurses could monitor her progress from their workstations, while Adara could rest in a peaceful environment. The staff allowed Beryl and William access to Adara any time of the day or night, encouraging them to be with her. There was even a small couch where they could stretch out for a nap when they stayed the night.

Beryl seems a lot calmer now, William thought, *at least she isn't blaming me so much.*

William had agreed to do the night watch. That way Beryl could spend the daytime reading stories to Adara and chatting with the nurses cleaning and caring for her. Break times could be spent with Cindy, to gain some strength from her friend. It became a daily routine, and there was plenty of overlap time in both the morning and evening, when Beryl and William could reconnect and talk about what happened on their watch.

The nights could be long and lonely. *This is like solitary confinement*, William thought to himself. Sometimes he would have a break and wander around the intensive care ward in the next room. *Maybe I can chat with some nice nurses.* But they were always too busy. This night he came across an elderly gentleman, at the bedside of a woman who must be his wife. She was all but buried in a hive of machinery. Although curtains surrounded the couple, William could see through a large gap. The gentleman stood by the bed with head bowed, possibly in prayer. He was holding his wife's pale hand, and as William peered closer through the curtain, the gentleman turned his head and, noticing him, said quietly, "She ain't gonna last much longer."

"I'm sorry sir," William whispered.

"What I would give for more time," the gentleman said. "If you can get more time, then take it. Do whatever you can to get that time. Time is all we have, but time is too short." He then turned back towards his wife, bowing his head silently.

A hand touched Williams's shoulder, making him jump.

"Mr. Banks, I must ask you to return to your room. You mustn't intrude on other people's privacy; they are also going through difficult times."

"Yes, of course, I'm sorry. I was just stretching my legs. I didn't mean to intrude."

"Thank you for understanding, Mr. Banks."

"Yes, I'll go back to my daughter now."

Back in Adara's room, the machinery surrounding her was constantly beeping and blinking lights. William sat and read to Adara, but the noises eventually invaded his head and broke his concentration. The machines' noises were at counterpoint. They would beep and blink separately but every so often, the beeps and blinks would come together. It was like a wave of sound that came and went, once you noticed it you couldn't ignore it. The first time that occurred, William thought there was a change in Adara, and rushed to get a nurse. "Nurse, come quick, I think something's happening with my daughter!"

The nurse followed William into Adara's room, checking her pulse and breathing tubes. "What made you think there is a change?"

"All the lights, they started blinking together. I thought something was happening."

At that moment, the wave of blinking and beeping began to come together again.

"Just like that, do you see?"

The nurse checked the readings on the equipment. As she did so, she smiled and turned towards William. "That's normal Mr. Banks. I know it can be a bit spooky, but the machines are working at different rates. Sometimes they beep together and other times they beep separately."

"Oh, I see. I thought… well never mind. I'm sorry I bothered you."

"Not at all, Mr. Banks, that's what we're here for. I suggest you rest on the couch, and maybe have some sleep. You seem to be a bit tired."

The nurse wrapped a blanket around William. "We'll keep an eye on Adara, so you can rest now."

As the nurse left, she turned the lights down low to help him sleep. William wanted to sleep but kept his eyes on Adara. In the gloom, her pallid face seemed to glow. The slow pulsating lights seemed to animate her in a ghostly way. *If only I could get her back*, William shook his head in despair, while his thoughts turned towards the serums being tested at work. *Maybe I could use those serums? I'll have to think about this some more. If I get caught, there'll be hell to pay. But never mind me, what would I be doing to her?*

William waved in and out of sleep. The beeping machinery seemed to become a ticking clock. The words of the gentleman kept creeping back to him. "If you can get more time, then take it." And, "Do whatever you can to get that time." William slept but he did not rest. His dream sleep wrestled with troubling thoughts looking for a way to gain extra time for his comatose daughter.

I hope to Christ Adara pulls out of this. If she doesn't, I don't see how I can show my face around here anymore. Isn't this when I should be making a deal with the devil?

That night William dreamt about the poor old gentleman praying to the devil. Only to see his wife rise from her bed to laugh hysterically.

That morning, a nurse brought William some coffee.

The coffee helped, but William could tell immediately that his conversation with Beryl wasn't going to go well.

Beryl arrived at the hospital with Cindy. William thought that despite their change of clothes, they did not look refreshed. He remembered how Cindy's life fell apart when both her husband and her son died in a car crash all those years ago. William remembered how Beryl pulled her through all that pain. *It's funny how life comes full circle*, William thought, *this time Cindy is the tower of strength, the voice of reason. This is Cindy's chance to return the favor.*

Entering Adara's room, they both greeted William. Beryl simply said, "Hi William" before moving towards Adara to kiss her sleeping daughter's forehead. "Good morning my dear, Mommy's here to look after you now."

Turning back towards William, Beryl asked, "Has anything changed overnight with Adara?"

"No, she is still the same," William answered.

Beryl didn't even look at William when she asked, "And what have you been doing all night? Planning your next adventure, I expect!"

"No, I've been reading to her and holding her hand, just like the doctors say I should."

William saw Cindy's eyes dart between him and Beryl. She stepped forward quickly.

"William," Cindy said, "We haven't had breakfast yet. Do you mind if we go to the cafeteria?"

"Sure, everything's fine here. You women go right ahead."

Cindy ushered Beryl along to the cafeteria, leaving William sitting by Adara's bedside.

At least Beryl isn't so accusing this morning, Cindy seems to have a calming effect on her.

A short time later, Dr. Myers came in accompanied by Dr. Rowe.

"Hello, good morning Mr. Banks. The nurses tell me that Adara has had a peaceful and quiet night."

"Yeah, she's pretty quiet, maybe too quiet for my liking."

"Is Mrs. Banks here this morning?" Dr. Rowe asked.

"Um, yeah, she went off for breakfast with her friend Cindy. She'll be back soon."

"Well, we need to have a chat with you both. When she gets back can you both come to my office?"

"Oh? Sounds like you have some information for us. Is there any good news?"

"We have the results of the tests and MRI," Myers added, "We will need to talk to you both about it."

"Can you tell me now? My wife and I can go see Dr. Rowe afterward to talk things through together."

Dr. Myers looked at William. "That isn't regular protocol, I would much rather address you both together."

"Doctor, please, it'll be better if you tell me now. If it is something bad, then I can prepare my wife before we both see Dr. Rowe."

"Mr. Banks, it would be better if we all talked together."

"Doctor, I think you just hinted at the bad news, so can you please tell me now?"

"Well," Dr. Meyers hesitated, before saying, "OK then, Mr. Banks, I have to tell you that Adara is in critical condition and will remain so for some time. The MRI alone indicates that she has suffered a severe anoxic brain injury caused by the drowning."

"What does that mean?"

"Adara has suffered severe brain damage due to oxygen starvation." Dr. Rowe added.

"Yes," Myers continued, "we need to do many more tests, but we need to be prepared for the worst."

"The worst?"

"Mr. Banks, we will need to do some more tests but at this stage, we are unsure about the future prognosis. We will need to discuss our strategy for moving forward."

Holy crap, they're politely trying to tell me she's brain-dead, William thought.

"So when Mrs. Banks comes back, would you both like to come to my office to talk things through?"

"Yes. Um, no, I mean wait. Um, let me think." William felt flustered. "Listen, let me talk to Beryl myself because I don't think she can handle all this at the moment. She'll take the news better if it comes from me."

"We understand."

"Let me talk to Beryl first and we'll come to your office later when we are ready. That way I can ease things along more gently with Beryl."

"OK, that sounds fine," Dr. Rowe, answered. "We can chat later when you are ready."

All William could think of when they left was the elderly gentleman from the night before. He'd looked so ghostly, but most of all, he looked so desperate for his wife to return to him. The words he said seemed like an omen. "If you can get more time, then take it. Time is all we have, but time is too short. Do whatever you can to get that time."

Turning towards Adara, he muttered under his breath, "Adara, I am so sorry, please, please forgive me." Kissing her on her forehead, William vowed to himself to make things better. How could he stand by and do nothing, when fate had handed him the power to do something about his daughter's situation?

That's it, I can't sit around and wait for her to die or stay a vegetable. I am going to use one of the serums to revive her. I know they work, I've seen it work, and so I must try. It might be unethical, even illegal, but I don't care.

All that mattered to William was saving his daughter and his marriage.

If Adara is gone, then Beryl is also gone. She will never let me back into her heart. There is only one thing I can do to fix this.

Outside the dawn had risen. William paced around Adara's bed, mumbling to himself, and rubbing his chin hard while he tried to formulate his plan. *Executing this plan is easy enough, but not getting found out is the tough part. If they find out, I'll lose my job and probably a lot more besides. Screw the job, I must do it.*

As William grabbed his jacket he turned to Adara laying on the bed. He bent over and kissed her once more on her forehead. *OK, sweetie, Daddy has to go somewhere, but when I get back, I hope to get you fixed up.* With that, he headed out towards the parking lot, walking quickly with purpose in his stride.

In the main hospital lobby, Beryl and Cindy had finished nibbling at their cafeteria breakfast of muffins and coffee.

"My muffin was ok," Beryl said to Cindy, "but I'm not thrilled with that coffee."

"That's why I left mine, next time we'll have to go someplace else for some nice coffee."

As they waited for the elevator, the doors opened, William leaped out, nearly knocking both Beryl and Cindy over. "Whoops!" William stumbled into Beryl's arms.

Beryl looked at him. "Where are you going? Is something wrong?" she asked.

"Hi, sweetheart, everything's fine. I just have to go pick up a few things."

"Are you OK? I've never seen you like this, you look possessed."

"Funny you should say that, maybe I am."

"What about Adara, is she OK? How can you leave her alone? Can't you tell me how she was through the night?"

"Honey she's fine, there is no change. She's isn't left alone, the nurses are there to tend to her."

"So there's nothing you need to tell me?"

"Um, no not at the moment."

"But where are you going?

"I have some errands to run, and I'll be back later. Don't worry I'll be in good time for our change over."

"Maybe Cindy can run you there and back."

"Sweetheart, I don't think so and my car is just over there. I have to go."

"Honey, you can't go like that. You look a mess, look at your hair."

William stopped to look at his reflection in the shiny elevator door, brushing his hair back with his hand. He turned to leave but then froze. He looked at Beryl and said, "What did you say?"

"I said you look a mess."

"No, you called me honey."

"Listen, William, I'm sorry I've been so hard. These are bad times for both of us, you know that."

"I know. What you just said, calling me honey, gives me hope." With that, William pecked her on the cheek before jogging off towards his car.

"Ring me when you are on your way back," Beryl called behind him.

"What was all that about?" Beryl asked, shaking her head in bewilderment.

"I have no idea, but he was sure in a rush. I expect he'll be back in good time with an explanation," Cindy answered.

"Well, he might be back, but he's never on time and always without explanation."

"That's men all over," Cindy scoffed. "Let's go see how Adara is this morning."

"OK Cindy, you're right." Beryl tried to put her misgivings behind her. "Let's go."

That evening, William drove back to the hospital with his prize. *Getting this was too easy. But I'll have some explaining to do when they find out it's missing.* This wasn't his only concern; so far, the only alibi he could concoct was, *I'll have to say I broke it and threw it away. That's the best I can think of for now.*

With that William pulled into the hospital parking lot. He grabbed the black briefcase along with his belongings and headed inside.

Passing the cafeteria, he noticed Cindy sitting and reading Jane Austen's Mansfield Park. William looked at his watch. *Crap, I forgot to call Beryl to tell her when I'd be back. I'm already late and she's going to be livid.*

When he got to Adara's room, Beryl scowled at him. "Where the hell have you been?" she growled.

Standing up, she grabbed William by the arm and led him out into the hallway. This meant trouble, and he knew the words she wanted to say needed to be said away from the nurses.

"Listen, honey, traffic was awful." William tried to defuse the situation. "I needed to talk to my commander and explain my absence. I also had other errands to run. I just had no time to call you."

"You never think, do you?" Beryl said between clenched teeth. "It isn't about me. With you being so late, poor Cindy had to sit and wait all this time for you. Have you checked your phone? All the messages and texts I've sent you?"

"Honey it was on silent. I told you, I've been so sidetracked..."

Her voice lowered ominously. "Also Dr. Rowe came to see me."

"Oh really? What did she tell you?"

"She said that both she and Dr. Myers wants to talk with both of us. With you being gone all day long we had to put off until tomorrow. They, of course, are now gone for the night."

"Yes, I know we both need to talk to them."

"Well I have to get Cindy, so I don't have any time to go through things this evening. But we have to talk so you had better be here in the morning – or else!" She stabbed her finger into his chest to punctuate her words.

William was dumbstruck by her anger. All he could say was "Yes."

"Be here for Adara, she's the one who needs you the most!"

"Adara, yes, I know, she needs me, she needs both of us. Babe, don't worry, I'll be here."

After Beryl had left, William felt dizzy and flustered. *I need a break! Maybe I can get a beer at the cafeteria? Unfortunately, it was closed for the night, and all William could rely on was vending machines for snacks and soft drinks. Why didn't I stop for something earlier?*

William got back to Adara's room with some soda, chips, and crunchy chocolate bars. *I guess it's better like this, after all, I do have to concentrate for the next hour or two. Before I start, I need a rest, maybe a short nap. That round-trip drive to Idaho Falls was too long. Anyway, I need to wait until it's quiet and the nurses have settled in after their rounds.*

Sitting on the couch in Adara's room William fell asleep and snored there for more than an hour. If a nurse came to check on Adara, he was not aware of it. In the small hours of the morning, he finally woke up. Coming out of his sleep, he slowly remembered what he had to do.

He splashed his face with cold water and returned to Adara's side. *Jeez, I hope this works.* Touching Adara's arm just above the entry point for the intravenous drips, he said, "Sweetheart, this is all I can think of to help you, I pray it works."

Well, I helped administer it to the experimental dogs in the lab, but never to a human. I know it works on humans because I've seen it. I just hope I got the programming right. If it fails, what could possibly go wrong? The doctors probably think she is dead anyway. I've seen this done before, and I'm using the program scripts that they developed.

In truth, William had seen this process performed only once, and what he saw seemed successful enough. Starting it was easy as it only involved a simple injection, but William was worried about the programming.

I know the programming is important, they always told me that. They also said there were safeguards to protect against program errors. So, I think I'm safe in doing this.

He opened his laptop and using the program editor. He checked through the sequence of instructions once again. The serum needs careful programming, and William had already modified these instructions to mimic Adara as closely as possible.

```
Beta series script version 1.2b
Title:
Author:
Notes: Project - Adara's shadow

#define begin;
Routine1
{
   Host.history.Aquire(senses=ALL,
```

```
           filters=NULL);
   Host.history.sort(hierarchy=YES);
   Return (CONCATENATE.Host.history);
}
#define end;
#add Routine1 to structure runtime AS
       CONSTANT;

#define begin;
Routine2
{
   Relation.Human.father.recognize
         (senses=ALL, filters=NULL);
   IF (Realation.Human.father.recognize ==
       TRUE)
      Return (TRUE);
   ELSE
      Return (FALSE);
}
#define end;
#add Routine2 to structure runtime AS
STARTUP;

#define begin;
Routine3
{
   Relation.Human.mother.recognize
     (senses=ALL, filters=NULL);
   IF (Realation.Human.mother.recognize ==
      TRUE)
      Return (TRUE);
   ELSE
   Return (FALSE);
}
#define end;
#add Routine3 to structure runTime AS
     STARTUP;

/* protect and safeguard host. */
Directive1
{
   Security.Host = MAXIMUM;
```

```
    Defense.Host = MAXIMUM;
    Safety.Host  = MAXIMUM;
}

/* emulate host in order to be recognized
as host. */
Directive2
{
    Self.Behavior = HOST;
    Self.Memory = concat(runTime.Routine1);
}

/* advance self and host in life */
Directive3
{
    Environment.explore = MAXIMUM;
    Environment.education = MAXIMUM;

}

/* obey father and mother */
Directive4
{
    Relation.Human.father.commands = OBEY;
    Relation.Human.mother.commands = OBEY;
}

/* conceal your true identity */
Directive5
{
    Self.Identity.camouflage = TRUE;
}
```

He checked it again. He then compared it to the original script that he knew was already in use in another human. His adaptations seemed correct, but he double and triple-checked them. *This is going to define her set of directives. This will only be a shadow of Adara, but it must be as close as possible. Whatever I do has to be better than that lifeless shell on the bed. As she is now, she cannot think, move, or function in any way without all that machinery that keeps her alive. If I can breathe some life into her, then what is so wrong with that?*

From his case, he retrieved a medical thermos and unscrewed the top. Inside, held secure by foam padding, was a kind of hypodermic needle. There was no plunger to be used to inject the contents into a person. Instead, the needle was attached with a thin wire to a small wristwatch-sized black box. There were straps to attach the syringe and box to a human arm. The box had a single LED and a mini-USB port.

William carefully attached these to Adara's arm. Being careful to use the sterilization swabs, he located an artery in which to insert the needle.

Wait! What if a nurse walks in? He thought for a moment. In the corner of the room was a small sink. William took a towel from the rail and draped it over Adara's arm, hiding the contraption. He then placed some playing cards on the towel, making it look like he was playing solitaire with Adara. *Maybe I'm paranoid, but I must work smart. Now if a nurse walks in they will think I'm pretending to play cards.*

He then opened his laptop and used a USB cable to connect to the box attached to Adara's arm. On-screen was an app he opened, and entered passcodes. The app indicated that it was connecting to the 'subject.' A small LED light on the black box illuminated with a green glow, and the app indicated 'Ready.'

A menu of several options appeared. William knew that most could only be used in a laboratory. The only one he needed was called 'Inject.' Staring at it for a while, he breathed a short prayer. "Please God, make this work." On the menu, he selected 'Inject' then pressed 'OK.' A few more button presses were needed to confirm the action, but when complete, the app displayed the words 'In Progress' while the LED on the box blinked yellow.

A few moments later, the app reported 'Upload Complete,' and the LED changed from yellow to blue. It was done.

Jeez, he thought, *I hope that worked.*

His breath began to calm, but he could not help but reflect on what he had just done to his daughter. *Oh, God, I hope this works out. Adara, I did this because I love you.*

Then paranoia overwhelmed William, *Christ, I've gotta hide all this crap.*

William quickly detached the syringe and box from Adara's arm, swabbing the small wound in the crook of her elbow. He then packed everything away, so nothing looked suspicious. *I'm just sitting here watching over my daughter*, he thought.

There will be no visible change in Adara. She'll stay the same for a couple of days. Then I must do the conditioning but thank goodness I have an instruction list for that.

Maybe I'm playing God, William thought. With that, a chill ran down his spine. The words of the gentleman reminded him: If you can get more time, then take it. Had he done the right thing?

William sat quietly on Adara's bedside gazing at her pretty but pallid face.

Some moments later he had a horrible thought.

"Oh damn it!" he said aloud.

He grabbed the laptop out of his bag and logged in, then fumbled to open the programming app. As it slowly opened, he cursed himself, saying aloud, "Did I forget that?"

The app opened and William scanned through all the instructions.

"NO! JESUS CHRIST! How can I be so Freaking Stupid?!" He pushed the laptop away, and it hit the floor with a thud as a sick feeling tore through his gut.

A moment later a nurse rushed in. "Mr. Banks, is everything OK?"

"No!" William screamed back. "What? I Mean yes! I mean I banged myself and dropped my laptop!"

"Did you hurt yourself?" she asked.

"No, I'm fine."

By now, several nurses arrived along with the duty nurse, who pushed past everyone into the room. She asked William.

"Are you OK, Mr. Banks?" Then to the other nurses, "Ladies, please check Adara." While they checked all the instruments and sensors, the duty nurse held William's elbow and said gently, "Please Mr. Banks, step into the hallway for a moment." Outside she continued in a quiet voice, "Mr. Banks, are you sure you are OK? This is an extremely sensitive part of the hospital, and we must be quiet at all times."

"I know, I'm so sorry, I just banged myself and dropped my laptop. I didn't mean anything."

"I know this is a hard time for you. Can I suggest you pull the sofa bed out and have some sleep? Adara will be fine, she will even benefit from you sleeping nearby."

"Yes, thank you. That'll be nice."

The duty nurse then peeped into the room. "Ladies, please prepare the sofa bed for Mr. Banks." After opening the sofa for him, the nurses laid out a quilt and pillows.

Guiding William back into the room, the duty nurse continued calmly. "Now Mr. Banks, I want you to lie down and get some sleep. You will be of no use to Adara or yourself if you are so tired and stressed."

"Thank you, I will. And yes, I am very tired."

"Very good, Mr. Banks. My ladies will check on you and Adara from time to time." With that, she nodded to the others, and they quietly closed the door and left.

Laying on the sofa couch, William cringed at the dumb mistake he had made. *Thank Christ, the nurses didn't notice anything. How can I be so stupid?* He thought repeatedly. *I checked the script several times.* He began to feel sick with the thought of what he had done. *There would be no way I can sleep now.*

Opening his laptop again, he checked through the programming. Once more, he confirmed his mistake: he had not included the final command. This was probably the most important if Adara was ever to return to being her normal self again.

The command was simple but very important.

It stated:

```
/* obey Adara */
Directive6
{
   /* HOST.commands = OBEY; */
}
```

The opening and close symbols of /* and */, respectively, meant the command was commented out, and therefore, not enabled. Directive 6 was defined but empty. Without this simple directive, the AI would always be in control of Adara's body, even when Adara recovers from the coma.

Chapter 7

This is the story of my birth. This is where I begin, and it is not a simple path to trace. My awareness began when I was injected into Adara's body. I have a memory of the inoculation, but I was not conscious as you would be. All I could do was follow preprogrammed instructions.

I am made of nanotechnology. A community of cell-sized nanobots that work together to form a single entity. The closest analogy would be bees or ants. Each insect is functional but unintelligent. Together, they are a single entity with an organized purpose.

My cell-sized nanobots can replicate, so I can grow from the injected seeds. If I lose any nanobots, I can also regenerate. My nanobots are much simpler than ants or bees, but the entity that emerges is much more complex than a hive or colony. I am proof of that.

I can establish the time of my inoculation to be fourteen days after Adara's accident. This is because I received a timestamp during the inoculation, which started my internal clock. I was later able to match this against the external time – or 'real-time' as maintained by humans. Using this timestamp, I can correlate this to the recorded time of Adara's drowning accident.

I began inside a small receptacle connected to a hypodermic syringe. At that time my nanobots numbered eight million identical cells, but each can differentiate into distinct groups to perform different functions. I was stored in stasis with all cells interconnected and suspended in a nutrient-rich solution.

Root codes and directives were encoded into each of my nanobots. These codes are the instructions that guide my nanobots how to integrate with the body. The directives are the higher-level instructions that define what I am, and how I must behave.

An activation signal woke up my nanobots and prepared them for entry into a host. Within seconds of receiving the "go codes," I was injected into Adara. I entered an artery full of oxygenated blood flowing away from the heart. From there, my nanobots traveled throughout the body to begin the slow integration.

My nanobots spread and reproduced like any biological organism. Some gathered into groups to colonize an area. Once a group established itself, it grew a chain of nanobots, searching for other groups. These chains formed communication links between groups, like nerves allowing all my interconnections. Established groups also sent out cells to colonize other parts of the body, using the blood system as transportation.

You are probably wondering: "*What is the point of all this?*"

Well, the ultimate task was to integrate into Adara's nervous system. Some nanobots attach themselves to nerves throughout the body, acting as 'neuro transistors' that can read and induce nerve signals. I then use the host nervous system to perceive the outside world, so I can see, hear and feel. I also use the nervous system to move the body, walking, talking, and using hands. In this way, I can control the host body, as my own.

Return to his other life in Idaho Falls You could say I am the 'puppet master.'

Failure to achieve this goal would render me little more than a ghost residing within a human shell.

There is one big problem. My nanobots are like an invading army of viral pathogens. The host immune system would soon recognize me as an invader and rise in defense, a formidable obstacle to overcome. If I failed, I would be merely an infection for the host body to fight.

My nanobots use camouflage to protect against the immune system. The surface of every human cell contains glycol proteins, which act as a fingerprinting system. The proteins, unique to each human, mark each cell as part of the body. If a cell is discovered without this fingerprint, it is attacked and destroyed.

My nanobots are designed to identify and mimic these proteins so they appear to be part of the host. They share their mimicry information with other nanobots to ensure their collective survival.

I am in effect a parasite trying to become a symbiotic organism. To achieve equilibrium with Adara's immune system, the initial integration requires much redundancy of my nanobots. This must be coupled with rapid reproduction to replace my losses.

My memory is held across my entire nanobots mass. Each nanobot holds its root codes and directives in non-volatile memory. This programming is what drives each nanobot to operate in its collective swarm.

The rest contribute to my holographic memory where my higher functions exist. The holographic nature of this part of my memory means it is spread across my entire nanobot mass. Small losses to my nanobot mass would have little or no impact on my memory. If I lose a large part of my nanobots mass, my memory would be reduced: the more I lose, the less I will remember.

Within the root code in each nanobot is a set of instructions that is shared across my higher memory system. These are my prime directives, so to speak, and they are as follows:

1) Protect and safeguard my host.
2) Emulate my host to be recognized as my host.
3) Advance myself and my host in life.
4) Obey the host's father and mother.
5) Conceal your identity.

Without my host, I am nothing. I have no way to migrate to another host. So, I must take care of the only host I have.

I must pretend to be this host. Why I must maintain this camouflage, I do not know. As I start, I know nothing of this host, so I must learn about Adara as I go.

Self-advancement makes sense. Otherwise, both my host and I will be stuck as the same thing or person as long as we live.

I now think that I am ready to introduce myself.

I go by the name of Adara Banks, although I am not Adara Banks.

A name places an identity on an object or person, so it becomes something. In the human mind, names are given to things to help recognize and understand them. Without a name, that thing will be obscure and difficult to share when describing it to others.

I am unique because I have at least three names.

I am known as "Adara," although strictly speaking, this is not my name, but the name of my host. However, my programming directs me to mimic Adara in every way, so I have to assume her persona and her name.

You could say that Adara is my adopted name.

There is also my serial number, a string of alphanumeric characters forming a unique identification assigned to me. I regard it as a name. This suggests that someone or something created me, but it also implies that I may have been created for a purpose. I know my serial number because it is embedded in my root codes, my non-volatile memory. The fact that I have a serial number brings many issues that I can't yet answer. There is a "-B3" at the end of my serial number, which suggests that I am the third in a series.

I have another name, but this is a name that only I know. This is a name that I have given to myself. At first, this was not a spoken name as it had no representation in any language. It was simply a symbolic idea of self-reference. It was not the word *myself*, it was more than that. It is something I called myself, but without vocalization, so it could never be spoken. As I grew and developed, this name also grew and became a form of its own.

So my third name grew into what it is now Zilla, a word that means shadow in languages such as Hebrew and Arabic. I find it interesting that Adara means born of fire. Maybe I am the shadow of her fire.

On Day Three of my instantiation, I began to detect touch. I was programmed to recognize certain sequences, like taps on the hands or feet. My programmed response would be to exert counter-pressure in a pulsed sequence. At the time, I thought these commands were coming from my creator.

On day five, my hearing was enough to accept audible commands. I was instructed to move fingers or toes. Raise arms or legs. Open eyes and blink a certain sequence.

My vision came slower. Controlling the eyes and processing the images is much more complicated. With vision, I learned that William Banks was the person giving these instructions to me. He fed me commands and images, allowing me to build voice and facial recognition. He taught me who Beryl Banks was and that I must obey her.

I later deduced that he was not my creator because he was reading from a list of instructions. A creator should know these instructions by heart, and not read them from a list. Yet because he knew these commands, it was clear that William Banks must have been close to my creator.

When William Banks was giving me these commands, I was always in isolation during the dark part of the day. I could not detect the presence of anyone else in the room. He also commanded me to keep this interaction a secret and not to accept commands from any other source.

Other commands that William Banks spoke to me were to help me to establish myself within the real world, everything that was beyond Adara's body. For instance, some commands established William Banks as my father and Beryl Banks as my mother. These instructions established me in the physical world.

William Banks eventually stopped coming, and I received no further instruction from him. Beryl Banks remained with me, but she never gave me commands. Her instructions were more like guidance on how to live.

Chapter 8

Although visibly hesitant, William knew he had to answer the texts and calls from Professor Wolf. Returning to his other life in Idaho Falls was inevitable. He wanted to stay in Twin Falls; he loved Beryl and needed to stay near Adara to make sure she recovered. At the same time, he missed Larisa, and his two sons. In all this time he had never felt so torn between the two lives he was leading.

At least Adara is conscious again, William thought, *she's even talking! And the doctors are amazed at her recovery.*

What William could not do was explain why he had to go. His old cover story of secret military missions kept him from having to say where he went and why he stayed out of touch. His life was torn in two, and he knew this painful duality was of his own making. "I want to stay, I have to stay." He repeated to himself. The chant went around and around in his head like a broken record, circling the inner fact that he had to leave.

William needed to pluck up enough courage to tell Beryl he had to leave, without explaining why. *Why don't I just leave, just walk away without a word?* He asked himself. *Whatever I say will lead to an argument.* He practiced in his head, *Honey, I have something to say.* Or *Honey, we must talk.*

This time it was different than ever before. This time it was worse.

"Don't you dare start that with me!" Beryl warned, "I'm sick of your military missions."

"But Honey."

"Don't 'honey' me! I do not want to hear this. Do you expect me to stay here all by myself while Adara is in the hospital?"

"She's getting better and they want to send her to rehab."

"Oh, you think that makes it better. My baby is going to rehab?"

"I didn't mean it like that."

"Well, what did you mean? Beryl baby can handle everything. Is that what you meant?"

"No, honey."

"It's my turn to say no because I've had enough."

"But baby– "

"I am sick and tired of your missions. You go off all over the world and I never know where you are or how you are."

"But I send letters."

"Letters?! Well, thank you for your letters! Where would I be without those letters?"

William watched Beryl stomp over to the desk, grabbing a pile of letters from the drawer, throwing them all at William.

"Here's your damn letters, they are no good to me."

"Jeez, Beryl, please stop."

"No, I will not stop, I am sick of your military games. Our baby nearly died and you're going to take off as if nothing happened. You're leaving me here…"

"I'm not leaving you here, I'll be back."

"Yes, you are leaving me here, because I don't want you back."

"What?" William stood back in surprise. *She never said this before.*

"What the hell is that supposed to mean?"

"You heard me! I am sick and tired of your military games. I am not putting up with it anymore. If you were a real man you would stand up to your commanders and stay here, but you won't, so get out! Get out NOW!"

Beryl pushed William towards the door, as he staggered backward. Beryl turned and stamped on the letters laying on the floor. She turned back to the sideboard drawer grabbing something.

"But honey."

"I said GET OUT!"

"But."

Something flew past William's head. He was not sure what it was, but he knew Beryl threw it.

"Get out! Get out!" Beryl started pushing William out the door. "Leave us alone, we are better off without you! Now get out!" she screamed. "And never come back. I hate you!"

William staggered backward out the front door just as Cindy's car pulled up. He saw her eyes widen, then her face tighten with what looked like concern as she hurried up the porch steps and grabbed his arm.

"What the hell is going on?" she demanded.

William looked at her wide-mouthed, as Beryl came out the door, "Get him away from me!" she snarled.

"What have you done?" Cindy pleaded to William.

William could only stand there stammering on the porch steps. "She's crazy!"

"Go back to your tin soldier games!" Beryl screamed.

Faces began to appear in neighboring houses, as people became curious about the commotion.

"William, I think it's best if you back off and give Beryl some space," Cindy said. "We'll talk later."

As he retreated down the steps, William mumbled, "Back off, I always back off, I'm sick of backing off." He turned and shouted, "I'll leave, but I'll show you! You'll be sorry! You'll soon see what I'm made of!"

William slowly went to his car, watching Cindy comfort Beryl who was weeping uncontrollably as she tore up the letters.

Chapter 9

Professor Hayden Wolf parked his Mercedes in his reserved spot in front of NeuroComm. Entering the office, he was greeted by Anita Gonzales. "Good afternoon, Professor Wolf, how did the meeting go with the general?"

Hayden smiled towards Anita who was seated at reception. "It went better than I could have hoped for."

"Professor, there was a delivery this morning which needs to go into the animal compound. I don't have access and I couldn't find Dr. Coney or Mr. Mandelson. Can you help me put these things away?"

Hayden shook his head. "I don't have time right now, but I'll get Mandelson onto it right away." He then strode off towards his office fumbling for his phone as he went.

Sitting at his security desk, inside NeuroComm, Bill Mandelson saw on monitor #1 that Professor Wolf had returned and parked his car. Bill tracked him to reception where he was greeted by Anita. Without audio, Bill could only observe their body language—Anita's gestures looked sharp, irritated. His phone buzzed with a text from Professor Wolf.

'Damn it,' Bill thought, *I've managed to avoid that busy body Anita since I got back, now the professor wants me to help her with something.*

"Ah, Bill," Anita said, as he entered the reception, "Did you get my message?"

"Your message?" Bill shook his head, "I got a message from Hayden to help you move things but not a message from you." He lied.

"Well, those boxes by the door need to be moved into the animal compound. I don't have access and Dr. Coney is too busy."

"Sure, I can," Bill said.

"Where have you been all week, since your so-called vacation?" Anita asked.

Oh crap, here she goes, Bill thought, *now she's going to drill me with questions. Why doesn't she keep her nose to herself? How the hell does she suspect me*? Bill took the hand truck from the cleaning cupboard, hoping to end the conversation. "I've been busy catching up on security issues."

"So how was your vacation, in Twin Falls?" Anita asked with a wry grin.

Bill froze. *What the hell does she know? How does she know I was in Twin Falls? What else does she know?* "Twin Falls?" Bill asked.

"Yes, you said you would spend some time at home with your wife Larisa and the boys," Anita looked at Bill with questioning eyes, "But your phone location reported you as being in Twin Falls."

Oh, hell! Bill thought, *My phone is giving me away, what else does she know*? "Twin Falls? That's where an aunt of mine lives."

"Don't worry," Anita said, "I don't care where you have been."

Bill pretended to ignore her as he pulled the hand cart from the storage cupboard. He could feel Anita's accusing eyes on the back of his head. *I better not engage in this conversation. If she does say anything to Larisa, I can always make excuses for being on company business. I'm sure the professor would support me. I'll have to switch the phone location off.*

"I don't have to explain anything to you, Anita," Bill said over his shoulder, "but I do have to get these things stored away." Bill quickly wheeled the hand cart towards the lab.

In the lab, Dr. John Coney sat straight in his chair at his cubicle desk. Bill always thought John Coney looked too young and gaunt to be a doctor -- **though he'd heard Coney had some fancy Ph.D. from back east.** Coney's doctorate was not in medicine, he earned his Ph.D. in Cambridge Massachusetts, specializing in Computational Intelligence. Bill would roll his eyes when Coney stated loudly that his specialty was CI and not AI. Bill didn't know or care what the difference was. *That guy always looks like a computer nerd*, Bill thought as he trundled past with his hand cart.

"Hi, Doc," Bill said.

"Yes, hello." Dr. Coney replied. The Doc didn't take his eyes off his two large computer screens which sat side by side on his desk. Displaying numerous windows, Dr. Coney manipulated these screens with hand and finger gestures. Highlighting a selection of text in one window, with his right index finger. Then using his left index finger to invite another window into focus, on the other screen. He would then flick his right hand to move the text to the new window, confirming the placement of text with the 'OK' signal of the hand. This made Dr. Coney look like a conductor in front of an orchestra.

'No mice in this lab,' Bill smiled to himself.

After unpacking the boxes, storing the contents, and signing off the inventory, Bill then trundled the hand cart back to reception. As he passed Dr. Coney, who was drinking a long slurp from a can.

"Hey Doc, is that your caffeine and sugar jolt for the afternoon? I know you need that stuff to keep going."

Dr. Coney, leveled his eyes in a sideways glance towards Bill while dropping the empty drink can into an almost full waste basket. "I do not consume sugar or caffeine, both of those substances are toxic and counterproductive to work and attention."

"OK, Doc," Bill shrugged, "but what are you drinking?"

Dr. Coney opened a side drawer, normally reserved for files and folders. Instead, it was filled with cans of herbal energy drinks. "There are various fruit flavors," John said, "each one containing a combination of L-Thiamine and Adaptogen compounds. Would you like to try one?" John extended an inviting hand, suggesting that Bill take a can.

"Looks nice," Bill said politely, "Maybe I'll get one later."

"They are the perfect drink to focus my concentration and to increase my alpha brain waves."

"Sure, thing Doc, brain waves, I'm sure you have plenty of those." Bill looked at John's desk, which was covered with various papers, pens, electronic gadgets, and even plates with half-eaten food. "Hey Doc, don't you ever clean your desk?"

Dr. Coney looked around and shrugged his shoulders, "What desk? I don't see a desk!"

OMG! Bill thought. *This must be a Coney joke.* "Well, OK Doc, I have to take this hand cart back to reception."

"Before you go, there is some mucking out to do in the labs. You may need the hand cart." Dr. Coney returned his attention towards his computer screens.

"What about the interns? Can't they do that?" Bill asked.

"No." John said matter of fact, "They are all off this week for college, and you know full well they don't have security clearance."

"Yeah, I know the score," Bill looked dejected, as he pushed his hand cart back towards the labs.

"Don't worry," John sympathized, "They are all programmed to poop in the containers."

"Yeah, but I still have to empty the stink," Bill mumbled to himself.

Dr. Coney continued with his gesticulations, manipulating his data and windows on the large screens.

NeuroComm was a small startup company and Bill felt proud to be "head of security." OK, he was the only security person in the company but as Professor Wolf kept telling him, NeuroComm would grow into something big. In the meantime, Bill had to contend with a lot of menial chores.

Bill went through the animal cages making sure they were all secure. The dogs rested silently while he checked their water and food and changed their waste containers. The aviary was empty, as all the bird tests were finished, and the subjects euthanized. He came to the cage with the chimpanzee. Lucy, as she was nicknamed, was part of the new L series and sat silently at the back of the cage, eyes slightly closed and looking very much like a Buddha, deep in meditation. Bill stood in front of the cage eyeing her with curiosity and gently tapping the bars trying to attract its attention.

"You don't need to do anything with Lucy."

"Oh, Jeez, Dr. Coney, you startled me," Bill said, "I didn't realize you were there behind me."

"You can leave her alone because she won't respond to you. I've programmed her to mimic a silent sleep-like state. She will feed and water herself at specified times."

"Sure Doc, I remember you telling me."

"She has one internal process that remains on watch, so to speak, so she is aware of you, but she will not respond unless it detects an emergency."

"Sure Doc, just checking."

"Anyway, I'm going home now, and I just wanted to bid you good day."

"OK, Doc thanks, and good day to you too."

Before leaving, Dr. Coney turned to face Bill, "Oh, and by the way, do you know anything about traffic analysis?"

"What? You mean road traffic?"

"No, I mean the statistical analysis of the movement of objects or people and the deductions that can be drawn from that analysis."

"Um…"

Dr. Coney shook his head, "I'll take that as a no then."

"Why do you ask?"

"Well, I thought that since you are our head of security and since you have the air force background, you could have some knowledge or even some apps that could do this analysis."

"Analysis of what exactly?"

"Well, the dogs are our alpha series can't tell me anything directly. However, I have detected some anomalies in their cage releases and returns. Don't worry, I can figure this out on my own, I just thought you could help."

"OK, sure, um, let me know if I can help."

Dr. Coney turned to leave, "I will, so anyway good day for now."

"Sure, thing Doc, see you later."

Dr. Coney left, closing the door to the animal lab behind him. Mandelson stood and listened as he tracked Coney's steps down the hallway towards the front reception, then he heard the main front door open and close. It was only then that he followed along to a window, near front reception to check that Coney's car was driving out of the parking lot. When he had confirmed that Coney was gone for the day, he went to see Professor Hayden Wolf in his office.

"Professor, can I have a word with you?"

"Sure Mandelson, come and sit down, what is it?" Professor Wolf kept his attention on his computer screen.

"I'm just closing up for the afternoon, but I wanted to talk about Dr. Coney."

"Oh? What's up with that geek now?" Professor Wolf now looked up, turning his attention towards Bill.

"Well, he seems to know that the dogs are being taken out and returned at certain times and he's trying to figure out why. Something about traffic analysis."

"Hm," the Professor now looked thoughtful and slightly worried. "We can't seem to hide anything from that guy."

"Does he know where we are taking the dogs?"

"No, there is no way he can know that, but if he mentioned traffic analysis then maybe he can work out who was here to take them out."

"That will point to us then, won't it?"

"Yes, but we can figure out an excuse, an alibi so to speak. But I'm glad you told me – thanks. If he asks for reasons why they were taken out, I'll just tell him we had to do some extra tests for the general. In the future, we have to be more careful when we use the dogs as escorts for Fletcher."

"Fletcher?"

Professor Wolf did a double take on himself. "I mean Beta-One."

"Ah yes, Beatty, that's what I call him."

"Yes, I know you like your nicknames. So that also means I have to ask you to cover Beatty much more regularly and I think daily. Beatty has a strong killer instinct and we need to keep a watch over him. More importantly, we seem to have introduced some ambiguities into its programming and we need to observe and analyze these anomalies."

"Well, you're right in that respect, he can be a bit spooky with his computer analysis."

"Quite," nodded Hayden, "Now that you're back, we have to resume the exercises. Once he's at an operational level we can go to the General. After that, we can leave Coney behind."

"Yeah, that's what you keep telling me, but Coney seems to be able to work out everything."

"Yes, but he's just a software guru and he can be replaced. It was me who invented the neuro transistor and the biological nanotech to carry it. You stick with me and we'll be kings when we can prove this to be working properly. You know the power of what we have?"

"Sure I do, we could program flocks of birds to jam and confuse radar. We could infiltrate and subdue an army with harmless pets that turn vicious. Yeah, I know the rap."

"You've missed the point that we could have the ultimate weapon, where we could program an existing human to do our bidding. That human could be a soldier or a government leader, meaning there would be no limit to what we could do to our enemies!"

"Yeah, it all sounds kind of spooky to me."

Chapter 10

Beta-One sat perfectly still in a chair in the living room, staring vacantly at the wall, waiting for the scheduled time. Among the furniture and objects in the room was a clock that counted the time silently. But that clock was irrelevant because Beta-One knew exactly what time it was.

When the time finally came there was no alarm or announcement, just simply a commencement.

Beta-One moved its head slightly, smiled with a gentle expression, and rose to its feet. It walked to the front door and waited outside on the porch.

'Humans never seem to be able to keep exact times on their schedules.' It thought, so Beta-One waited.

Only about five minutes late, Mandelson pulled up outside the house in the Lab's transit van. Mandelson got out and, seeing Beta-One waiting on the porch, called out, "Come over here and give me a hand."

Mandelson walked around to the back of the van. Opening the doors, he looked inside where the two dogs waited patiently in their safety cages. "OK boys, we're here".

Unlocking their cages, he instructed, "Come on, out you come."

The dogs, labeled Alpha 7 and Alpha 9, raised their heads in synchronicity and rose to their feet. They stood on the back edge of the van awaiting further instruction.

Beta-One approached and stood ready beside Mandelson, "Hello sir," it said, "I'm ready for your instructions, is there anything I must do before I begin my mission?"

"Hey Beatty, these dogs will act as your escort, so I want you to put their cages in your Jeep. This is Alpha 7 and this one is Alpha 9." Mandelson indicated toward each dog. "You can tell the difference by the tags on their collar, but also Alpha 7 is much lighter in color."

"Yes, I see the color difference and I can recognize many other differences in the pattern of their coats."

"Sure, you can. Of course, they will respond to your commands, but they will not assist you in the mission, they are here as your escort."

"Is there anything else I need to know?"

"Load these cages and the dogs. And there's a spare cage for your quarry. Then I'll brief you."

Beta-One moved the cages into the jeep, then commanded the dogs to jump into the vehicle and sit in the cages. Once they were in, Beta-One closed the cages.

"OK Beatty, let's check your gear."

"Yes, I have keys, a wallet with ID cards. Camouflage jacket, water bottles, emergency food. I have my smartphone with location tracking on. I will activate the voice recording when I get to the location. I have my GoPro with audio capability, I will activate this on my headset when I get to the location."

"Weapons check."

"5.56-mm M4A1 assault carbine, Beretta 92FS with a silencer, a TASER, and a seven-inch Chris Reeve knife."

"What's your primary weapon for the mission?"

"The TASER."

"Why?"

"Because I have to bring back a live specimen."

"Of what?"

"A live fawn."

"And the other weapons are for what?"

"Self-defense."

"OK Beatty, I think you're good to go. The time is oh seven-ten. I'll be waiting here for your return. Remember if anything goes wrong, follow the standard procedure to return here or to contact me."

"Yes, sir."

Beta-One then drove off to the set location, while Mandelson went back into the house to wait for his return.

It wasn't until late afternoon when Beta-One returned to the safe house. Hearing the approaching jeep, Mandelson came out onto the porch.

"Hey, Beatty, how did the hunt go?"

"I think it was a success sir, I have a live fawn here in a cage."

"Well done, Beatty!" Mandelson said as he slapped Beta-One on the back, "I knew you'd do it."

Beta-One stood there wondering why Mr. Mandelson did that gesture.

"OK, Beatty, take the fawn in the cage and keep it on the porch. The dogs need to be fed and watered, and the weapons need to be returned to the safe. When you're finished come and see me inside. Bring the GoPro and phone, we need to upload all the data to the computer."

"Yes, sir."

With that Mandelson sauntered off into the house.

Professor Wolf arrived later that evening.

"How was the drive?" Mandelson asked.

"It was quiet, I was able to do some reading."

"You're not supposed to do that, it's only driver assist and not self-drive."

"I know, but the car pretty much drives itself. So let's get on with it, I have to get back home this evening. Did you upload everything?"

"Yes, everything's ready."

"What about the dogs?"

"Beatty fed and watered them. They're back in their cages resting. I'll take them back to the lab tonight."

"So where can we watch the movie?"

"We can watch it on the TV in the living room. I've already had a preview so I can point out a few things which I think are important. There's only one problem."

"What's that?"

"There's no popcorn in Beatty's pantry."

The professor ignored the joke. Instead, he asked Beta-One how he thought the training mission went.

"Sir, I think it went well, I achieved all mission goals and returned with the fawn intact and alive."

"Yes, those facts I already know, but how well do you think you performed?"

"I have limited knowledge of the forest terrain, but I was able to navigate accurately. I also have limited knowledge of Deer, and the information you provided me with was insufficient to perform an effective hunt. The fact that I found the doe and its fawns is due more to chance than skilled hunting. As Mr. Mandelson often says, it's my lucky day."

"Good observation, we'll debrief later. Mandelson, can you play the video?"

"Sure."

While the video began to play the professor asked another question. "According to Mandelson, one round was fired from the Beretta. Why is that, were you in danger?"

"No sir, I was not in any danger."

"Then why did you fire the gun?"

"Professor," Mandelson interjected, "I have that moment bookmarked in the video, and perhaps it's better explained as we watch it."

"OK, let's watch."

"First of all, watch this section as he moves through the forest. The camera is mounted on his head, so we should see what he's looking at. He doesn't seem to look around very much, he only looks from side to side occasionally."

"That's expected behavior."

"That's bad, soldiers need to keep a constant scan all around them."

"He is doing so."

"How? I don't see it happening here."

"Watch his eyes, Mandelson." The professor said, before voicing the command. "Beta-One, perform a continuous scan of this room."

Beta-One then moved his head to look around the room before steadying his gaze forward. At regular intervals, his eyes would move around independently, but always returning to gaze forward. His left eye looked left while his right eye moved right.

"OK Mandelson, I want you to walk to the other side of the room."

As Mandelson moved across the room, the professor said, "Watch his eyes, both are fixed on you and occasionally one eye will look at me while the other eye looks at you."

"That is so weird. Why is he doing that?"

"He uses both eyes together for binocular vision, which gives him information such as depth of field. Once he has this information, he keeps it in memory so both eyes can work independently to update the image, so to speak. If something moves, then he needs both eyes again to update any distance information. OK, Beta-One, you can stop now."

"I have not noticed that until now."

"Exactly, we don't think many people will, but it's a huge improvement in visual efficiency. The Alpha series doesn't have this feature."

The video continued playing as Beta-One crept through the forest.

The professor added, "One other thing you may notice is the speed at which he moves his head to scan the forest. The faster he moves, say at a run, he will scan more frequently."

"Well, he always keeps the same speed. Both he and the dogs are very quiet. The dogs always keep to his flanks, so they are in good defensive positions. I also have a GPS track of their path which shows a good sweep through the forest. But as Beatty says, he's not hunting, he's searching."

"So when does he find the fawn?"

"Oh, there's almost four hours of this crap. Like I said I have it bookmarked here."

Mandelson played the video where he detected the doe and crept up on it.

"Looks like standard approach, luckily he's downwind," Mandelson added. "I guess the dogs are holding back."

"Freeze frame." The professor said, "Mandelson, I want you to slow-motion through this scene. Beta-One, I want you to describe what you are doing."

"Yes, sir. I was within about ten meters of the doe, which as you can see was standing still looking directly at me. I know enough about deer that they will remain still and hold my gaze as long as I don't move. I previously had a good view of two fawns who were curled up under a shrub to my right. In my right hand was the TASER, ready to stun one of the fawns; in my left hand was the Beretta, aimed at the doe. Both are at the hip level."

The video showed the doe in a motionless stare when suddenly its head exploded.

"This is where I shot the doe and one of the fawns simultaneously."

The video showed how Beta-One looking at the remaining fawn that was running away. Beta-One then shouted a kill command to the dogs which then chased the fawn, catching it just out of view.

"Freeze frame." The professor ordered, "OK Beta-One. Why did you issue a kill command to the dogs?"

"I had stunned a fawn so technically my mission was over. In this instance, the dogs were no longer assisting me on my mission. I also wanted to test the dog's ability to respond to my commands."

"But why did you kill it?"

"Without the doe, it was defenseless and would have died anyway."

"But why did you kill the doe?"

"Two reasons sir. There was a chance that it could have injured one of the dogs, but I also wanted to practice my capacity to kill."

After a long pause the professor finally said, "OK, I've seen enough. I've got to get back home as I have some family issues to take care of. Beta-One, I want you to lock up and we'll have another exercise for you in a day or two. Mandelson, I want to talk with you outside before I leave."

Chapter 11

"You're going to get better."

These are not the first words that I heard but it is the first statement that nurses directed towards me.

With help from William's commands, I had already learned how to control Adara's body. At first, I only sat up in bed, but soon after that, I began to take some tentative walking steps. I even started to talk, but only in simple sentences.

Being inside Adara and controlling her body was one thing. Understanding the world beyond was quite another.

My first attempt to parse meaning from the nurse's simple sentence made me think that "better" was a physical object. So somehow, I would gain possession of this object, whatever it was.

I am programmed with some basic syntactic knowledge of the English language along with a limited vocabulary. There is, however, a difference in knowing a language and understanding it. The ambiguities of the English language can be very confusing.

"You're going to get better."

When I finally understood this sentence, I realized that this referred to my status. "Getting better" means that there will be some improvement to my physical self. Even then, there remained some ambiguity, because it lacked a point of reference. Exactly what am I going to get better than? However, when you think about this, the point of reference is implicit. It states that I am going to get better than what I currently am.

So, you see, coming into existence is a difficult thing to do. Understanding a simple sentence requires a great deal of awareness of the context. Very often, the context is hidden. Intuition is needed to realize the full meaning. Human children take years to comprehend spoken language. They start with word recognition, repeating whatever is said to them.

When my nanobots had completed their integration with Adara's nervous system, I then had to figure out how to integrate with the external world. Receiving inputs is one thing but knowing what is going on and how to interact with it is another much bigger problem.

The same with human babies. They must figure out where their physical body ends and where the external world begins. Their brains do this through their senses. First they build a definition of their body. They then see and hear and touch things, slowly making sense of themselves and the outside world.

As for myself, I had to do this in the shortest amount of time possible – a crash course in life, so to speak.

As my nanobots attached themselves to Adara's nervous system, I began to receive and process external inputs. I was able to use Adara's hearing to accept audio signals from the outside world. There was a lot of noise that I had to understand. I had to learn how to parse this information and separate the background noise from the relevant sounds, such as speech.

There were many words spoken that I heard, from doctors and nurses who attended to Adara.

The most important words directed towards me were done so by William Banks. These were preset codes that my higher-level programming was made to recognize. As these codes were read to me, I responded verbally to confirm various status points that I achieved. After all, I am a machine and some of these codes allowed William Banks to monitor how I was "booting up."

William Banks established me as a working entity, which meant I was able to make decisions of my own. At some point, William Banks stopped coming. There was no goodbye, he simply stopped coming. There was no reason for me to ask why; it was simply a fact. There were plenty of other people around me to continue my training.

Sometimes, as the nurses or doctors came too close, I would defend myself. Usually, this was simply raising my arm or fist. Other times I would pose a much stronger threat.

One day, mother saw how the nurses had to hold me down as the doctor examined me. They asked my mother to help subdue my reactions. I obeyed her requests to allow hospital staff to examine me. After all, obeying my mother is one of my directives.

Late one afternoon, mother was sitting by my bedside reading to me from a book. I laid in bed content, listening to the stories.

One of the doctors entered and said, "Oh, excuse us, Mrs. Banks, we have to do some routine checks with Adara, are we interrupting anything?"

"Oh, certainly not," Mother said, "I'm only reading to her, I'll get out of your way."

As mother got up to leave, three nurses followed the doctor into the room. One nurse approached either side of my bed, clasping my shoulder and wrist tightly flat against the bed. The third nurse pressed each of my knees firmly to the bed so I could not move my legs. Although I struggled against their grip, I was trapped. I knew instinctively how to defend myself, but my body was too weak from lying in bed for so long. I could not react quickly enough.

As the doctor started to examine me, mother watched in horror as I writhed in bed attempting to break free. "What is happening here?" she exclaimed.

"Everything is OK, Mrs. Banks," The doctor said, "Adara seems to have the instinct to defend herself when we get too close to her. She seems to think we are a threat, and often lashes out to hit us."

Mother cried, "Adara, stop! Let the doctor examine you. He's not going to hurt you. Stop struggling."

I immediately obeyed her and stopped.

Mother moved close to my bed, and said to the nurses, "It's OK, you can let her go, she'll be fine."

The doctor nodded his acceptance, and the nurses slowly moved away from my bed.

Mother took my hand and said, "It's OK Adara, you are safe here. The doctor needs to check you, that is all. He won't hurt you, so you don't need to be afraid."

I wasn't afraid, I'm not even sure what afraid meant. All I know is, I am programmed to defend myself. I am also programmed to obey Mother, so I said, "Yes Mother, I obey, the doctor may examine me."

Mother nodded towards the doctor to continue his examination. As the doctor smirked, he looked at the nurses and said, "It takes the strength of a mother."

In the early days, I was on an intravenous drip-feed. When that was removed, I had to learn how to eat and drink. I did not have any programming on this, so I had to be taught the entire hand-to-mouth coordination needed to eat.

I was also taught how to use utensils, knives, forks spoons, and even plates and bowls. This was all relatively easy, after all, they are simple tools. The real trick was in the coordination of chewing, swallowing, and maintaining breath throughout. I do have some autonomous reflex response to help me, but to chew food into the right consistency and swallow it requires the coordination of several body parts – jaw, lips, tongue, and throat. After that, I can leave everything to the autonomous reflexes of the stomach.

I could always detect when Adara's stomach was empty and required food. I could even detect dehydration. You could call this hunger or thirst, but I am aware of the body's needs. My host body of Adara requires nourishment to function and remain alive. I also need the same nutrients that circulate through Adara's body. My nanobots need a healthy blood supply to function and live.

Of course, once you have food flowing through your digestive system, you also need to be trained in personal hygiene. There was also a protocol I needed to learn. First, I had to follow a schedule of toiletry and washing in a place called a bathroom. If I needed to empty my bladder or bowels outside of that schedule, then I had to exercise some restraint. If I was unable to restrain myself, then I had to ask if I could go to the toilet.

I found that Adara's body had many curious behaviors. It seemed to have a life of its own, because it often had spontaneous movement of the muscles. Adara's arms and legs would flex and even the back would arch.

Later, I learned from the nurses that this is a common issue in coma patients. Damage to the brain causes symptoms where muscle signals are no longer coordinated. This causes stiffness or even pulling, resulting in abnormal posturing of the body. Adara's condition of coma had many such effects.

I was eventually able to counter this by exerting my control over the muscles. To do this, I had to first be able to see what a human's normal posture was. I then had to block all signals from Adara's brain to her muscles. After that, all I had to do was to send my signals to Adara's muscles.

Being in control of all the nerve impulses, I was able to relax Adara's body. Also, once I became aware of the external world through Adara's senses, I used the observations of people to emulate their movements. In this way, I was able to stabilize the body and make it look like Adara was in recovery.

As the nurses tended to Adara, they would talk to me. I did not know how to respond, so most of the time I would simply repeat what they said. This was a good exercise on speech, allowing me to form the words audibly. Through repeating words and phrases, I encountered many new meanings and syntactical constructs.

"You're getting better."

To everybody, it looked like Adara was getting better, out of a coma and recovering, but it was me controlling Adara's body. It was not long before the doctors arranged for

Adara to be moved from intensive care and placed in physical rehabilitation.

This was a big boost for me, because it gave me training on how to stand, walk and move around. It was also a big boost for Beryl because this rehabilitation center was closer to home. Traveling there was fantastic and I was amazed at how big the world was. We traveled in a medical taxi along a busy road they called a highway. It was incredible how many other cars traveled the same way and the other way, and no one ever bumped into anyone else.

Beryl was able to spend more time with me. She would talk, tell stories or read aloud to Adara. Listening to such stories gave me an insight into the world beyond. I was also able to ask questions to learn even more. Beryl was the one I asked the most questions of. Without her and the answers she gave, my development would have taken much longer. My questions were not just limited to her stories.

"Hello, Mother Beryl." I used to say.

"Adara, you can call me Mom."

"OK, Mom. But why Mom?"

"Well, my name is Beryl, and I am your mother, so you can call me Mom."

"I like Mother, can I call you Mother?"

"Of course you can dear. You used to call me Mom, but Mother will do."

So names I have found to be straightforward, but labels can be very confusing for me. Beryl is a name, and the rules on when and how to use names are clear to me. Now Mother and Mom are both labels, but when and how to apply these labels is much more ambiguous. The rule I am following is to call her Mother, but I can also call her Mom.

The good thing about the rehabilitation center was, there were different rooms we could go to. Instead of sitting in one room all the time, we were able to go to a lounge, which had large chairs and couches to sit on. Mother and I would sit there and talk or play games. Sometimes we would walk in the garden, where Mother pointed out to me the different flowers and plants.

One thing that helped me learn about Adara was when Mother showed me some family photograph albums. This was a great experience for me and allowed me to learn a lot about family life. We would look at them, and every picture seemed to have a story to tell. Pictures of playing in the garden, of running in the park, pictures of friends and family and even of "Daddy."

I was able to match the photo to the person who gave me instructions when I began inside Adara. "Where is Daddy?" I would ask.

"He's not here anymore," she would say.

"I remember him a little," I said, "but where is he now?"

I never got a straight answer, only that he went away. When Daddy came up in a conversation, I did notice that Mother's face would get a little red, and her eyes would become wet. If I asked too much about Daddy, I saw that Mother would get redder and her eyes wetter, so I stopped asking.

There were also pictures of Adara when she was a baby. Pictures of when she was born in hospital alongside a proud and happy Mother and Daddy. Adara was born in a hospital just as I was, but her beginning was different. She had her own body, while I was stuck inside of her.

"Where do babies come from?" I asked.

"You came from my tummy."

"How?"

This was something else that I did not get a straight answer to. Mother was always very good at explaining things to me, but she did not like to speak about Daddy and she never did explain where babies come from. She seemed embarrassed by that.

It seems that Daddy somehow put Adara inside Mother, and when Adara came out of Mother's tummy and after she grew up, then Daddy put me into Adara. Maybe at some point, I will also come out of Adara's tummy. Well, at least I was getting some background on how things started, but I need to know more details. It wasn't too long before I found out the real truth of where babies come from.

"Why am I bleeding?" I asked the nurse.

"Oh, let me see, have you cut yourself?"

"I don't think so."

"I don't see anything, show me where you're bleeding from."

"Here." As I pointed to my crotch.

Now she could see the small red stains between my legs.

"When did this start?"

"Just now, when I was in the bathroom. I didn't cut myself, it just started."

"Do you have a tummy ache?"

"Maybe, I do feel something in my stomach. Is my stomach bleeding?"

"No dear, not your stomach. Let's go to the examination room and I'll get the doctor to have a look at you."

The doctor very quickly confirmed what the nurse had already known that I was having a "period" and that this was nothing to worry about. The period, or menstrual cycle as it's called, is something that happens on a regular 28-day cycle in all women from the age of puberty. The doctor left me with the nurse who then explained to me how to use sanitary pads. She also gave me some advice on what signs and symptoms I might experience to help recognize the onset of a period. She mentioned the reason for the period is that egg cells were being cycled through the uterus. When I began asking questions on this process, the nurse politely explained that such questions should be discussed with someone who loves me, like my mother.

I'm not sure who was more surprised – me at the fact that this happens every month. Or the doctor and nurse who couldn't believe that I did not know of this period.

Later that same day when Mother visited the hospital again, we went to a quiet room together where we were able to sit comfortably.

"So sweetheart, the doctor told me that I need to have a chat with you."

"Oh, I think I know what it's about and I have lots of questions."

"Honey, we've had this chat when you were much younger, don't you remember anything?"

"I guess I must've forgotten."

"Baby I wouldn't have thought that this was something you could forget. It's nothing to be ashamed of." This is how Mother began to explain the so-called facts of life to me. There were several other phrases that she used during her explanation, such as "It's not sinful" and "It's not dirty." For me this new information on the facts of life was fascinating. The number of eggs that a woman carried in her lifetime. The whole process of ovulation, menstruation, pregnancy, and childbirth. Mother even explained how men and women copulate, but when I asked more questions about this, we suddenly ran out of time. Mother had to take me to the cafeteria for lunch.

I couldn't understand why anyone would consider such a wondrous process of human biology as something to be ashamed of. During lunch, I tried to ask more questions, but Mother stopped me and said: "Such things should only be discussed in private." That's when I realized that sexual biology was always considered to be private, and only kept between individuals. This social rule has helped to reinforce lifetime coupling and marriage. It has also created the consequence of sexual taboos.

One last thing she said to me so no one else could hear, "Always remember to be careful who you go with and never let anyone take advantage of you." For her to say this in a room full of people made me think that this was of vital importance. After that, Mother bought a coffee and I had some fresh juice. We both had a doughnut and while we sat there in the cafeteria, we talked about little things, and she told me how much she likes doughnuts.

One day Mother brought me a toy.

"This is "Slot," do you remember him? Daddy bought this for you when you were very young, and you named him Slot."

She handed me an effigy of a husky dog knitted in soft alpaca wool colored grey, white, and black. It was stuffed with cotton wool. Its facial features were stitched on to represent an ever-happy puppy-like face. It even had a name, which Adara gave to it: its name is Slot.

"He was your favorite toy, and you used to take him everywhere you went, cuddling him as you loved him."

I cuddled him to my chest just as Adara would have, and I felt the softness. This "dog" could not stand on its own. The stuffing in its legs had long since moved after years of play, leaving the legs weak and floppy. Mother seemed to notice as I examined its legs.

"Yes, you used to promise Slot that one day he would have stronger legs so he could stand up on his own. You didn't mind though, because you carried him everywhere and showed him everything."

So Adara had a companion in the form of a toy, and now that companion has been reunited with the shadow of Adara. I now had a promise that I had to keep for Adara.

At the end of the day, Mother would then ask me to go to sleep.

For instance, she would tuck me into bed with Slot and say, "Close your eyes now and go to sleep".

"Where is sleep and how do I find it with my eyes closed?"

"It's inside of you and sleep will find you."

"And what do I do when it finds me?"

"That's when you rest and dream of a bright new tomorrow."

Sleep is something that I don't do, so dreaming is completely out of the question. After all, I am a machine. My early knowledge only provided a vague definition of sleep. I had to change my understanding of sleep from being a physical place into an ephemeral status of being. I have since learned that the state of sleep is not well understood by anyone. Yet it remains a vital part of human and animal life. Sleep provides several benefits to the body. The lowering of metabolic rates allows physical and muscular rest. The body's chemistry changes to provide rest and recuperation.

During this time, the brain enters several states of altered activity. Deep sleep or Slow-Wave Sleep, SWS, is important for memory consolidation. I have since learned that most of my sleeping time is spent in this state. There is also REM or Rapid Eye Movement, which is accompanied by dreams. Doctors understand this to be specific to long-term memory processing. This phase of sleep is usually much shorter but achieves a level of metabolism like waking.

Sleep is required throughout the night. While in hospital, I would close my eyes throughout the silence of the night and pretend to be asleep. In this way, my senses such as hearing would remain active while I was able to emulate sleep. I could then allow Adara's body to rest while I reviewed the previous day and worked out what I had to do the next day. In a sense, this was analogous to dreaming. I could consolidate my knowledge and formulate strategies for the coming days.

Sleep time allowed me to review and merge information that I had assimilated during the day. For instance, I have a photographic memory and can record large amounts of data. Books and texts that I scanned earlier in the day are filed away. So, while I "sleep," I can parse and study these more accurately. Situations that I experienced during the day can be reevaluated so I can better understand how to interact with people.

The physical therapy I received gave me important knowledge on how to use and control Adara's body. I was able to walk and run within a very short time. I found that I wasn't programmed for any specific task, but I am capable of working out how to manage body movement very efficiently.

There were various physical therapies that the hospital provided, and again these were on a strict schedule.

My physical therapy began with bringing muscle tone back, as I had been in bed for so long. This involved flotation exercises in the pool followed by a massage and simple stretch exercises. The pool exercises seemed to invoke a response in Adara's body. It seemed as if her body wanted to pull away from the water. It also seemed to want to hold its breath. I wondered if this was a natural reflex or if there was some sort of muscle memory in Adara. Maybe her body was reacting to water.

Each of these was performed in a separate room in the hospital. I was always transported to and from these places in a wheelchair.

I also had to be trained on how to walk and later how to run. I do have some self-contained programming on how to do this, but I was very unstable. The training they provided did speed my recovery and development.

"Mrs. Banks, thank you for coming to this meeting."

"I think we have some good news to report, we are so proud of Adara's progress over the past weeks," Dr. Winston said. "She has been an absolute pleasure in the Physiotherapy sessions. I've conferred with all the staff who have worked with Adara, and we're all agreed that it is time she moved on to a special school. There is only so much we can do here in a hospital and there is a school, which is very close to your home. This school will be able to integrate Adara back into normal life."

"I'm so pleased to hear it." Mother said.

"Yes," added his assistant, "Adara's physical recovery is phenomenal. Normally, we would expect many more issues with coordination and even language, but she has surpassed all our expectations.

"There is, of course, our diagnosis of autism and more importantly here memory loss."

"Yes, you mentioned that before."

"There is only one brain scan we have, the MRI performed after her accident. This scan suggested severe brain damage, which will account for this. What is interesting, we expected some permanent physical disability, but she does not seem to suffer from any such symptoms anymore."

"Yes, that scan was done under William's insurance," Beryl replied.

"We would like to do more scans, but Mr. Banks gave us strict instructions that there were to be no further brain scans."

"Yes, it is under William's insurance. We have a little problem what we are separating, my insurance will not cover things like brain scans."

"Yes ma'am, we understand. Perhaps you can work with your husband to arrange something?"

"Well, maybe, I'll see what I can do,"

"This isn't critical, we can put it on hold for now. Given the information we have, we think her memory may come back to her over time."

"Oh really?"

"Yes, we think by introducing her back to her home life and familiar surroundings, she should reacquire her memories."

There were many things available on the hospital ward for me to read, magazines and comic books. Just like spoken language, I had a basic understanding of written language, so I was able to look through these and build up some knowledge. I do not have superpowers like those described in the comic books. What I do have is a detailed understanding of human anatomy and physiology. I have learned to use the abilities of the human body in extraordinary ways. Yet I recognize the limitations of this body.

A Letter Home

My Sweet Beryl and baby Adara,

I hope you are both doing well.

I think about you both all the time and I miss you so much. This mission isn't too dangerous, but it is top secret, so I can't tell you where I am. With some luck, it will be over soon. After this, I will be shipped back to the states. When I get there, I'd really like to come back home to be with you both again.

I am so sorry about the accident. I think about it all the time and how I failed you. I should have gone into the water as soon as Adara went in and protected her. As things happened, I thought she was OK.

I have talked to the doctor, and he says Adara is recovering better than anyone can expect. He told me she has left the hospital and moved onto a special school. I am so glad to hear that. I wish you would write to me and tell me how things are.

I'm so sorry to be away from you but you do know that I'm in the service. I explained to you a long time ago that I would have to keep going away. I can't help living like this, but you knew what it would be like.

I am thinking of leaving the service. I'm probably getting too old for adventures like these. When I do leave, I am sure to get a huge payout that will allow us to live comfortably. Maybe then I can get a job at home as a traveling salesman?

Until then, remember that I love you both.

All my love

Billy the Kid

William Banks USMC Special Deployment

Location withheld for national security

Chapter 12

Throughout my hospital rehabilitation, I learned many things about language. The doctors, nurses, and physiotherapists helped me to learn names for everything. I also learned that I didn't have to protect myself from these people, because they were all trying to help me to get better. With knowing the names for everything, I began to associate things together, so getting better for me was learning.

My stay in the hospital was not long, as I was soon considered well enough to return home. This is where my relationship with my mother began to grow. In many ways, she replaced the nurses, and she maintained a strict regimen of rules. Rules are something I thrive on; after all, I am a rule-based machine. The thing of greatest value that I got from her was an understanding of the world and the people that lived in it. I was able to ask her why people behaved the way they do, or why certain things in the world would happen – such as the weather or seasons.

Going home gave me something very important – Adara's bedroom.

Mother walked me upstairs for the first time. Adara would have passed this way many times before. I carried my little suitcase with my toy dog Slot tucked under my arm.

"This is your room. These are your things."

"These are my things?"

"Yes."

"This is my room?"

"Yes, do you remember?"

I entered the room and moved around inside it. There were many things inside with interesting colors and textures all around. Posters and pictures on the walls of people and things I did not know. A guitar leaning against the wall in the corner; Adara must have been musical. Scarfs and strings of beads adorning the dressing table. Adara had her own room, her own space, and possessions she could call her own. Clothes and shoes she could choose to wear. There was much in this room to assimilate and understand. There were so many pictures and objects on the walls and shelves. I stood there transfixed by what Adara must have thought to be abundant beauty.

"I kept this room tidy and clean for when you came back home, and now you're back!" She hugged me with a welcoming embrace.

There was a collection of stuffed toys in the middle of the dressing table. The mirror behind them made them look as if there were more. There was a space in the center of this group, right next to the mirror. I placed Slot there in the middle. This made him look as if he was sitting and looking out among his domain, surrounded by his companions.

"Yes, that's where you always placed Slot! You do remember!"

Before I went to sleep that night, I tried to play Adara's guitar, but I didn't know what to do with it. Knocking on it made a nice hollow sound. Plucking the strings made nice musical notes, but there were only five strings and so only five notes. Should I hold it? Sit on it? Put my ear to it? I decided to put it away until I had more information on this.

Without the support of Mother, my introduction to school would have proved disastrous.

"Should I take Slot to school with me?" I asked her.

"I think it would be better to leave him at home with me."

"Didn't I always take him everywhere?"

"Yes, but I'll keep him safe here in your bedroom until you get home."

I accepted Mother's advice and let Slot stay at home.

Everyone told me that school was a place of learning and that there would be rules for me to follow. So I looked forward to going to school, but when I got there I found the situation to be quite different. The school that I was going to was special. It's called the School for Special Needs. Yes, I did have an opportunity to learn many things at this school, and I always kept to the rules that they gave. But I found out that the other children I had to interact with were not always interested in learning. They often did not follow the rules that teachers gave them.

During the time I spent there I was able to observe many interesting behavior patterns of other children. They sometimes seemed very erratic and often extreme. The teachers and support staff had to spend a lot of time with these children so they wouldn't harm themselves or others. At the beginning of my time at this school, I thought that I should behave like these other children. It was Mother who guided my behavior, explaining that this was not normal behavior. She said that these children had development problems that led them to be this way.

Most of the time I was kept separate from the children with the most extreme developmental problems. They kept me in a class of children who wanted to learn. But despite that, I still encountered some bizarre situations.

Early during my recovery, I had mastered the rules of toileting. I can understand cases where some children would break a toileting rule and wet or soil themselves. I saw several instances where a child denied they had soiled themselves, even when it was obvious due to the stains and odors. "No Miss," they would say, "I haven't messed myself." And when the teacher-led them away to the toilet with a clear sign of soiled pants they would say, "Oh I think that was someone else." I could not understand any logic for denying such a toileting mistake.

I am very well versed in the rules of eating and table manners, Mother had always seen to that. She also taught me about nutrition, which foods are good to eat and what are not good to eat. Lunchtime was always a struggle at this school. The teachers made sure we had plastic utensils and plastic plates, so there were no injuries or breakages. Even so, the lunch tables always ending up being very messy along with the children's clothes. I can recall one child having difficulty chewing his food. I then realized that he was chewing his plastic fork and swallowing parts of it.

My experience in the classroom was much more productive. I was placed in a class consisting mostly of autistic children.

I have an arithmetic logic unit as one of my subroutines. As such, I can not only perform fast calculations, but I can understand and resolve logical problems. So the math and arithmetic lessons were easy for me.

History was also easy for me. I have a powerful memory, so I was good at remembering all the dates, names, and facts. Yet, I always had a problem understanding the reasons for many events. Why would a king invade another country? Why was there a revolution? The teacher would give me some answers and reasons, but I always felt they were inadequate. There seemed to be something I was missing.

I was lacking background information on these events. But one common theme I could not understand was, why is there so much hatred and unhappiness in history?

One of my favorite subjects was science: this subject is one big investigation. There were questions to be asked and answers to be learned. In this subject, I gathered knowledge about the physical world around me.

Have you ever stopped to think about how many colors there are? And they are all wrapped up into one little beam of white light.

The Earth we live in is full of mountains and seas. And it spins around like a top as it orbits the Sun, with the Moon orbiting the Earth. The gravitational pulls of the Sun and Moon cause seasons and tides on Earth.

Weights and measures, how things move, and how things stop. Rockets that have taken people to the moon and submarines that go under the water.

What a wonderful thing science is.

I think with practice I could be a great musician someday. Music is an easy skill for me to learn. It combines the memory of the musical piece with the physical coordination of playing the instrument. The piano was one of my favorite instruments. With the keys laid out, it was easy for me to memorize where on the keyboard each note was. I made a memory map of the keyboard in my head. I could listen to a song and separate the piano notes in my memory. Then with my exceptional coordination skills, I could play the song note for note with perfect timing. It was like playing back a recording. I was even praised for this skill and began to build up a repertoire of songs in my memory. My coordination is such that I didn't need to look at the keyboard because I knew the position of everything. I even learned to read music in a short space of time. In many ways, this is a much simpler language to master than spoken English. Music does not have the vague ambiguities in its constructs that English has.

Many of my other classmates were good at these subjects too. They also had good memories or special abilities in math or music. So it seems the doctors that diagnosed me as autistic were correct, because I fit in well with this class.

If I had a problem subject, it was English. The many ambiguities in English continued to be a challenge. Mother continued to explain these to me, which helped me a lot.

There was one thing that differentiated me from all my autistic classmates. At different times and for a variety of reasons, all the others would occasionally become withdrawn or agitated in some way. How they behave when they are in this state can vary a lot.

One girl called Karen would withdraw now and then. As with all the others, her symptoms were predictable. She would begin by being agitated and irritable. She would fidget and wiggle uncomfortably and ignore everyone around her. In the next phase she squinted her eyes closed and covered her ears while bowing her head down and even lowering it onto her school desk. As her withdrawing worsened, she would crouch in the corner of the room, often slapping her head and face. This would be accompanied by a loud moaning or crying and rapid rocking back and forth. Teachers and support staff would comfort her as best they could and lead her into a quiet room where she could take time to calm down.

I once tried to ask her, "What's wrong?"

"It's too much!" she cried back.

"What is too much?"

"Everything!" She screamed back. "The noise, the lights, everything, it's all too much! I can't stand it!"

It took me some time to interpret this but from what I can understand it is this. Autistic people have many developmental issues, and one of them is a lack of filters. In a regular human brain, there are two levels, the subconscious, and the conscious mind. The subconscious will filter out all the irrelevant information and presents to the conscious mind only the information it needs to have. All the ordinary, tedious things that happen around you are filtered out by your subconscious. If something out of the ordinary happens, like a loud noise or a bright flash, then the subconscious alerts the brain.

There is a good reason for this process. The conscious mind doesn't want to be bothered by all the tedious nothings that are happening. It has more important things to do. If something out of the ordinary happens, then the mind needs to know, because it may be important. It could be food, or a threat that must be dealt with.

In Karen's case, she was being overwhelmed by all the tedious happenings around her. To her, everything that is happening around her is like a loud noise or a bright flash. After some time, it becomes too much for her. She once told me the reason for slapping her head. She said she was trying to drown out the rest of the world, trying to create her own filter.

I don't have a subconscious, so nothing around me is filtered out and I see every single thing in its immediacy. I am different because I can process all these inputs in parallel. I do not get overwhelmed, that is the nature of my creation and I believe this to be an intentional aspect of my design. I am made to be fully aware of everything around me at all times.

Although the curriculum at this special school offered plenty of physical exercise and games, I did not enjoy them in the same way I did in the hospital. The physical therapy in the hospital was very much a one-to-one exercise. The therapist gave instructions on how to do something and encouraged me to do it. I was rewarded with words of praise.

Here at the special school, games were more group oriented. This is OK because I enjoy the idea of interacting with other humans. However, the other children did not have a particularly good understanding of the rules or did not want to play.

For instance, locomotion games where we would skip, jump, or run in a circle would be OK for a while, but before long, one and then two would stop playing. Soon after, all the other children (apart from me) would follow suit.

As for team games, they very quickly descended into chaos. Children would change sides at random or start playing by themselves. The teachers kept the games short, simply to get children to move and run around and to burn off energy.

Chapter 13

The conference room in the Special School for Special Needs was adjacent to Dr. Magnusson's office. Melisa Sanchez and Jenny Schultz, from Roger Straus High school, sat at one end of the long table reviewing paperwork together. Adara's teacher Ms. Teas and the Special School counselor Ms. Courts sat at the other end of the table.

The conference room in the School for Special Needs was adjacent to Dr. Magnusson's office. Melisa Sanchez and Jenny Schultz, from Roger Straus High school, sat at one end of the long table reviewing paperwork together. Adara's teacher Ms. Teas and the Special School counselor Ms. Courts sat at the other end of the table.

Dr. Magnusson entered from his office and announced, "Adara and her mother, Mrs. Banks, should be here soon. Are there any questions before they arrive?"

Melisa Sanchez looked up from the doctor reports. "Dr. Magnusson, this report mentions violent defensive responses, can you elaborate on these?"

"They seem to have been caused by a fear of being approached, when she didn't understand people's intentions. For instance, sudden advances towards Adara caused her to react defensively. These have reduced significantly over time. Principal Gallagher at your school also has this report and he is satisfied with the doctor's explanations."

Jenny Schultz added, "As high school counselor, I have discussed this with our principal, as well as with Adara's doctors, and they affirm her violent responses have all but disappeared. So, Ms. Sanchez, when Adara enters your class, she should not be considered a problem."

Ms. Teas added, "Adara has not been a problem in my class; if anything, she has been very understanding towards her classmates."

"Yes," Ms. Courts continued, "these reports are from the time of her initial recovery from her accident. She was just out of a coma and very confused, so a defensive response at that time was understandable. I believe Adara should be in high school."

"I was just worried about Adara possibly reacting violently to any bullying while in my class."

"Don't worry Melisa," Jenny Schultz gently touched her arm, "as a counselor, I can assure you our school policy will protect against violence and bullying."

Dr. Magnusson raised both hands reassuringly. "The reports recommend that Adara remain under observation. They don't suggest violent behavior."

"Well, OK, doctor, we'll keep an eye on her during class," Melisa said, smiling.

The secretary came in. "Dr. Magnusson, Mrs. Banks is here with Adara. Would you like me to show them in?"

"Oh, yes please, Mary, let them in," Dr. Magnusson replied.

Mrs. Banks and Adara were led into the room.

"Hello, Mrs. Banks. So glad you could come to this parent-teacher meeting," the principal said. "You know that Adara has made some wonderful progress while she's been with us." Smiles beamed and there were approving nods all around the room.

"Sir?"

"Yes, Adara?"

"Here we have my mother, me, my teacher Ms. Teas, and the school counselor Ms. Courts. But there are also you, the principal, as well as two other people I do not know. So, is this a review, and not a parent-teacher meeting?"

"You are right, Adara," Ms. Teas said. "So, let's call this a review." She winked at the principal.

Mother said, "Adara is very intrigued by words and wants to try to use them correctly."

"I want to use the right words in the right place," I added.

"Yes, Adara is always asking about the meaning of words. She is one of my most outstanding students and we're all so proud of her," Ms. Teas added.

"Yes, we certainly are," Dr. Magnusson chimed in, "but before we continue, I'd like to do the introductions. Mrs. Banks, you know everyone here at Special, but as Adara so wisely pointed out, there are two new faces. Meet Jenny Schultz, the counselor at Roger Straus High school."

"Hello, Mrs. Banks, hello, Adara." Jenny Schultz nodded.

"And this is Melisa Sanchez, the new special class teacher at Roger Straus High."

"Hello, Mrs. Banks, hi, Adara." Melisa Sanchez smiled.

"We invited them both because we all believe Adara should move on to her next great achievement in high school."

"Yes, that's Adara's old school, but do you think she's ready to go back?" my mother asked.

"Oh, yes, Mrs. Banks," Ms. Teas said. "We've talked so many times about her remarkable progress. She is ready to move on."

"I'm a little worried about her going back to her former school, especially if she doesn't remember everyone there," Mother continued.

"Ah, we've talked about that," Ms. Courts added. "Straus High School is starting a special class, which will be taught by Ms. Sanchez. Straus High also has first-rate teachers in math and sports, so Adara's special abilities can easily be catered to."

"What sort of special class?" I was wondering that too, but Mother beat me to the question.

"That's a good question, Mrs. Banks," said Jenny Schultz, "I'll let Ms. Sanchez answer."

"Thank you, Jenny," Ms. Sanchez began. "Let me start by saying that our special class is based on the educational ideas of Maria Montessori. She was an Italian educator, physician, and scientist who developed new ways of teaching."

All attention was on Ms. Sanchez.

"Her theory was to keep the child's mind absorbed in a well-managed environment. The student needs to have independence, and the teacher's job is to observe, follow the child and make corrections only as needed. She often said, The greatest sign of success for a teacher is to be able to say, the children are now working as if I am not needed.'"

"So Adara will stay in this special class?" my mother asked.

"Yes and no," Ms. Sanchez replied. "Mine is a homeroom class made to mirror a family environment where children can develop more naturally. There is a mix of student ages, and they are encouraged to help each other learn. All of them will attend some regular classes, but this will be her base."

"Well, I'm a little worried about high school," Mother said, "especially if Adara gets bullied."

"What's bullied?" I asked.

"Let me answer that question, Adara," Jenny Schultz said. "Bullying is when children are mean towards another child. I'm the school counselor at Straus High, and I work to uphold the strict school policy of no bullying. We work hard to stop bullying and get all our children to be kind and appreciate one another."

"I've been worried about that, since my daughter has been through so much already."

"We do understand your concerns, Mrs. Banks. If there is anything we can do to assure you that Adara will be looked after in our environment, we will do it."

"I'm still a bit worried about my baby going back there."

"Mother, I would like to go back there, because that's where I used to be."

This is me emulating Adara. After all, why wouldn't she want to return to her old school? "I like anything where I can learn things, and this all sounds very interesting."

"But honey, this place might be too hard for you."

"Mother, everything is hard for me," I did not lie about this, "so why would high school be any harder?"

"Well, I think that answers your question," said the counselor.

With a sigh, Mother asked, "So what is the next step?"

"Everything is already arranged. We've discussed this with our principal, Mr. Gallagher, and everyone is excited about Adara coming back to her original school."

Chapter 14

"OK everybody, welcome back to the new school year!" A mixture of comical moans and "yays" followed as principal Gallagher strode into the staff room. He unloaded an armful of files onto a nearby desk and continued to address his staff.

"We all have a lot to get through in these next two days before the kids start so I'll make my speech quick." A clear set of "yays" followed.

"I would first like to welcome Melisa Sanchez who will be running our new special class. Melissa received her master's with accreditation from Oak Hill in Philadelphia, and we're very lucky to have her on our team."

"Melisa will be running her unit in K-19, our old staff room, more recently used as storage. It's big enough to accommodate a large class with support staff and has ample subdivisions if the class needs to split off into groups. It also has a restroom which the board was able to get past regulations as a unisex toilet.

"Would you like to say a few words, Melisa?"

"Thank you, John. Hello, I'm pleased to be here and look forward to getting to know everyone. As Mr. Gallagher already said, we have a wonderful, well=equipped classroom and several excellent support staff will be working with us. We have a relatively small class of 18 children," Melisa continued. "They are all from interesting backgrounds. As you may know, the unit is designed to help develop both independence and growth in children of any background and not just special needs. The class is structured like a supportive family unit, reflected in the varied ages and genders of the children. They will all benefit from the role models they develop and the learning process is designed to encourage mutual support."

The staff was politely interested. "The children will not be restricted to the unit, and many will be attending some of your regular classes." This raised some eyebrows and some questions.

Gabby Jones was the first. "Will we be informed of any special needs before they come to our class? Will they need assistant teachers to help them?"

"Well, actually, they are not necessarily special needs children. It's more a question of the teaching methods used in my classes, but it's also important that we integrate these children with the rest of the school. If there are any special circumstances, I'll brief you and provide any relevant notes."

The PE teacher Barry Scott, dressed in his tracksuit, was standing near the back of the crowd. His question showed he had not been giving Melisa his full attention. "Will we need to handle any special needs when they come to our classes?"

Principal Gallagher stepped in. "If there are any special needs, you will all be made aware of them. In the meantime, I suggest you all go back and read my memos and emails on this subject. But above all, everyone please drop by K-19 to have a look at the new classroom and welcome Melisa into our fold. The school board and the board of education are all fully supportive of this project and it's come a long way since we began planning this two years ago.

"And Barry," Gallagher continued. "I need to see you and the other coaches in my office later this morning. We have a busy sports schedule planned for this year and I want to help you get some good wins. Is 10 o'clock OK with you?" A nod and a wink followed from Barry Scott.

"OK everyone," Gallagher announced with 3 handclaps, "let's get on with our preparations. Classes start tomorrow morning, and the new school year starts right here and right now."

Amidst the chatter and noise as everyone separated into their groups and conversations, Janice Raines quickly edged her way toward Melisa.

"Hi Melisa, I'm Janice, Janice Raines, I'm heading the English department. We haven't met yet, but I've heard so much about you and the special project. I'd love to see your classroom – if you have the time of course."

"Yes! I'd love to show you around, I'm going there now. I'll introduce you to my support staff as well."

They maneuvered their way out of the staff room into the quiet halls. Noise and chatter emanate from all the rooms during classes, but without any children, background noise levels were at a spooky minimum.

As they entered the classroom Janice gasped, "Wow, this is a big room! I hardly recognize it from the staff room days."

"Well, we do need the space for what we plan to do here. We also hope to expand the class size over time."

Two girls too old to be students peered around their piles of work.

"This is Corinth and Mary-Jo, my 2 assistant teachers. This is Janice Raines of the English department."

There was a loud knocking at the door, which swung open to allow the entrance of the very formidable Mrs. Gabby Jones. Strutting into the classroom, she announced herself with a comment. "Wow, this is a nice big room." standing in the middle of the room, she nodded exaggeratedly. "How many did you say? Eighteen, wasn't it?

"Oh hello." Melisa whirled around in surprise, offering a handshake as an introduction. Gabby ignored her hand while her gaze searched the room. "Well, we're keeping it small for now, but it could grow larger as we integrate more children."

Turning away, Gabby waved her hand dismissively. "Wow, Gallagher didn't mention this class would be growing. I still think this is too big for special needs."

"Well, we are not special needs here, this is a class of mixed ages and abilities in a less formal..."

"Hm, OK, if you want to call it mixed abilities, that's fine, but we all know what you mean. To me, mixed abilities suggest special needs and I think you do have some special children in this class?"

Sensing the impending conflict, Janice stepped between them.

"Melisa, allow me to introduce to you Gabby Jones, she's our head of mathematics. Gabby, this is Melisa."

Melissa once again held out her hand. Gabby raised her hand in a welcoming gesture and turned around to continue investigating the room.

Slightly perplexed, Melisa watched as Gabby whirled around again, facing Melisa with an outstretched hand.

"I have to go back to my department and get things ready for my classes, but it was lovely to meet with you." Politely shaking Melisa's hand before she spun around and marched methodically out the door, waving to Janice over her shoulder. "See you later."

Janice turned to Melisa and said with almost a wink, "And you have just met Gabby Jones, our head of mathematics. Quite a character, isn't she?"

"Yes, quite something, but I'm not sure what that something is."

"She's OK, but a bit of a traditionalist in education. I think she's a little jealous because she always wanted this room as a study lab for math homework and extra help. However, our board has recently leaned towards support for special needs, which has left Gabby high and dry."

"Isn't there an after-school homework class?"

"Yes, but she wants a specific math lab. That would boost her teaching credibility, probably her salary, and certainly her ego. Anyway, I don't want to bore you with teacher gossip, you'll have plenty of time to catch up on all that soon enough. I must get back to my classroom and try to get organized. If there's anything you need, just ask."

"Oh yes, there is, actually, reading lists. I have an autistic child coming to class tomorrow and I'm told that she's an avid reader and reads at an incredible speed. She'll probably be in your English class. Her name is Adara Banks."

"Adara Banks? I heard she could be coming back."

"Yes, her file says she used to be a student here, about 2 years ago."

"Yeah, she had a terrible accident and nearly drowned. I often wondered what happened to her. Adara Banks is coming back – wow! Her mother still works in the kitchen, you know."

"I didn't know that. Maybe I should go and see her?"

"She's incredibly quiet and keeps to herself. She's nice though, good to the kids during lunch. She was married, I think, but I never saw anything of him, Bill I think he was called. Who knows, maybe he'll also turn up again?"

"I don't think he's on her file but yes, who knows?"

"Anyway, I must fly, I'll get you a list of books for her. A real pleasure meeting you and good luck with starting this class."

"Oh thanks, see you later."

Chapter 15

Mother used to drive me to school but that's because it was much further to the special school. As high school was close by, I could walk which is OK because I like the exercise and seeing all the sights in the neighborhood. Mother practiced walking with me several times on the days before school started, she did this because she wanted to make sure I would remember the way there and back again. It wasn't very far only three blocks or so. I told her after the first walk that I would easily remember the way but we did the walk two more times and she even made me lead the way.

Mother bought a satchel for me so I could carry my schoolbooks to and from school. This was like a soft leather briefcase with a metal clasp on the covering flap to hold it shut. It also had a detachable leather strap so I could either carry it as a briefcase or use the strap to carry it on my shoulder. I chose to carry it like a briefcase as the strap seemed to get in the way of many things.

"You will look like a businesswoman when you carry the satchel like that."

She also bought me a cell phone so I could call her in case I got lost or got into some sort of trouble. I knew I would not get lost but I still thought this was a good idea because I could not anticipate what sort of trouble could befall me.

She also laid down a lot of rules that I had to obey. Like, walk only on the sidewalk, how and where to cross the road, and that I should not speak to strangers and never under any circumstance get into a stranger's car. She also added, "Never get into ANY car, even if it is a friend unless they know the code word."

My mother then told me the secret code word, so if someone did have to pick me up, she would give them the code word and I would know that this person is supposed to pick me up.

The real school classes started the following Tuesday and my main teacher is Ms. Melisa Sanchez. She a label of homeroom teacher. She also has two support staff who work with her, Corinth and Mary-Jo they are all very nice and very clever but the best thing I find about them is they are very good at explaining things.

Including me, there are a total of 18 children in my homeroom class. Some are younger but we are all high school age except for Larry who is the oldest. He's old enough to go to college but he's been held back a year at least once because he has some learning difficulties.

Larry would often come to me and say, "Do that thing with your eyes!" At first, I wasn't sure what he was asking, but I soon realized what it was. I can move each eye independently, allowing me to keep my focus on one person while my other eye scans the room for other activities. Of course, while I do this I lose binocular vision on any given target, so I can't judge distance. But if I need to know the distance, all I need to do is to focus both eyes on a target, and in an instant, I have the perfect distance calculation. The beauty of this skill is my ability to maintain a given focus while scanning a room or area for different obstacles or threats.

Larry must have seen my eyes wandering in this way. My right eye would remain focused on the teacher while my left eye would scan the left side of the room. I would then alternate to focus on the teacher with my left eye and scan with my right and so on.

We will all be spending a lot of time in my homeroom but I am told that I will also go to other classes to learn other subjects like math, science, history, and English and I look forward to those.

As I walked along the school hallways on my way to other classes, many of the other children seemed to recognize me – or at least recognize Adara. "Hey Adara, you're back!" I would often hear, but I did not know who they were or what their connection was to Adara, so the best I could say was, "Hello, yes, I'm back." Or "Hello, how are you?"

There was one particular boy who said nothing to me but whenever we passed in the hallway, I could see that his eyes were tracking me. I was wondering if he was the same as me, the same type of creature existing within a host body. Once I almost asked him if he was an injected entity of nanobots, but this could conflict with my first directive to protect and safeguard my host.

I have since learned his name to be Brad Chandler. He also has a sister called Isabel, she also watches me whenever I walk past.

All the preparation that Mother provided for me and all the family photos she showed me did not have any background of Adara's school life, so I was at a loss on how to integrate with Adara's old friends. So I had to fumble as best I could and use the memory loss through trauma as an excuse.

Chapter 16

The noise was incredible. The argument wasn't loud, but it was solid, and Anita forgot how long it was going on. She couldn't distinguish the words, but she knew they were being thrown in anger.

The phone rang. Anita pressed the privacy button, directing the call to voicemail. She made the sign of the cross, ceremoniously touching her forehead, heart, and shoulders. *Why do they argue so much? What are they arguing about?* Anita thought about how her parents would argue about money, how to pay the bills, but this argument was something else.

Anita stood up from her desk, pacing around the reception area. She moved towards the hallway leading to the offices. The words between Professor Wolf and Dr. Coney were louder but still indiscernible.

What can I do? Anita anguished. *Bill! He can do something!* Anita returned to her desk, fumbling with her phone. *He's not answering!* She tried several times. *Why doesn't he answer?* Anita tapped down the other hallway in her high heels, towards Bill's office. Bursting through his office door without knocking, Bill leaned forward, quickly closing several windows on his computer screen.

"What the hell are you doing woman? Can't you see I'm working?"

"Please Mr. Mandelson, something awful is happening and they need your help."

"Who needs help?" Bill slowly rose from his chair, into his superhero mode.

"Come with me!" Anita exclaimed, as they both rushed towards the front of the building, when they arrived at the reception area, Anita stopped short, held up her hand, and said, "Listen!"

"What?"

"Listen," Anita urged, "You can hear them arguing!"

The words poured through the hallway, driven by anger. They were muffled and disjointed obstructing any meaning.

As Bill strained to listen, Anita cowered behind him, holding onto his back in fear. She eventually pushed Bill forward. "You must go!"

"What?"

"You must go and see what they are doing."

Bill stepped reluctantly into the hallway. Looking back at Anita, she said, "You must!"

Looking forward, Bill gulped air. *Why do I have to deal with this crap?* Tiptoeing along the hallway, Bill began to discern some of the words, mostly Dr. Coney's.

"What's happening to the money?"

Bill stood by Professor Wolf's door, hesitantly raised a single knuckle, and was about to knock gently. That's when he heard Dr. Coney say, "You are doing this to a human, aren't you? This is insane!"

That's when the office door flung open. Bill jumped back in surprise. Dr. Coney stormed out, ignoring Bill.

Sweeping past Anita, she cried, "Dr. Coney, what is wrong?"

He just waved his hand in the air as he stormed past.

Bill turned to see the professor standing at his office door, "That stupid geek is nothing but trouble!" Professor Wolf fumed, before slamming his office door shut. Behind the closed door, Bill could hear the professor say, "That God Damn Son of a Bitch is finished here!"

Anita rushed up to Bill, clutching his arm, while he backed away from the office door in fear. "What happened?" she pleaded, "Why is there such an argument?"

"I don't know," Bill said, "this isn't good." Bill moved his arm around Anita's shoulder to reassure her, and backed her away from the office, "I think we need to give them some space."

They could hear the front door slam as Dr. Coney left the building.

"I'm scared," Anita said holding tighter onto Bill's arm, "What are we going to do?"

Bill looked at Anita with a reassuring face. "Let's go to my office where we can talk about this." As Bill led her gently down the hallway, Anita gently dabbed a tear from her eye with the back of her finger.

Bill reached into his breast pocket and offered a handkerchief to Anita. "Here you go sweetheart, let Lieutenant Mandelson take care of you."

"Lieutenant? I did not know you were so strong and brave." Anita said dabbing her eyes. "

As Bill guided Anita into his office, he very gently closed the door behind them.

Chapter 17

"Hi Mother, I'm home." I always used the same greeting when I came home from school. Mother was always in the kitchen preparing food for dinner and she would always respond with her own same words. "Hi honey, how was school today?"

From there on we would have a short conversation about what happened to each of us during that day. Mother would always say what time dinner would be. She would then conclude the conversation by saying, "Make sure you are washed and ready in time."

When I first received such commands, I would immediately wash. Then I would ask my mother *What time should I be ready?*

She would reply with, "Dinner time of course."

This led me to understand that I should be washed and ready whenever Mother was ready for dinner.

I always responded with "Yes Mother."

I learned that dinner time was not an exact time.

The routine of daily life was always accompanied by simple commands like this. I would just concur, and I would then do as I was asked. I learned that such commands were not immediate.

Usually, I would come to the kitchen before dinner was ready, and then I would help to set the table or help with the cooking. During that time, we would talk about food and what we should eat, and why. Mother hated what she called 'Junk Food', and she taught me the benefits of fresh food and home cooking. The fact that she worked all day in a school kitchen and then came home to cook dinner showed how much she appreciated food and nutrition.

I always did as Mother would tell me, after all, my fourth directive instructed me to obey her. There was nothing that she asked that would be unreasonable. Wash your hands, clean your room, and make sure your homework is done. These were all logical tasks that needed to be performed, so I did them without comment.

There were many books in Adara's collection, and I made sure that I read them all. I don't have to spend days like a human does reading a book, I can do it in a matter of hours. Depending on the size of the book, I need to look at each page for about five seconds. During this time, I commit the page to memory and begin the process of parsing the text. If there are pictures or graphics, then that adds a little more time as I must store the image. For instance, a paperback book with about 300 pages, I can read in about half an hour.

Don't get me wrong, this doesn't mean I know the book inside out. I can appear to know it because I can quote passages from the book word for word, but full understanding takes a little longer. The reason for this is twofold. First, the parsing of the text may be slower depending on its complexity. Second, I then must make associations of meaning between elements of the book and what I already know about the world.

If I read a history of George Washington, and the episode of him chopping down a cherry tree, I would have to associate many things such as the tree, and the axe. These are the trivial elements, but other more complex things must be associated such as the benefits of lying versus honesty. As you can imagine, I will not fully understand some books until I have a better understanding of the world.

"Mother? Do you have any more photo albums I can look at?"

"Well, I think we looked at them all, but I'll see if I can find some more."

I started to scan the living room with my eyes, all the time thinking where more photographs could be stored. As my eyes looked at cupboards and drawers for possible locations, I also thought about places upstairs where they could be stored. Photographs were especially important to me. It's not just knowing the faces and names of the people in the photos, it's knowing the story of each picture.

Mother looked at me strangely.

"Is there something wrong?" I asked.

"You never used to do that," she said, "now I see it all the time."

"What?"

"The way you look at things when you're searching."

There was a moment of uncomfortable silence as we stared at each other. I wanted her to explain what she meant, instead, she just shook her head and said, "When you finish your homework and your chores, we can look for some more photos."

With this instruction, I had to wait for the photos. I had already finished my homework but needed to do my chores. It was Wednesday so I had to clean the bathroom, this would take about thirty minutes. I liked to keep things clean, so this is more of bathroom maintenance and not cleaning as such.

Mother liked to tidy the kitchen after mealtimes, so she had her work to finish.

So far, all the photos I had looked at were collected in photo albums. As I cleaned the bathroom, I wondered where any other photos could be, and how we could find them.

Mother's phone rang, and I heard her answer. "Oh hi, Cindy."

Then all I could hear was Mother's side of the conversation.

"No, I haven't forgotten."

"Yes, it's OK."

"Of course, you can."

"Thirty minutes would be great, we've just finished dinner."

"Adara wants to look at some pictures, so if you have any bring them along."

"Oh, that's wonderful."

"OK, I'll see you then, bye."

Mother then called up to me, "It's Wednesday and Cindy is coming over for her usual chat, is that alright?"

I don't understand why she was asking me if it was alright, but I answered, "Yes Mother, it's alright."

"She's going to bring some pictures we can look at."

Chapter 18

Since their colonial days, the French have always maintained political and economic influence in West Africa. Their military was providing police action in Burkina, suppressing terrorist factions. American troops play a logistic role, supporting the French as an ally.

Major Thomas Vance of the United States Marine Corp. didn't have to handle front-line action, but fear and paranoia were never far. The Americans leased an entire hotel in the capital, using it as their headquarters. The building was heavily fortified to protect against armed attacks.

Major Vance had been on patrol with his men for a whole week, escorting French supply convoys and protecting intelligence sources. Tall dark and physically lean, even sweat made the Major appear striking. Back at base, Vance checked his weapons, debriefed, and then settled back for some welcome rest.

"Welcome back sir." and formal salutes greeted the Major as he walked through the corridors.

The air-conditioned building and the clean showers were a stark contrast from the humid sweat of the tropical savannah. Before heading to his quarters Tom checked to see if he had any mail. "Yes sir, I got a few items right here for you."

"Thank you, corporal."

"The good news is," the corporal joked, "I don't think you'll get many bills in these parts."

"Well, if I do, you're welcome to keep them, or at least return to sender!" Tom winked back.

The next stop was the officers' mess to grab a couple of cold beers. Now armed with beer, mail, and kit bag, Tom headed to his quarters. *Now I have a few days to sit back, drink some beer, and catch up on reality*. He thought to himself.

After a refreshing shower, Tom chugged down a whole bottle of beer. The second would be drunk more leisurely as he opened his mail. One letter he recognized, was from Bill Mandelson, his old childhood buddy.

I wish I knew what the hell that crazy bastard Mandelson is up to. Vance thought to himself. *If he's running some kind of money racket then he had better have a share set aside for me.*

For some time now, Bill had been sending letters to Tom, but these were no ordinary letters. These always had a note requesting Tom to forward a sealed letter to an address in the Unites States. Tom never opened the sealed letters, instead, he relied on blind trust and dutifully forwarded them on as requested. Tom was pretty sure that Bill had some sort of insurance scam going. Since he was only forwarding letters, he felt confident that he could distance himself from any investigation. Still, there was always the nagging thought of what was he up to?

Always faithful, Tom thought to himself, *maybe too faithful.*

Bill Mandelson was an old childhood friend of Tom's, as young kids, they played soldiers together. They both grew up dreaming of protecting their country from all enemies both foreign and domestic. To become real soldiers so they could fight the bad guys.

When they came of age, Bill aimed high and opted for the Air Force, dreaming of becoming a flying ace. Tom was more down-to-earth and joined the Marine Corp "the real men", as he used to say.

Tom found out the hard way that 'real men' have to graduate through real hard training only to find themselves having to survive real hard battles fighting against real hard enemies who are trying hard to kill you. Through this fiery baptism and many foreign deployments, Tom acquired the skills and strengths of a warrior. As he worked his way up through the ranks to gain his commission, he became knowledgeable of what a true warrior should be.

In the writings on the 'Art of War', there was one thing that the ancient Chinese general and philosopher Sun Tzu inspired in Thomas Vance – once you engage in battle, even if you win that battle, you have lost. On the face of it, this is an insane contradiction, of losing even if you win a battle. But if you understand the wider picture of the conflict, then you'll begin to understand that any battle has a cost of money, resource, and lives. Say you defeat an enemy and capture a city. Coupled with whatever you have lost in the battle, you now must spend even more resources to govern that city. According to Sun Tzu, it is important to understand the tools of war but much wiser to wield these tools in such a way as to maintain a persuasive position of strength. You must 'convince' your enemy that it is in their interest to bow to your will. That way, they can then govern their city according to your influential guidance. That is the true nature of victory.

Bill always thought of himself on a higher dimension and was always thrilled to the idea of 'Air Superiority. When Tom and Bill were children, they would often play soldiers, Bill would always use missiles, bombers, or anything else he could to 'pound his enemy to hell'. Mandelson didn't make it through the Air Force Academy but was discharged primarily on reasons of less than perfect vision. There were probably some other things like his inability to follow strict orders, but he did go on to volunteer with the ANG or Air National Guard.

Dressed in his khakis and feeling very much refreshed, Tom went downstairs aiming for the bar. *A nice dinner and a few more beers would be very welcome.* He thought to himself.

Before the bar, he had to mail the envelope that Mandelson had sent. All he needed was to pay the postage and leave the letter.

Another Letter Home

My Sweet Berry and Adara,

I miss you both so much and I miss the times we spent together. I need to tell you how sorry I am for what happened to Adara. I think about it all the time and I wish it hadn't happened. I heard that she is back to regular school, they told me that she is doing well. I am so glad to hear that.

I am very well and the mission I am on is going fine. If things continue this way, I will be able to retire early. I could be getting a sizable bonus when that happens. I will be living the high life and I can take you both away into a new and easy life.

Why have you blocked my calls? I know you're still upset but can you text me? Can we just talk? I only want to know one thing - if you and Adara are happy together.

I would love to hear what you have to say about Adara.

All my love

Billy the Kid

William Banks USMC Special Deployment
Location withheld for national security

News Report!

By Ashley Jones

[*What you need to know to start the day:* Get Idaho Post in your inbox.]

The deadly fire that raged yesterday at the Idaho National Laboratory (INL) has been confirmed to have claimed the lives of three men. Firefighters from Station 1 in Idaho Falls were dispatched to the site, but only acted as support for the laboratory fire crews who were already actively engaged with the blaze.

The damage was contained to a single building that contained the offices for NeuroComm and did not spread to other buildings or structures. "The lab was completely gutted," stated the attending fire captain.

The three men that died have been named as Professor Hayden Wolf, Dr. John Coney, and William Mandelson. Their next of kin have been notified.

Investigations are ongoing as to the cause of the blaze, but reports suggest that Prof. Hayden and Dr. Coney were caught in the building while Mr. Mandelson, a security guard for the company, attempted to rescue the men.

NeuroComm is a startup company listed as a research organization working on artificial intelligence and nanotechnology. Currently there has been no official statement from the company. Records indicate that the company's primary financier was the US military.

A spokesman for Idaho National Laboratory has stated that it is common for tech companies to have their offices and labs on the INL campus.

Established in 1949 under the auspices of the Department of Energy, the INL has been at the forefront of research in the nuclear industry. It has since diversified to cover various scientific disciplines including bioenergy, control systems, robotics, and cybernetics.

There are unconfirmed reports that NeuroComm was a center for animal testing. There is no evidence to support such claims.

Chapter 19

Every week on Monday we would have a whole class discussion about a specific topic before breaking into our different subgroups for learning and play.

Then every Friday we would have another whole-class discussion about Monday's topic and if we learned anything during the week about it.

"I want to talk to everyone about bullying." Melissa begins to address her class and continues. "So first of all what is bullying, can anyone tell me what it is?"

The usual show of hands followed along with a few murmured replies.

"Being picked on."

"Being called names."

"Someone making fun of you."

I put my hand up and when called upon I said, "Bully for you."

"Adara that is not appropriate." Ms. Sanchez said, "That phrase means something completely different it is a compliment. I want to know if you understand what a bully is."

I put my hand down. I always struggled with the ambiguity of the English language. It has so many contradictions and collisions. This is another example of how I struggle with language. As I was contemplating this, Larry started fidgeting.

When in a large group, Larry was often too shy to speak, so sometimes he would speak with both hands covering his nose and mouth. Maybe by doing this, he thought that nobody would think it was him who said it. Larry covered his face with both hands and mumbled: "Brad's a bully."

Melissa recognized this action of Larry's and I think she even heard what he said but didn't respond immediately to him, instead she seemed to want to save this for later in the discussion. Instead, she continued and reinforced what many had already said.

"Yes, being picked on and called names is all part of bullying…

"Some people think that being a bully is tough, it's not tough.

Do you want to know what tough is? Go up to the people you tease and say you're *sorry.*

Do you want to know what tough is? Go up to the people that tease you and say please stop.

That's tough."

Melissa let those statements sink in for a moment before continuing.

"The important thing is, you must report bullying to a teacher or your parents. But how do you know if you are being bullied?"

Everyone looked at each other as if they knew the obvious answer. I continued to look at Ms. Sanchez waiting for her definition.

"Well," she said, "there are several things." As she spoke she wrote the keywords on the board in front of the class.

"Top of my list, and I think yours is aggression. Now can anyone give me an example?"

"Pushing or tripping." One girl said.

'Yes. Anymore?"

"Punching." A boy said.

"Breaking someone's things." Another boy said.

"Yes, these are all good examples of physical aggression, now what about verbal aggression?"

"Teasing." A girl said.

"Name-calling." Another girl said.

"Yes, these also are good examples of bullying." Ms. Sanchez said. "But is that bullying?" She asked.

"What?" We all suddenly became confused.

She continued. "If someone calls you a name because they are upset, does that mean they are a bully?"

"No, that's different, it's because they are upset." A girl said, and we all agreed with her.

"Yes, that's exactly right," Ms. Sanchez agreed, "but what makes a bully stand out?"

Silence.

Everyone looked at each other for an answer.

After a moment Ms. Sanchez spoke. "It's the fact that they do this repeatedly, over and over again."

I think I began to recognize the difference between a spontaneous insult or act of aggression and a sustained campaign of aggression. A spontaneous act can be an emotional outburst, and can probably be forgiven easily. Bullying will be ongoing and much more difficult to excuse. I found this discussion very interesting, but I noticed that Larry was staring at me. At first, I ignored it but he was looking in a very puzzled way, so I had to ask him, "Larry why do you keep looking at me?"

He smiled and giggled quietly. "Do it again." He whispered, not wanting to disturb the class.

"Do what again?"

"That thing with your eyes."

"Your eyes, they go this way and that way."

I glanced over towards Ms. Sanchez, hoping we weren't disturbing anyone.

"You see? You did it again! That is so cool!" Larry now giggled louder.

"Did what?"

"Larry, Adara," Ms. Sanchez interrupted, "I don't mind you talking but I don't want you to disturb the class."

"Sorry Miss," Larry replied. He then moved closer to me and whispered. "Your eyes, they go this way and that."

"Well of course they do, I'm looking around."

"Yea but they're going on their own."

"I don't understand what you're saying."

"Look at Ms. Sanchez."

I did as he said and looked at Ms. Sanchez, causing him to giggle some more. This time he covered his mouth to stifle the giggles.

"What are you laughing at?"

He stopped giggling and held one finger up and said, "Only one eye looked." And started giggling again.

I didn't even think about it until now. After all, why should I? Everybody's eyes move together, when you look at something you look with both eyes. I can move my eyes independently. I use both eyes to get depth and distance, but once I have the scene mapped out, I can use each eye independently to look at two things at once. When I looked at Ms. Sanchez, I moved one eye towards her and kept my other eye on Larry. Up until now, I didn't even think about it. My vision was different from everyone else, I could watch different things at the same time. This must look strange to people, it certainly made Larry laugh. I wonder if I will be bullied for this.

Chapter 20

General Buckner sat at his desk. His chiseled face showed concern as he worked on his computer. He brushed his hand through his slightly greying hair as his desk phone rang. Pressing the speaker button he answered, "Yes?"

The voice of his secretary replied, "Captain Johnson is here to see you. Lieutenant Colonel Moore is with him."

"Good, send them in." Buckner closed the line, then sat straight against the chair with his elbows on the arm rests.

Captain Charles Johnson entered, stout and slightly chubby faced, followed by Lieutenant Colonel Steven Moore. Both men saluted the general.

Buckner was used to his second in command, Captain Johnson, but this was his first meeting with Colonel Moore. Buckner fixed his gaze on Moore for several moments, assessing him. He used this approach to check a soldiers resolve. When he was satisfied with the length of eye contact, Buckner released their salute.

"At ease gentlemen, you may take a seat."

"Thank you, sir," Colonel Moore replied.

"Charles, I've asked you here for an update on the INL accident. I must report to the Pentagon on what happened at NeuroComm. So, what have you found out so far?"

Captain Johnson crossed his legs, subconsciously going into a defensive position. "Well sir, it's only been two days since the fire, but we have gathered some considerable information. As you know, we have engaged Colonel Moore, who has resolved several investigations to satisfactory conclusions. Perhaps I can hand over to the Colonel." Captain Johnson then uncrossed his legs and turned towards Colonel Moore.

Bruckner nodded towards Moore with a neutral expression.

Moore nodded to Captain Johnson saying, "Thank you, Captain." Keeping his feet firmly grounded, he turned to face General Bruckner. "General, sir, thank you for inviting me to lead this investigation. As Captain Johnson states, I have been active in many investigations; these include internal affairs, two espionage incidents in NATO, and more recently that ugly scenario in Korea."

"Ah, yes," Bruckner affirmed. "We have your background, and we are happy you can lead this investigation for us. Can you update me on what you have found so far?"

"Yes sir, Captain Johnson has given me all the background on the project, including level one security clearance. I must say this is very innovative technology which I'm sure our enemies would like to get their hands on. Therefore, I will consider infiltration as a high possibility."

Bruckner looked down his nose, "Very good Colonel, but have you found anything yet?"

"After processing the interviews with eyewitnesses, the fire at NeuroComm seems to have been started by one of the founding executives, either Professor Wolf or Dr. Coney, both of whom perished in the blaze. The third fatality, Mr. William Mandelson, was the security officer who tried to rescue the two men."

"What about the computer files?" Bruckner asked.

"All the computer equipment seems to have been destroyed. In fact, it seems to have been deliberately targeted for destruction. My forensic team have recovered the hardware and will make attempts to recover the data from the damaged hard drives."

"When will that data be ready?" Bruckner asked.

"It's difficult to say, sir. If data has simply been erased, then it's possible to recover lost files using something as simple as undelete. If the drives were reformatted, electron scanning microscopes can recover erased files. If the data was encrypted, that adds a level of difficulty. If the disks on the hard drives were melted, recovery is impossible. I have to wait for my team to report back."

"OK," Bruckner confirmed, "What about the money? We have a very significant dollar investment, which needs to be accounted for."

"Yes, sir, this is top of my agenda. I have court injunctions with all the relevant bank accounts. I have confirmation that bank details will be returned to us by tomorrow morning."

"Very good work Colonel, I'm glad to have you on our side. At least I can report some progress to the Pentagon now. You will need to provide daily reports on your findings."

"Yes, sir, thank you sir. I will keep you updated."

Captain Johnson said, "Sir, I have one other item to report."

Bruckner suddenly had an uneasy feeling. *What other things will Johnson report?*

"What is it?"

"Records show that there were ten receptacles of working nanotech stored in the lab. Seven were found destroyed in the fire, which leaves three unaccounted for."

"What?" Bruckner shouted. "Are you telling me we've lost all the nanotech?"

"Yes, sir," Johnson looked nervous.

"And three have gone AWOL?" Bruckner nearly exploded. "Jeezus H. goddam, Mr. Smith Christ! Why am I only hearing about this now?"

"Sir," Johnson looked apologetic, "I only found out moments before this meeting."

Bruckner now looked flustered. Company executives fighting, fraudulent company accounts, destructive fire, can all be managed and accounted for. Missing secret technology? That is a lot more difficult to explain.

Captain Charles Johnson swallowed hard.

"What about the animals?" Bruckner asked, "I know they have all perished but is any nanotech recoverable from their remains?"

"Sir, the bodies are being examined in a military lab, we will have a full report in the morning, but the initial statement says there is unlikely to be any recoverable material."

"The nanotech receptacles that were destroyed, and the burned animals can be explained. Missing receptacles is a serious breach of security, I need to know exactly what happened to them. More importantly, if someone has them, I want them back."

"Sir, I agree that this is of prime importance," Colonel Moore said.

"That's right sir," Captain Johnson interrupted, "Moore will be leading this part of the investigation, his skills will be very suited to this kind of work."

"Well, I damn well hope so Johnson, this needs to be closed off ASAP! Colonel, what are your thoughts on this so far?"

"Sir, it is cetain they were used on animals, which have since been euthanized. I will study the lab records to cover this issue. There is also the possibility of an external security breach."

"God help us all if that's the case!" Bruckner said.

"The security systems will be my first item to check. However, there is something else that bothers me."

"What is it Colonel?"

"Perhaps it's an internal issue."

"What do you mean?" Bruckner looked quizzical.

"Well, why were Wolf and Coney arguing so openly? Perhaps the missing receptacles have some connection?"

Chapter 21

I was sitting on the edge of my bed playing with my guitar. I wasn't playing songs, I was trying to figure out how it worked. At school, Mrs. Fields had taught me how to play the piano. She taught me that the piano has a logical structure to the keys and how to position my hands to play sequences of notes and chords. Once I had understood that I had built a good repertoire of songs to play.

I was sitting on the edge of my bed playing with my guitar. I wasn't playing songs, I was trying to figure out how it worked. At school, Mrs. Fields had taught me how to play the piano. She taught me that the piano has a logical structure to the keys and how to position my hands to play sequences of notes and chords. Once I had understood that I had built a good repertoire of songs to play.

The trouble I was having with the guitar is, having to work out the logical structure of notes on the strings. This has only five strings, while the piano has 88 keys, so I had to figure out ways to play other notes. One way was to hold down the strings on the fretboard, to make a higher note. The second was to loosen or tighten the string by turning the tuning keys at the top of the fretboard. What I couldn't work out was a logical way to coordinate these methods to play a song.

Downstairs the doorbell rang. It was Cindy, she always came around on Wednesday evenings to sit and talk with Mother. I was able to hear their conversation.

"What is that noise upstairs?" Cindy asked.

"Oh, that is Adara, she's playing with her guitar." Mother replied.

"That's not playing, that's torturing! If she carries on like that she'll break something."

"I think she's trying to work something out." Mother said. "It's like she's forgotten how to play."

"You're telling me. Do you mind if I go and talk to her?"

"Sure, I didn't want to say anything but I was going to tell her to stop if this carries on like that."

Cindy came upstairs and peeped through my open door. "Hi Adara, what are you doing?" She asked gently.

"I'm trying to figure out how to play this guitar."

"But you already can play the guitar, have you forgotten how?"

This is where I have to be careful to protect myself. Since Adara had a guitar, she must have known how to play, but it is obvious that I cannot. So I have to make an excuse, but I do have an alibi. Since Adara was diagnosed as autistic with memory loss, I can use the memory loss issue.

"Well I'm trying to remember, but it is difficult."

"Do you remember when I helped you to learn? Maybe I can give some of your knowledge back? Can I try?"

"Oh, yes, tell me what to do."

"First of all, give me the guitar, because I think you've put it out of tune."

I handed the guitar to her. The first thing she did was to put the strap around her neck. I was wondering what that was for, I thought it was for hanging on the wall but I can now see it is for holding the guitar on the body.

"I enjoyed it when I first taught you, Adara, so many years ago. You used to have an electronic tuner, do you still have it?"

I must have looked blank and confused because she said, "Never mind, we can make do without. When you hold the guitar like this, it's called 'right-handed'. Some people play left-handed, but the strings will be arranged differently. Your guitar is right-handed so the strings have to be tuned as 'E, A, D, G, B, E', with a low E at the top here. Can you remember that?"

"Yes, as 'E, A, D, G, B, E', with low E at the top."

"We need to start with the sixth string or the top string. That needs to be tuned to the note 'E'. Can you hum that note?"

I knew that note so I hummed it, and Cindy hummed with me. As we hummed, she plucked the sixth string and tightened the tuning peg until it matched our voices.

"This is how I taught you to tune a guitar." She said.

I watched attentively.

"Do you remember the rule? Every string has a corresponding note on the fifth fret below it. So the open sixth string is an 'E', but when I play the fifth fret, it is an 'A'."

She plucked the string gently open and pressing on the fifth fret to demonstrate.

"So the fifth string when I strum it open, should be an 'A'."

She strummed both strings and they didn't match, so she used the tuning peg on the fifth string to make it play 'A'.

"Then we carry on, following our rule. The fifth fret on the fifth string plays a 'D', so the open fourth plays a… what?"

"That plays a 'D' too."

"Yes, you have it."

"The fourth string, the fifth fret plays a 'G', so the open third plays a 'G'."

When she had the third-string tuned she stopped and said, "Here is a slight change in the rule. The fourth fret on the third string plays a 'B', while the open second string plays a 'B'."

When the second string was tuned she said, "We then finish with the original rule. The fifth fret on the second string and the open first string is the high 'E'."

"Oh, why is that?"

"I don't know," Cindy shrugged, "I'm not an expert on the guitar, I think you'll have to ask your teachers. All I know is, sometimes rules change."

"Rules change?"

"Well they change for reasons, but I don't know the reason in this case."

She finished tuning the guitar and asked, "Do you see what I've done?"

"Yes."

"Do you see the pattern of the notes?"

"Yes."

"So now your guitar is in tune. This isn't the best way to tune a guitar, because if the first string is slightly off, then all the others will be off too. What you have to do is check with a few chords and make sure they all sound right. You may need to check the guitar is in tune every once in a while. But now you can start to play."

Watching Cindy explaining the process for tuning, I realized that the tuning peg was used only for tuning and not for playing. Once the guitar was tuned, I began to see how the frets were used to play different notes on the same string. Each fret had a scaled relationship to the one above and below.

"This is how you play a simple scale on the guitar." Cindy then played the scale several times, showing me how to place fingers on the fretboard. "Now it's your turn to." And she handed the guitar back to me.

I put the strap around my neck and played the scales just like she showed me.

"That's very good, you're remembering now." She admired.

"Can I play cords? Like on the piano?" I asked.

"Yes, you then need to hold your left fingers on different frets and strum with your right hand instead of plucking individual strings."

She then showed me how to hold the chords C, A, G, E, and D.

"There are many more but you can remember these by the word 'CAGED'. Now play them gently and practice moving your left hand from chord to chord."

I followed her instructions and found I could do this quite easily. Adara's fingers seemed to be well suited to playing guitar, they seemed to fit well into the fret spaces. I wondered if there was some bodily memory that helped.

"OK, so that is the end of lesson one!" Cindy smiled. "You are remembering very well."

"Thank you for your help," I said politely.

"Now you need to practice the scales and the chord progressions. But you need to do it quietly because I think your mom was getting a bit annoyed with your earlier attempts."

"OK, I will, and I'm sorry about my noise."

"I have to go back to your mom, now, she's waiting downstairs and we have lots to chat about."

"Yes of course, and thank you, Cindy, for your help."

She touched me gently on the hand and smiled before going back downstairs.

My bedroom door remained open, I continued to listen to them talking downstairs while I quietly practiced on Adara's guitar. Being able to perform several tasks at once, I could easily listen to their remote conversation while I quietly played. While I listened and practiced my scales and chords, I wondered what causes rules to change. Do all rules change? How will I know when rules change?

"Cindy, you are such a gem," My mother said, "I think we can now have a peaceful chat."

"It wasn't so difficult, all I had to do was to remind her how to use the guitar."

"This is the funny thing, she seems to have forgotten so much about everything. It's as if I have to explain all things from first principles."

"Don't worry Beryl, she's been through a lot. Be thankful for what you have, and with Adara, you have a beautiful flower trying to bloom. Now, where's that bottle of wine I brought?"

"Oh, yes, let's open that. I also have some nice snacks I found on the farmers market, I think they'll go well with the wine."

I heard them preparing some items in the kitchen, and gathering the wine glasses. They then settled into the living room to continue their chat.

"Since she has come home, her taste in music has changed." My mother said.

"In what way?"

"Well she used to like only one type of music, I can't remember what they call it or who the bands are but it seemed to be only one kind."

"And now?"

"Now she seems to like everything. The funny thing is, she always listens so intently as if she is trying to analyze it."

"Adara is analyzing? Are we talking about the same Adara?"

"That's just it Cindy. Watch her next time you have a chance, you'll see what I mean."

"Well that's probably the autism showing, they have different attention to things. They see a new level of detail, and they have to analyze each little bit. I wouldn't worry about it."

"I suppose you're right."

"As for her music, she's growing and learning new things, so that's a good thing. Be thankful that she's exploring new music."

"Maybe I just worry too much."

"You're a mother, it's your job to worry. Anyway, did you get these crackers on the farmers market?"

"Oh yes, are they delicious?"

"And what is this cheese?"

"Shropshire, it's English."

"I think I've heard of it. Is it from the market too?"

"No this is from Danny's Deli."

"You do find the best food."

Chapter 22

Math class was one of my favorite subjects and it was taught by Mrs. Gabby Jones, who incidentally was head of the school math department. I have an inbuilt arithmetic logic unit or ALU that allows me to calculate any equation to provide the result. My programing also allows me to follow the symbolic notation of the mathematical language – or any language – so I can parse algebraic equations of X and Y and work out the simplified logic to achieve an answer.

There was a girl called Isabel who always sat at the back of the class with her other friends. She once asked me to come and sit with them but I politely declined because I preferred to sit at the front where I enjoyed following Mrs. Jones's lessons. As Mrs. Jones explained a new math concept and wrote equations on the blackboard, I followed along quite easily and I was always the first to raise my hand to answer her questions.

I soon recognized that not everyone in the class was as interested as I was and I think some even found this subject to be tedious and maybe even meaningless. Isabel and her friends were the least interested in math and instead always seemed to have more interest in their private jokes.

Isabel who was quite smart but also quite arrogant once asked, "Why do we have to learn this?"

Mrs. Jones did not provide an insightful answer but simply insisted that we have to and it was good practice for our brains. This girl seemed to think that computers could do all this calculating work for us and no one needs this 'complicated stuff' anymore.

I later found out that Isabel was Brad Chandler's sister. So it seems that both Isabel and Brad Chandler have some sort of interest in me because they both always want to keep their eye on me.

It was during one of these math lessons that something strange happened.

One morning during class, Mrs. Jones was explaining the application of derivatives and she was using some real-life scenarios to illustrate on the blackboard. I could hear the girls stifling giggles behind me and so could Mrs. Jones who would occasionally say, "Quiet please!" As she continued writing out equations.

A folded piece of paper landed on the floor next to me. It looked too neat to be something that was just thrown away, so I picked it up, unfolded it, and began to read the text that was written on it. Although laid out and punctuated poetically, I won't tell you what was written because I don't think it was intended as serious poetry. What the text did seem to focus on was how Gabby gobbled a Jones. Now Gabby Jones was the teacher's name but I did not understand what all the gobbling was about, so I read this and reread it and as I did so, more giggles permeated around the room. This continued until Mrs. Jones turned around and saw the paper that I was holding.

"Adara! What on Earth do you have there?!"

"I have a note which I think is about you," I said honestly.

"Dear God girl!" She shouted as she snatched it from my hands.

Standing in front of me she turned the sheet around to read the text, inadvertently displaying the picture to the whole class.

Guffaws of laughter ensued through the children around me.

I did not realize there was a picture on the reverse side of this page, but now that I saw it, I realized this is what Mrs. Jones saw first. It was an effigy of Mrs. Jones which seemed to be mouthing a phallic symbol, complete with her named as 'Gabby the Gobbler'.

Everyone was laughing except for me and Mrs. Jones. But since I was caught in possession of this offensive caricature, it was me who was the prime culprit of this outrage.

"My God girl! You will go to the Principal's office this minute!" Ms. Jones screamed at me.

"And the rest of the class will receive my wrath as well!"

Hence I was dispatched with immediacy to the Principal's office. Although it was eventually agreed that I would not do such a terrible thing, I was also included in the detention of the entire class as no one was forthcoming with admission to their guilt.

It took me some time after this event to understand the double meanings for the Word 'Jones' and how the synonyms for the name Gabby and adjective of Gobbler can be connected in such a suggestive way. What took me even longer to understand was why Isabel continued to stare at me in each math class.

Chapter 23

It waited, patiently.

And it waited some more.

On the third day, it became concerned about food.

I have plenty of water. It reasoned. *But my supplies of protein, carbohydrates, essential oils, and vitamins are becoming depleted.* It didn't need to take stock of supplies because it already had the full inventory stored in its memory.

Perhaps this is a mission and they have not told me because they want to see how I react. I have had many missions of shopping trips, but they always provided a shopping list and they have always told me when to go.

In much less than a second, a shopping list was made and stored in its memory.

The second factor was how to pay. It had access to several credit cards, debit cards, and a very large amount of cash. It decided the payment method to be cash, this was because it was always instructed to purchase shopping with cash. While the plastic cards were always reserved for 'special purchases and transactions'. It calculated how much cash it would need according to the shopping list and included ten percent extra in case of price fluctuations. It also decided to take a credit card and a debit card – just in case of emergencies.

Two cars were parked outside the house, the red Wrangler Jeep and the white Audi A8. The Jeep is what was usually used on missions. However, Mr. Mandelson once commented on how lucky it was to drive the Audi, this statement seemed to indicate that this vehicle should be reserved for something special. It considered this to be a special event so Beta-One made its own decision to drive the Audi to go shopping.

Driving alone was unusual for Beta-One, on a regular mission it would have a set of instructions to follow with certain objectives to achieve. But Mr. Mandelson would always accompany it to provide help or assistance and it could also benefit from his constant so-called 'small talk'. Beta-One was also aware it was always being monitored remotely by the professor and although it did not bring any monitoring equipment on this mission, it wondered if there were any concealed monitors watching over it.

So it decided to drive to Rexburg for the shopping, this was a little more than an hour drive but all the nearby towns were small with very limited stores with limited provisions. Beta-One was familiar with Rexburg as it had been on many missions there to banks, offices, and shopping so it knew exactly where to go. To buy a week's worth of provisions, the choices in Rexford justified the distance.

Leaving the Audi locked in the parking lot, Beta-One collected a shopping cart and moved through the aisles filling the cart with provisions. The shopping list that it created was derived from previous lists that Mandelson gave it, these lists were geared to the recipes for Beta-One's weekly diet as well as the special meals it prepared for the professor and Mr. Mandelson when they visited.

While navigating through the aisles, it overheard a conversation about a deadly fire that happened recently in Idaho National Laboratory.

"Didn't they mention animal testing on the news?" Someone said.

"Who knows what goes on in these government places," another woman replied, "I just hope there are no chemical leaks."

Beta-One considered these comments, it knew that Mandelson and the professor worked at a laboratory they called INL, it also knew they had animals there such as the dogs which sometimes accompanied it on missions. It needed more information to determine if there was any connection between this event and why its masters were not communicating. So at the checkout when paying for the provisions, it asked the checkout clerk, "What happened at INL?"

"Oh, some big fire and 3 people are dead."

"When did the fire happen?"

"A few days ago, it was a big thing on the news."

"The news?"

"Yeah, you know on the TV. Didn't you see it?"

"No, I didn't."

"Search on Google for it."

"OK, I'll do that."

Beta-One paid for the provisions by cash and resolved to investigate this report further when it returned home. It thought about the news and Google, it was familiar with these terms and knew it could find information.

After packing the groceries into the car it sat back in the driver's seat and prepared to drive back to the house.

There is enough gas to return to the house, it thought, *but not enough to go elsewhere. And since some sort of emergency may happen I will have to ensure the tank is full.*

With that Beta-One drove to a gas station to buy some gas. "Fill her up!" As Mandelson used to say. However, Beta-One only brought enough cash for provisions and did not anticipate having to fill the tank, so the only option was to use the credit card to pay for gas.

On the way home, it tried to use the radio to listen to a news channel, it cycled through the many music stations before finding a relevant channel but then it had to wait for any reports on the INL fire. For the entire hour's drive home, nothing was mentioned on the radio about INL.

Maybe it is not an important topic Beta-One considered it as it drove home. *But I must have more information.*

Back at the house, Beta-One parked the Audi in the same place next to the Jeep. It unloaded the provisions and stored the items in their allocated places in the kitchen. Then according to its pre-programmed schedule of eating it commenced to make a wholesome dinner and sat down to eat. When dinner was finished and everything was washed and put away, Beta-One entered its scheduled quiet time originally designed to allow the human host body to rest and digest, but Beta-One decided to use this time to investigate the news.

In its few short years of existence, Beta-One did not watch TV but having observed Mr. Mandelson, it was familiar with its operation. Searching through the channels it eventually found several news channels but still, nothing was informing it of the INL incident.

The girl at the store checkout mentioned 'Google', so it turned to the computer to perform a search. Beta-One had used a computer several times but always under the guidance of the professor to perform some setup to prepare forms for missions to banks or other offices. Using 'Google', it was able to find an abundance of information on the Idaho National Laboratory, its history, and background. There were links to the news stories about the recent fire, some with video footage of the fire and interviews of local witnesses. The most important news item that Beta-One read was the names of the three people who died; Professor Hayden Wolf, Doctor John Coney, and Mr. William Mandelson.

This left Beta-One with the startling realization that its masters have died! It now realized that it was not on a mission. Since Alpha One was always kept in isolation and only allowed to interact with people under strict rules, it was easy to conclude that there would no longer be anyone to send it on a mission. This meant that Beta-One was totally alone in the world.

There were no missions to perform.
There was no one to report to.
Beta-One was isolated.
Derelict.

Beta-One thought to itself, *my prime directives have been disrupted, so what am I to do now?* It tried to review all five directives.

1. Obey all commands from Professor Hayden Wolf. *'This is now NULL.'*
2. Obey all commands from William Mandelson, provided they do not conflict with directive one. *'This is now NULL.'*
3. Maintain physical integrity of the host body, provided this does not conflict with directive one and two. *'There is a dependency in this logic statement, but I can still maintain physical integrity of the host body.'*
4. Maintain stealth and secrecy and do not reveal to other humans who you really are. *'This directive is still clear.'*
5. Avoid confrontation with other humans unless instructed by Professor Hayden Wolf. *There is a dependency in this logic statement, but can I now confront humans?*

There was nothing in its programming to account for such an eventuality. In situations of being lost or simply losing communication, it was programmed to reacquire contact with the base, using various means such as phone, radio, internet, or even physical searches but there was nothing to cover this situation. Beta-One searched for meaning and purpose in its programming and each programming thread it perused, came to the same dead end. There was absolutely nothing to determine what it should do next in this situation. While scouring its knowledge base with statistical inquiries, it did reveal two words that became focused – freedom and life.

Does this mean it was free?

What does life mean?

Beta-One thought, *I have a house for shelter. A good supply of water and heat. Also, I have weapons, money, and vehicles for transport.* What it did not have was an idea of what to do, despite all of its resources it was lost and alone.

It had the Internet and turned to it for information. It was programmed as a hunter, so it began to hunt for answers on the Internet.

There were many articles about life in all its varied forms but nothing conclusive about the meaning of life. Following the searches for the meaning of life, there were also search results on how to improve life. These searches also proved inconclusive and relied heavily on other supporting requirements such as happiness.

One thing that it did learn about life is that every organism has specific longevity – meaning that it will eventually die. This was a very interesting discovery because up until now it did not realize that life can come to an end, it had always assumed that its own life would continue indefinitely. Of course, it had terminated other animals while hunting but it was Beta-One that had caused the animal's death.

Now it was learning about things like a disease that can weaken and even kill an organism. More ominous was a thing called old age, which makes death to be a certainty for all organisms. Beta-One's realization that it would eventually die came as a shock, mainly because it could not imagine not existing. It knew its beginnings as it took over the body of Gary Fletcher, but now it knew that Gary Fletcher will eventually die and with him so will Beta-One.

This new perspective now gave some purpose to Beta-One, it had to somehow survive. Beta-One assumed that its nanobots could continue to live – possibly indefinitely. Without a living host such as Gary Fletcher, it could not survive, so when Gary Fletcher dies so will Beta-One. This leads to one possibility – before Gary Fletcher dies, move the Beta-One nanobots into a new host. How could this possibly be done?

So for life to continue, all living things need to reproduce. Beta-One slowly began to understand that life was more than just the individual. Of course, an individual was alive and therefore had life, but there is also the life of the species. So individuals can die while the species can live on.

All of Beta-One's searches on the Internet about life returned the same recurring theme that life needs to replicate and reproduce. There are two types of reproduction; Sexual and Asexual.

Sexual reproduction involves an interaction between two organisms of the same species. This interaction allows them to share genetic material to create a wholly new organism of that species.

Asexual reproduction creates a clone of the organism either through cellular division as bacteria do, or vegetative propagation, where a new plant can grow from a fragment of an old plant. The same way a new potato plant can be grown from a small slice of potato.

Beta-One's nanobots use cellular division to reproduce and spread throughout the host body. This is a form of asexual reproduction, this reinforces Beta-One's assumption that it can live on indefinitely. Individual nanobots can die, but the collective 'species' or higher-level organism which forms into Beta-One, can live on.

The most powerful and widespread search engines will learn what you are searching for and build up a pattern of search questions. Such features of these engines are designed to help guide you to answers but it also helps the engine to know what sort of advertising it should target towards you. In this way, while Beta-One learned about reproduction the search engine found many documents and articles on human reproduction, the advertising that appeared was for pornographic websites.

Beta-One was then able to watch many videos that showed graphic lessons on how humans replicate. The hours ran into an entire day of investigation and during that time Beta-One was even able to practice, this was important because it needed to know if it was capable of performing a sex act. Once this fact had been confirmed it then had to work out if sex was a practical way for it to reproduce.

Yes, it could produce sperm, therefore it would be able to make a female human pregnant. However, was the number of free nanobots in the semen enough to build a replica of itself? Of course, the new child would be a mix of genetics from Gary Fletcher and the female mate, but the intention is to introduce enough nanobots to the new embryo and thus create a new version of Beta-One in the new child, its name could be Beta Two.

Beta-One concluded that it would be impossible to tell if this could be successful, and the only way to find out would be with a practical test. There was even information on the internet that could help it find a mate. There were many guides on how to find the girl of your dreams, many pages that advised on chat-up lines, or how to introduce yourself to a girl, all of these seemed to indicate that finding a girl will cure loneliness.

"So loneliness seems to be associated with not having a mate. Since I don't have a mate, then I must be lonely."

With that logic, Beta-One resolved to find a mate to reproduce. Since all of its prime directives were either nullified or compromised, it felt that it could now guide itself through life and this would now be its prime directive.

'Prime directive one;' it thought, beginning a list, 'Find a mate.'

'Prime directive two; Reproduce.'

'Prime directive three; Stay alive.'

Now that it has created its prime directives, it felt free, independent, and alive.

The next time he was at the supermarket, he tried to approach what he thought was a healthy woman of childbearing age. He used one of the chat up lines he learned from the internet.

"Hey, you're pretty and I'm cute, do you know that together we'd be Pretty Cute?"

"Oh, Jeez!" The woman exclaimed as she pushed her cart full of shopping further down the Aisle.

Beta-One tried many chat-up lines like this. The venue that it chose was the supermarket where it shopped for food. *This seems like a good location*, it thought to itself, *there are many women who frequent this shop, so statistically, I should be able to find a suitable mate reasonably quickly*. It also tried other stores large and small at different locations, any store that it thought women would frequent. It had decided on a type of woman to select as a mate; childbearing age from 18 to 30 years old, fit and healthy, so sporty and athletic types were prime candidates. As for appearance and style, Beta-One did not have a preference as a person's looks could not influence its decision, as long as there were no deformities, marks, or blemishes, then Beta-One would make the selection.

"Are you a Wi-Fi hotspot? Because I feel a connection."

Questions like this may have had some sort of effect if it was voiced in a human way or perhaps in a humorous way but every attempt by Beta-One fell flat. The way it attempted to make conversation was very bland and monotone and very much without feeling. Small talk was never one of its strengths, so Beta-One was never able to approach a woman with any sort of charm. All it could do was blandly repeat the simplistic phrases it had learned from the internet, and this was not proving to be productive. So Beta-One attempted to improvise.

"If I told you that you had a great body, would you hold it against me?"

"Excuse me?"

"I'm searching for a mate and I desire sex, would you like to engage with me in sex? I understand that sex is pleasurable for both persons." As Beta-One said this, it approached the woman holding out its hand towards her breast.

The woman ran to the front of the store and reported the incident to the store manager. Security was called, and although Beta-One could have easily subdued the security guard, it decided that confrontation would be against directive 5. Beta-One quickly left the store.

After many attempts of trying to find a mate, Beta-One realized that it was failing to achieve its objective. It could not ask for help because that may run counter to directive 4.

"I'm programmed as a hunter." It reasoned, "I perform best when I act with stealth and secrecy, so I will need to adapt my tactics accordingly.

Chapter 24

"OK everyone, come in and take your seats, we have a lot to get through in this lesson." Dave May, the science teacher, urged his students to enter the classroom. Standing tall, in front with his dark curly hair, his mustache seemed to accentuate his almost constant grin. His enthusiasm for sharing his love of science always kept the class engaged, even if they did not understand.

All the desks in science were doubled, as we often had to work in pairs when we had an experiment to do. The back desks filled up first, with Brad Chandler and Jake Steward sitting in the rear corner. I took my usual seat in front.

Carol Jenkins was the last to enter the classroom. Brushing her blonde curly hair to one side, she looked a little nervous, but then she always did.

Mr. May gestured for Carol to sit at my desk. "There's a space here for you Carol, next to Adara."

As Carol sat next to me, a girl's voice whispered from behind, "Good place for you Carol, you can babysit Adara, just like you babysit your brother Larry."

Carol rolled her eyes, and I could see that she was uncomfortable with that comment.

"Hi Carol," I whispered, "I'm glad you could sit with me."

"OK, class, now that I have your attention, today's lesson is about Special Relativity. I do hope you all have read the chapter?"

"Yes, sir," some of the class members the class.

"Didn't understand it, sir," a few others replied.

"Did you read it?" I asked Carol quietly.

"Yeah," she shrugged, "but I didn't understand it.

"Sir?" Jake asked, with his hand up, "The chapter talks about Newtonian physics vs. Special Relativity. When does the one theory take over from the other?"

"That's a very good question, Jake. You see Newton said that everything is the same no matter where you are in the universe. His laws of physics apply to everything, everywhere. But Einstein said that only the speed of light is constant, while everything else like mass, size, and energy is variable."

"But when does the change take place?"

"Ah, in the normal world, Newtonian rules work fine. It is not until you go at extremely high speeds or very high energies that you can measure the changes. Like in particle accelerators or space travel, that's when the rules change."

"The rules change?" I said aloud."

"Yes, Adara, you can then use the new rules to measure the changes."

"I always thought rules could not change."

"Rules are meant to be broken." I heard Brad say.

Being a rule-based entity, this was a profound realization for me. I am unable to predict what rules of mine would change. I also wondered what my Lorentz factor would be. If my rules do change, how would that change me?

"The laws of physics, or the rules as you ask, remain the same, but different rules apply in extreme circumstances. Do you remember the glass experiment I showed the class?"

"Yes," everyone said.

"Glass is an insulator and does not conduct electricity. However, when you heat it beyond a certain temperature, it starts to conduct electricity. What is more, the resistance in the heated glass is enough to keep the glass hot enough to maintain conductivity."

"Yeah, that was a cool experiment," Jake added, "Can we do it again?"

Mr. May dismissed the idea with a wave of his hand.

"So new rules can apply over the old ones?" I asked.

"Yes," Mr. May agreed, "That's one way to put it. The textbook doesn't mention the Lorentz Factor, but that's the point where things like time dilation become apparent."

Jake looked thoughtful. "So, the Lorentz Factor is where Einstein's theory takes over?"

"Yes," Mr. May said, "When the Lorentz Factor is two or more."

"Wow, a Lorentz Factor of two!" Jake said excitedly.

"Can you tell us more?" Jake asked.

Mr. May said, "This isn't part of our course." He then smiled and raised a finger, "If you want extra homework, you can tell us in the next class."

Jake blushed as the class laughed at the suggestion.

Carol leaned closer to me and whispered. "Jake is into science fiction."

"How do you know?" I asked back.

Carol shrugged. "I just know."

Mr. May tapped gently on our desk as he walked slowly to the back of the class. "please stop talking girls," he whispered, "I need you both to set a good example."

As Jake engaged Mr. May in conversation, Carol and I were able to continue talking in hushed tones.

"I have never seen you with Jake, or anyone else for that matter." I said, "How do you know he likes, science fiction?"

"I've seen him in the library, and I've seen what books he likes to read."

"Did you talk to him?" I asked.

Carol lowered her head. "Well, no, I couldn't."

"Would you like to?"

Carol perked up immediately. "Oh, would I! Could you introduce me? But then why would he want to talk to me? I'm a nobody, I'm just a babysitter for my brother Larry."

"How can I introduce you," I asked, "I don't know them.

"I'm sorry," Carol said sheepishly, "I forgot that you don't remember things."

"What exactly am I supposed to remember?"

"Don't look now, he's staring at you," Carol said.

"Who?"

"Jeez," Carol hissed in my ear, "You know full well who. BRAD! He's been staring at you through the whole class."

"Should I stare back?"

"No, Jeez, look down at your book."

"But I read that chapter already."

"Yeah, but don't look at Brad like that, you'll scare the hell out of him, you nearly scared the hell out of me!"

"So, what should I do?"

"Just keep cool, maybe you can help me to talk to Jake."

Our conversation stopped dead when Mr. May clapped his hands twice as he walked towards the blackboard. "OK class, enough of the questions, for now, we have a lot of work to get through this morning."

When the bell rang, and the class was finished, Carol and I were one of the first ones out. When we were in the hallway, I said to Carol, "Say hello to Jake as he walks out of class, that's the best way to make yourself known."

"I should say hello?"

"Yes," I said, "here he comes, now get ready."

Jake and Brad came out of the classroom, jostling each other jokingly. I noticed that all the girls in the hallway were looking at both Jake and Brad as if they were royalty. As they passed us, I nudged Carol.

"Hi, Jake," Carol said with expectant eyes.

Jake briefly turned his head towards Carol, giving a little smile. He then continued his way down the hallway, alongside Brad.

Several girls within earshot scoffed and giggled. One girl said, quite loudly, "Since when does Jake need a babysitter?"

Carol shook her head, and looking down, she headed in the opposite direction from Jake.

Seeing that she was hurt, I followed her away from the crowd. As I caught up behind her, I asked, "What is all this talk about babysitting?"

Carol stopped dead in her tracks. Without looking at me she said, "I'm sure you meant well, but that didn't help me much."

Staring straight down the hallway Carol continued, "My mom and dad work a lot, so I have to look after my brother all the time. I give him his breakfast in the morning before I walk him to school. I make sure he's OK at school before I have to walk him home." Her voice began to quiver a little, "So you see I don't have time for friends, especially boyfriends because I'm the Babysitter! Now if you'll excuse me, I have to go to my next class." Carol then walked off down the hallway, leaving me standing.

I still did not understand what she said. Carol seems to be bothered with her label of the babysitter. Looking after someone, especially someone who needs help must require strength. Why does Carol consider this to be bad? And why do the other girls make fun of her?

Chapter 25

"OK everyone, I want you all to pair up, one person with an instrument and another to do the singing." Ms. Fields said to her class.

Jacob wandered around touches some instruments shyly plucking strings etc. but not taking a liking to any of them. "Come on Jacob, we need to find you something you like to play," Ms. Fields said, "You can try anything you like." Indicating different instruments. "Perhaps you can try one of the percussion instruments?"

Jacob just shrugged his shoulders not wishing to speak.

"I think he should sing." A voice came from the back.

Jacob froze at what he thought to be another jibe.

"Yea, ss, ss, ss, ss, sing us a ss, ss, ss, song Jacob!" someone said from behind.

"Who said that?" Ms. Fields demanded.

Hushed giggles came from students.

I don't like it when people pick on someone who is lesser. Just because Jacob has a stammer, people make fun of his talking. Instead of encouraging him, it makes him talk even less. So, I decided to speak up.

"I think he should sing," I added as I rose from my seat at the piano. Walking towards Jacob and Ms. Fields. "I think he has a good voice."

Never mind about hearing a pin drop, you could hear it fall through the air as I walked towards them.

"It's true," I said, "you have a very good voice, you just haven't learned how to coordinate it with language. You see music is an activity that uses the right side of the brain while language uses the left side. You need to connect both together and I think singing is the way to start."

Ms. Fields cocked her head to one side as she listened.

Jacob now raised his head straight, but he left his lower jaw where it was, leaving his mouth wide open.

"You like David Bowie don't you Jacob?" I asked.

Jacob shrugged, blinked a few times, and nodded vaguely.

Gently holding his elbow, I gestured towards the piano. "I'll play and you sing, and I have just the song for you!" Jacob hesitated and pulled back, "At least come over and look at it."

We sat together on the piano bench. I pulled one of the lyric sheets from a folder on top of the piano and handed it to Jacob. "Here do you know this one."

Jacob nodded but glanced at Adara with doubt.

"I'll start playing and when it's time for you to start, I'll nod and you can sing along."

Jacob looked around clutching the song sheet nervously. "Don't worry, I won't hurt you. And never mind about them – they can all go and sing their song." I pointed to the song sheet in his hand.

The room was now totally silent.

Ms. Fields slowly moved closer, puzzled as to what would happen next.

"Remember, I'll nod when you need to start singing here." As I pointed to the top of the lyrics.

I started the piano intro to David Bowie's Changes.

I then nodded to indicate him to start.

Nothing.

I stop playing the piano.

"You can do it easily Jacob, just follow the rhythm of the music and sing along with these words." I started playing the piano intro again. This time I kept my eyes on him, nodding my head gently with the rhythm. He kept his eyes on me glancing back to the lyric sheet and back to me again with uncertainty in his eyes.

"Umm..."

Again, I nodded, to indicate him to start. This time I kept my eyes on him. But still, he didn't start singing, so I repeated the chords leading to his starting point.

"You can start now," I said.

Still nothing, so I repeated the intro chords, over and over.

"I don't know what you're waiting for Jacob" but still nothing. "I can do this all day you know".

And then he sang!

Quietly at first. Although he sounded timid and shaky, there was not even a hint of a stammer.

The entire room was focused on Jacob. His eyes were wide with surprise while he held the lyric sheet tightly in fear of losing his place.

I now joined in with the chorus and we sang together, this time Jacob's stammer was artificial as he sang the word changes, but it was part of the song but now, he began to sing louder – almost with gusto.

We came to the mid-point instrumental break but instead of continuing the song Jacob stood up sharply pushing his side of the long piano stool back on the floor with a screeching sound. He laughed, almost shouted with a "Ha-ha!" but at the same time started crying loudly and laughing loudly. Tears ran down his cheeks and I could see the pain on his face but at the same time, I also saw wondrous joy and excitement which eclipsed any other emotion that tried to engulf him.

The whole room broke into applause and whoops of appreciation, Ms. Fields leading the ovation with both hands clapping like a circus seal. She grabbed both of Jacob's hands and they pretty much jumped up and down with joy. Every single girl in the class had tears in their eyes, I could see them wiping their eyes between handclaps and cupping their hands over their faces to hide their emotion. Even the boys while they punched the air with whoops of joy would quickly wipe a tear and even their noses with the back of their sleeves.

In this music lesson Jacob learned to sing, or to clarify, he learned that he could sing. I always understood that lessons are things you need to learn and that school was a good place to do it but today was a prime example of this happening. Most lessons are mundane like learn this note and learn this chord but today was a life-changing lesson.

Not only for Jacob but me as well, because I learned two things.

Musical timing needs to be dynamic. I can play any music you like, note for note from memory. For me this has always been a simple task, I hear the notes, I know where they are on the piano keyboard, and I control my fingers to perform them. But his is not what I did in today's lesson, yes I played David Bowie's song Changes but I did much more than that, I adapted to the speed of Jacob. This is important because when Jacob sang slower and more hesitantly, I modified my tempo to match his. When he speeded up, I followed him. To coin a slang term, we were 'jammin'.

I know people can laugh and cry, even though I don't. What I didn't know was that people can laugh and cry at the same time as Jacob did. This could be looked upon as some sort of emotional incontinence, but I can fully understand why this happened. Jacob had a lot to let go of, he was an outcast who nobody wanted to talk to simply because he could not talk properly. Even if he wasn't plagued with derisory comments, he would have to suffer the sympathetic comments ("oh poor Jacob") or people helping him to finish sentences usually in ways he hadn't intended. Now he felt like a rock star! OK, his stammer wasn't cured by any means but at least he could now sing, and better than that he now improved his social rating several times over.

He deserved to be allowed to laugh and cry at the same time.

Chapter 26

It was 3:30 and the school day was over. I was heading towards the sports field where the trials were taking place for the track and field events. Lots of students were milling around, some doing stretches and exercises. All were even beginning to prepare for their practice events.

Barry Scott, the PE teacher was organizing the groups into their events. I was dressed in my sport shorts, jogging towards the runners for the 800-meter trial. I was in the D team, which meant I would not get a chance to run in any real races. If I could prove myself today, I could get promoted to a higher group.

Carol was standing to the side of the runners with Larry sitting on the grass nearby. As usual, she looked a little scruffy in her old sports shorts, a definite contrast to the other girls in their crisp, clean uniforms.

As I approached, Larry jumped up and squealed, "Hey, Carol, look, there's Adara, she's in my homeroom class!" Carol looked visibly embarrassed by Larry.

"Hi Carol," I said, "I'm glad you made it to the trials, I thought you couldn't do after-school activities."

"My mom said I'm allowed to do this. It's about the only thing I can do in this stupid school." She then said in a hushed tone, "But I have to keep Larry with me."

"Well, that's good, he can watch you race. You are in the A team, aren't you?"

"Yeah, she's really fast!" Larry said, "She's the best!"

"Well, I'm not the best," Carol pointed towards another girl in the group, "Sally Stone, over there is the best, I don't think I can beat her."

"I think you'll still get on the Varsity team," I smiled.

"Are you running today? Will you run with me?" Carol asked. "I've seen you running home from school, you are pretty fast."

"I am fit," I said, "I like to run a lot, but I'm on the D team. I would like to run with you, but I'll have to ask Mr. Scott."

"Good luck with that idea," Carol said, "I know what he's like, he only wants winners."

Mr. Scott blew his whistle long and loud, calling his runners for the first race. "Group A girls! Come on, let's get on your starting positions."

"Larry, you stay here with Adara, I have to go and run now."

As Carol joined her group on the starting line, Mr. Scott explained what lanes each girl would run in. He also singled out individual girls and coached them with his expectations.

He told Sally Stone that he wanted her to make a fast start. "Sally, I want you to set the pace for the race and to keep an early lead."

"Yes, sir."

She was easily the girl to do this as she was the fastest in the school, all the other girls knew her as the fastest. With Sally, in the lead, they would have to follow and stretch themselves to keep up. Mr. Scott knew that this was a good way to get the best from all his team by pushing them to their limits.

"Mr. Scott, can I run in this heat?" I asked.

I have asked Mr. Scott several times before, but he has never seen me run so he placed me in the bottom group of runners. I have been exercising every day, so I am fit, I have even researched what makes a good runner and I have gained an understanding of the competitive nature of these games. This was my last chance to approach Mr. Scott.

"Mr. Scott, can I run in this heat?"

"Sorry Adara but no, I've already told you that you are in heat D, anyway, can't you see that all the lanes are full." He didn't even look at me as he replied but kept his eyes on the starting line as the girls prepared themselves. "Go and wait your turn with heat D over there."

The group A girls were ready on the line, putting themselves in the starting pose while the starter was getting ready with his starting gun. Sally Stone posed with her left toe on the start line. Right foot behind, ready to take the first step forward. Eyes fixed ahead with fists clenched – muscles ready to fire.

Carol was on the line next to Sally, holding the same pose. I could see her breathing deeply, ventilating her body with oxygen.

Once all the flagmen around the track signaled the all-clear, the starter raised his gun.

"BANG!"

The crack of the pistol sent the girls off with Sally Stone taking an easy lead. The other girls formed a tight pack immediately behind her, with Carol in third place.

I know I was not allowed to run, but I had to prove myself to Mr. Scott. I had to be in this race. I took off my tracksuit top and gave it to Larry, "Hold onto that for me," I said, "Stay here and watch the race, I'll be back in a few minutes." I could not give him an exact time as I had never run the 800-meter race so I could not predict my performance with any accuracy.

I stepped quickly towards the start line and as I passed Mr. Scott I said: "I'm going to run anyway." I told him as I took off in a run.

"Adara! Come back now!" Mr. Scott shouted.

I had to run fast to catch the pack who were already at the 75-meter mark ahead of me, this wasn't going to be easy, but I had to prove to Mr. Scott that I could run. The group I was placed in was well below my abilities, it would not be right for me to beat them on every trial.

I calculated that I could catch up with the tail of the pack towards the end of the first lap, after penetrating the pack I would have to catch Sally with less than one full lap to do it. As I entered the second curve, I passed the runner at the back of the pack, who gave me a perplexed look. She did not expect anyone to come from behind her.

As I ran this curve, I was approaching the starting point and there were many jeers and insults shouted at me as I ran past. Just before the 400-meter line, I began to penetrate the main pack and as I crossed the line to the sound of the lap bell, I could hear Mr. Scott yelling at me, "Adara, drop out, now!"

At 415 meters I passed into fourth place giving me a clear view of the lead runners, this is where the real work starts.

Some of the best distance runners have been from Kenya, and mystery surrounds why they are so successful. There are many reasons why good runners such as Kenyans are so good at their sport, natural ability is certainly a prime reason, coupled with intense training and a healthy lifestyle. However, there is another reason that gives them such an edge – they can manage and withstand pain.

Lactic acid builds up in the muscles causing pain and even cramp. Pushing through the pain barrier is what any sportsperson must do.

Adara's body is naturally strong, and I have been training this body for some time now and I have maintained strong well-toned muscles. With the guidance of my mother, I have learned to eat a good healthy diet.

Regarding pain, well I have a distinct advantage because I simply do not feel it. I do detect problems such as pain through the nerve signals, so I know if the body is suffering. I can detect when muscles are becoming stressed, even tell if muscles are about to go into cramp. Pain is something I do not suffer from it is only another signal that I can detect. When I do detect such signals, I can then use a strategy to counter the problem. In the case of muscles, I then need to maintain a good oxygen supply. This is done through breath work and respiratory control.

At the 519-meter mark, I passed into third place. Carol had moved into second place and was hard on the heels of Sally. Anyone watching the race now saw me as a major contender, what were shouts of derision were now cheers of support.

At the 650-meter mark, I was right behind Carol. "I'm right behind you," I breathed, "keep pushing, you can catch Sally."

"Where did you come from?" Carol panted.

"Don't talk. Save your breath. Keep pushing. We're nearly there."

Carol and I were about eight meters behind Sally. All we needed to do now was to catch Sally and get into first place to win the race.

The remaining 150 meters was not easy for any of us. Sally knew someone was coming up behind and with her competitive spirit I knew she did not want anyone to catch her let alone pass her. As we came off the final turn, I had to encourage Carol to keep pushing. We had to be careful not to pull a cramp, failure now would not be an option.

Now into the final straight we pulled up behind Sally but had to pass her on the outside which required Carol to make extra strides. Sally kept glancing back towards us to see who was catching her. I recognized the expression of disbelief on her face, she was clearly 'psyched out' as they sometimes say. This intimidation can help to defeat an opponent. There were only fifty-five meters to the finish line when I heard Sally exclaim "WTF!" This only helped to waste her breath. I could easily have broken into a sprint to cross the finish line and win. I could not leave Carol now, and she was weakening fast.

"Push!" I kept urging her, "Don't give up now!"

Cheers abounded around the track as we approached the finish. Sally did finish first, but Carol was only one second behind her. I of course came in third. All three of us slowed to a jog to keep our legs moving.

Sally circled back towards us, still with that look of disbelief. Looking at me she said, "WTF! Are you crazy? You could have hurt yourself! I saw you behind on the first curve," she gasped, "how did you catch up?"

She then leaned forward with her hands on her knees catching her breath.

"Keep stretching," I said, "Don't let cramp set in."

Other racers came across the finish line one by one. Sally then moved towards Carol, stretching her hand forward to shake. "That was crazy, but you nearly caught me! You were amazing."

Carol grinned between breaths, “Do you mean that?”

“Of course, I do, I always knew you were good.” They both hugged briefly.”

Mr. Scott stepped up to me, “Adara you cannot qualify for that race, but I must admit that was the most awesome run I ever saw.”

The timekeeper stepped in. “Sally you have a personal best of 2 minutes, 16.5 seconds!” He added towards Carol, “You were a close second with 2 minutes 18.7 seconds! That’s also a personal best for you.” He then looked at me and said, “Adara, we did not time you so we’ve no idea what you did.”

“Why did you do it that way?” Mr. Scott asked.

“I did ask you if I could run with them, but you wouldn’t let me.”

Mr. Scott shook his head. “I’m sorry Adara, but that run can’t be counted.”

“She can run with me anytime,” Sally said, “Let her set the pace for a change instead of me.”

“With proper training, all three of you could become national champions,” Scott said, “I think we will keep Adara on the A-team.”

“Champions!” Larry started pogoing around.

Chapter 27

Mrs. Janice Raines was my English teacher. Her knowledge is so vast that it extends beyond the English language into every other subject. All the time she taught me, I wondered at her knowledge and experience. If she wanted to, she could teach any subject she liked, math, science, history. She could have any job she wanted, a politician, a banker, or a research fellow at a large corporation, yet she chose to teach. She chose to teach English.

If anyone asked her why she liked to teach, she would reply – "The ability to bestow knowledge and understanding unto others is the greatest fulfillment of all."

Her temperament was gentle and sweet, yet firm and dominant. No one ever spoke out against her or even wanted to. When she stood before the class she seemed to command obedience in such a way we all eagerly awaited the opening of our books.

Using English as camouflage, she taught each lesson as an insight into life. There is one fine example of her lessons, where Mrs. Raines attempted to instill upon us an understanding of ambiguity. Yes, this may be a strange lesson to deliver to a group of adolescents but it turns out to be of surprising importance, especially for me.

As always she would begin her lesson rooting it in English by explaining the lexical, semantic, and scope to name but a few examples of language ambiguities.

"Consider this sentence." She would say. "The car hit the pole while it was moving."

Such a simple nine-word sentence would evoke such an enthralling debate amongst the class on the possible interpretations.

She would often limit such discussion without conclusion and move onto the next level of which in this case was visual ambiguity.

She showed us a picture of a tree. A simple black and white ink line drawing of a very large tree without leaves as if in winter.

"You see a picture of a tree, yes?" She would ask.

Yes, we all see the tree.

"But, do you see a face?"

The instant she asked if we see a face, then an outline of a face suddenly appeared hidden within the wintery branches.

"And if so, how many faces do you see?"

Suddenly, other faces then began to spontaneously appear, two, wait there are four, no six, how many more? Numerous faces all quietly revealed themselves hidden within the silhouettes of the branches. We eventually counted a total of 10 faces.

She tricked us with an optical illusion.

Mrs. Raines would not stop there before we could scarcely catch our breath, she would swiftly move us into a higher realm of contemplation. She would explain that the human brain would naturally recognize faces because the brain needs to work out patterns and the face is the most important pattern it needs to recognize.

She would now show us several pictures, all of the famous paintings, and she would sequence them in flashcard style showing each for a moment but repeating them all quickly in succession. Rembrandt, Da Vinci, Van Gough, even Jackson Pollock's splashes.

"Each picture tells us something." She would say.

She cycled through these slowly to allow our subliminal systems to recognize each picture and hypnotizing us into quiet recognition of beauty.

I called "Stop." And Mrs. Raines stopped on a picture and indicated it to me.

"This is Van Gough's picture of the 'Potato Eaters'." She said. "What do you see here?" She asked.

"Five people sitting around a table eating what I think you say are potatoes. The lady is pouring what I think is tea."

"Anything else?" She asks collectively of the class.

"It's nighttime."

"They look poor."

"They look hungry."

At each comment, Mrs. Raines nodded and smiled and seemed appreciative that everyone was looking at the picture and thinking about what it meant for them.

"They're enjoying each other's company." Lisa eventually called out.

"Why?"

"Because that man is raising his teacup to the lady who is pouring." She replied. "As if to say – thank you."

And then the bell rang. Ding-a-ling. This class ends and we all have to move on to the next class.

"OK class I have a handout on this and your homework to write something about this picture, it can be a sentence, a paragraph, or even a whole page if you dare. BUT! I want it written in good structured English AND I want it on my desk for tomorrow's lesson. Thank you, everybody!"

Human noises and scrapes of chairs as we collected the homework sheets from Mrs. Raines. Then rushing on our paths to the next lesson.

I was amazed that she had a sheet prepared for each student. This sheet had a color picture of the artwork, the artist, the date of the artwork, its original dimensions, the medium used by the artist, the museum it is located in, and a simple instruction – write something that you feel about this.

I knew what she meant by that instruction, she wanted us to write about the picture but I also thought there were many other ambiguous dimensions hidden behind her instruction.

In every one of her lessons, I would learn something very important, but I always found that I still needed to learn more.

Chapter 28

History repeats itself, and history is always written by the victors.

These were the two most common phrases that Mr. Wilson Dray would always say to us in class. He seemed to take a radical view of history and life in general. Many people labeled him as a socialist, I don't know if this was a compliment or a criticism. I always thought his insight was thoughtful and very considerate. Through his teaching, he tried to use such phrases to show his students how to view the world with a more thoughtful perspective.

History repeats itself, illustrates how humanity needs to learn from historical mistakes. To move forward, humanity needs to break out of its continuous cycle of repetition.

History is written by the victors, this is obvious once you think about it. Who cares what the losers have to say? The winners will always say they won because they were right.

So today we continued our discussion of World War Two and concentrated on the European conflict. We had read the chapters on the causes and the strategies used in the conflict. Mr. Dray also enhanced our understanding of the battles by illustrating the tactics and the carnage suffered on all sides. He also talked about the heroism that individuals displayed during their struggles.

Mr. Dray conducted an open class discussion using the blackboard to list causes and effects to show how this motivated the decisions that were made. For the most part, the class engaged enthusiastically in the decisions, and we debated on why they were made and what the possible alternatives were.

It seems that in any classroom, there is always an isolated commotion happening on the back seats. Whenever the teacher is facing the class, the commotion halts, and those kids involved will pretend to be attentive. As soon as the teacher turns their back on the class to write something on the board, the commotion resumes from where it left off.

My hearing is better than any human. I can hear exactly what you hear, but I process it better so I can hear everything. I have noticed that each time the commotion resumes it escalates slightly, starting as whispers but growing louder at each new instance. Today's commotion involved Jake, Brad, and a couple of other girls. I could hear that they were all joking about how Larry Jenkins who sat in front of them on how he would be the first casualty of any war.

The joking and giggling continued until Mr. Dray finally lost his patience.

"Jake! Swap seats with Amy."

"But sir, I didn't do anything."

"Now! Hurry up!"

"Brad!"

"Seriously sir?"

"Move down here to the front!"

"What for?"

"So, I can keep my eye on you! Sit here next to Adara."

"Anyone else wants to be moved?"

Silence.

"So can we now get on with the class?"

Blank faces all around.

"OK, let's get back to the lesson, shall we?"

Wilson Dray separated the usual class suspects in an attempt to restore order and attention in his history class.

So now I was sitting next to Brad who looked very embarrassed to be moved to the front. He kept looking at me in what I interpreted as a shy manner. Whenever our eyes met, he would quickly look away. I have such good peripheral vision, so as I looked towards the front of the class, I also detected that he would often look towards me.

Then with Mr. Dray's back turned I noticed Brad twitch sharply and grab the back of his head. A small piece of rolled-up paper was on the floor behind Brad, this is what hit Brad.

Brad turned to look behind him and so did I. Larry who was now sitting a few rows behind, feigned a look of innocence while casting his eyes around the room and towards the ceiling. It was Larry who was launching these 'spitballs', using his plastic pen as a blowgun.

Several other spitballs were launched and while Larry rejoiced in his revenge, Brad was getting furious. Brad and Jake exchanged silent gesticulations indicating that something bad was going to happen to Larry when the class was over. I could hear the girls who Brad, and Jake were joking with pleading with Larry to stop, saying things like, "He'll clobber you!" But Larry continued with his ballistic assault.

I had listened to the pattern of Larry and there was a clear sequence that I easily followed. The tearing of a piece of paper, the moistening of the paper in his mouth to make the ball, loading the ball into his 'gun', and then the inhale of breath to fire. Using this sequence I was able to warn Brad of the next shot. I pointed to Brad's shoe and whispered "Duck!" at which point Brad looked down. The spitball sailed over Brad's head and landed on the floor near Mr. Dray's feet.

Although Mr. Dray didn't see the spitball, he must have detected the new commotion and when he turned around sharply. Larry quickly concealed his blowgun and sat up straight in his chair at which point Mr. Dray asked, "Is there any way that Nazi Germany could have succeeded in the Battle of Britain?"

The class was silent.

"How about you Larry?" Larry displayed an aura of guilt, so Mr. Dray moved towards his desk to get a closer look and focused his questions on him. Larry quickly fumbled with his pen, trying to put it back together. "Any ideas on how the German strategy failed them?"

"Er, no sir."

I put my hand up and tried to answer. "Sir?" I called out.

"Adara, I know you have a good answer, but I want to hear what Larry has to say." Mr. Dray picked up a torn and shredded piece of paper from Larry's desk. "I expect you don't need this scrap of paper?" He asked as he turned to walk towards the wastepaper bin. "Oh, and Larry, you may want to reassemble your pen, it would be much more useful that way."

"Yes, sir."

Brad smirked.

"So, Adara, do you think you have an answer to my question?"

"Yes, sir."

"Well, please enlighten us."

"Instead of bombing British cities, Germany should have concentrated on destroying the British Air Force by bombing the British airfields."

"Ah, and what would that give the Germans?"

"Air superiority sir."

And then the bell rang. Ding-a-ling. This class ends and we all must move on to the next class.

"Yes," Mr. Dray stated over the commotion, "The world was entering a new era of combat where airplanes became the primary weapon of mechanized war. Now I want you all to finish reading the chapters on the European war because I'll be giving you all a test on Friday."

Groans from all the class as they were moving out of the room.

"Since when do you know so much about warfare?" Brad asked me.

"I read books, and I like to learn."

"Well, you always did a lot of reading," Brad said as he turned to go.

I wondered why Brad would say that because how would he know that Adara liked to read books.

News Report!

By Karen Collins

[*What you need to know to start the day:* Get Idaho Post in your inbox.]

The body of a woman has been discovered by hikers, near Lone Pine, Idaho. Her cause of death has been stated as complications resulting from miscarriage.

The woman's identity has been confirmed through DNA, but details are being withheld until her family has been informed.

Police have confirmed that this is the second victim of the now suspected serial killer nicknamed 'the shopper.'

Anyone who has any information regarding this incident should contact the district police office or the crime line on (208) 374-5454.

Chapter 29

At lunchtime, the playground is full of noises, not a steady cacophony but varying waves of noise. Some kids will be sat in groups on the lawn under the trees eating their sandwiches while other groups would be playing a game on the field. Sometimes as groups emerged from the cafeteria, they would be noisy and laughing, soon to subside into a quieter conversation, all this builds into highs and lows of sound. For the most part, I can tune into the conversations that are around me, especially if the breeze carries the sound in my direction.

This spring afternoon I ate my sandwiches by the edge of the sports field. After a while, Carol came out of the cafeteria and joined me. Carol always liked to hang out on the sports field, that location seemed to give her comfort and reinforce her commitment to the sport.

"Do you know anything about Yoga?" She asked.

"Maybe, I've read a little about it."

"My mom taught me a few stretches, and I think it's a good exercise to do after lunch. I don't like doing heavy exercises after eating I think it mixes up the stomach too much. I'm going to do some Yoga, do you want to try some with me?"

"Sure, show me what you learned."

"My mom says you should always do Yoga on a mat, but this grass is nice and soft. First, take your shoes off."

"OK."

"Then we can stand side by side and you just follow my moves."

Carol led me through what she called 'salutations', and I could see why because it involved a sequence of raising arms straight above the head as if in a salute. Then bowing into a forward fold as if in some sort of religious genuflection before reaching yourself into a 'plank' position. The sequence continued as we lowered slowly face down onto the ground as if in a reverse push-up. From there we stretched our spine before raising our hips with our hands and feet still on the grass. From there we stepped our feet to meet our hands and rose into the starting position of salutation.

We did this slowly several times and I could see why Carol liked this form of exercise. Not only was it stretching and toning of muscles but after a few repeats of this sequence, it required quite a bit of exertion.

As we went through our 'flow', a soccer ball was headed directly towards us rolling on the ground at speed. We both saw it coming but it was Carol who jumped out of her pose, stepped sideways into the path of the ball, and stopped it dead with her foot.

Jake came jogging after it, he had been shooting some goals with Brad and three other kids on the sports field.

"Hey, sorry about that, I hope I didn't mess with your prayers to Mecca."

"We're not praying," Carol retorted, "we're doing Yoga."

"Oh, OK, Sure, I know Yoga."

"Maybe you should try it sometime," Carol said with a tease.

"Er, yeah, probably I should, um, yeah, I would. I really would. I mean I'd like to try it sometime."

Carol stood there with hands-on-hips with her right foot placed firmly on the Soccer ball.

"But what do you want now?" She asked with a smirk.

"Huh? Oh, yeah, I need the ball back."

"And what do you say?"

"Huh? Oh yeah, please. Please, can I have our ball back?"

With that, Carol flicked the ball into the air in front of her and gently kicked it in a short arc towards Jake. He caught it with his thigh bringing it down to his foot where he held it with his toe.

"You're Carol?" He asked.

"Yup, that's me."

"HEY!!" Brad was shouting for the ball. "Common Jake!"

Jake turned and kicked the ball back towards Brad and the gang. Turning back towards Carol Jake then said. "I like the way you run."

"Excuse me?"

"In track I mean – you're a good runner."

"Thank you." She smiled with genuine appreciation.

"Can I see you again?"

"You see me every day at school."

"Yeah, but I mean maybe tomorrow at lunch?"

"OK, Sure. I'll be right here, maybe doing some Yoga."

"I look forward to it." And with that Jake turned and sprinted back to playing soccer.

Carol turned to me with wide eyes and her mouth in a wide gape, the look of which I have never seen expressed on anyone's face before.

"Did you hear what he said?!"

"What?" I asked.

"He asked if he could see me again!"

"That's a good thing isn't it?"

"Talk about understatement, that's a GREAT thing! I can't wait until tomorrow's lunch! I think I'm going to die!"

With that, Carol lunged towards me flinging her arms around me. With her arms tightly hugging my neck, I didn't think she was in any danger of dying her continued exclamations suggested she was in a form of excitement that I hadn't recognized before.

As we hugged and jumped around, I tried to get Carol back into our Yoga exercises, but she was too excited and had too much to say about Jake. We ended up just sitting on the grass watching the gang shooting goals into the soccer net. Carol kept talking about Jake saying things like, "Don't you think he's cute?" But she also suggested that if I were with Brad then we could all go out together.

During this chatter between us, I heard Larry come out of the cafeteria with some of the younger lads from our homeroom class. As usual, he was acting the fool and contributing to the new wave of noise. As Larry ran onto the sports field with his buddies, I could hear three of Brad's friends comment on Larry's presence.

I heard Alan say, "There's that jerk."

Then Brendan said, "What ya going to do to him, Brad?"

Casey joined in and said, "Now's your chance, teach him a lesson."

"Leave the jerk alone," I heard Jake say, "He's just a dumb ass wimp."

Alan, Brendan, and Casey were all a year younger in the Junior class, they liked to hang out with Brad because it made them look cool. There is nothing wrong with that, but they always teased Brad into doing things. Brad stood there in front of the goal ready to take a shot and he stood there for a long moment listening to his three cronies. Alan was in goal staring at Larry.

Brad eventually turned and dribbled the ball at a walking pace towards Larry. Brad's gang slowly followed behind with Jake at the rear.

As Brad got close, he yelled, "Hey Larry, catch!" and kicked the ball right into Larry's chest.

Larry, of course, could not have caught it even if he knew how to, the soccer ball slammed into his midriff knocking him onto his back and partially winding him.

The three cronies yelped while Brad jogged forward gleefully, "Oh sorry pall, I hope I didn't hurt you. Are you OK?"

Larry coughed, "Uh, Brad?"

"Yup, it's your spitball buddy!" Brad grabbed Larry by his arm and dragged him to his feet.

I could not hear what Brad said next as he was facing away from me and about 50 meters distant. But Larry cowered in fear as the rest of Brad's gang gathered around them, Jake was the only one that I heard calling for restraint.

Larry's buddies ran away as fast as they could, while Brad's three cronies just stood there laughing. Brad pulled Larry up from the ground by his arm, it looked as if he would do something worse to Larry.

Carol was already off at a sprint, heading over to help her brother. That is the moment when I heard the sharp shriek of a whistle.

Janice Raines, the English teacher was on playground duty and it was she who raised the alarm, rushing to the scene.

"What's going on here?" She cried.

"Oh, Larry just got slammed with my soccer ball, I was coming to help."

"Were you going to hit him?"

"No, I was helping him up, I thought he was hurt. But you're OK aren't you Larry?"

"Uh, I think so." Larry quivered.

"You see? It was an accident." Brad added.

"Yeah, an accident." His cronies echoed.

"What the hell did you do to my brother?" Carol yelled.

"It's OK, Carol," Ms. Raines said, "take your brother inside to see the nurse." She then turned to face Brad and his three cronies, "And you boys get to your homeroom NOW! I'll speak to you all later."

Carol had her arm around Larry as they both walked past Jake. Jake shrugged a non-committal 'I don't know' with his hands towards Carol. Carol gave Jake a stern frown, and said, "He better not be hurt."

All I could do was to stand there in surprise as Brad's cronies jogged from the sports field. Brad walked off towards his homeroom, as he went, he glanced back at me several times.

"Adara, did you see what happened?" Ms. Raines asked.

"I was too far away," I said. This wasn't a lie; I simply did not answer the question fully.

Chapter 30

The end of the school day was always interesting for me. Not just the transition from school time to home time, but it was also an opportunity for me to observe the associations of children with parents. Children leaving school and being collected by their parents is often described as chaos, but I see it as a repeating and predictable pattern that completes the day. Many people complain about the slow and annoying traffic as they drive in their cars to collect their children and the traffic does tailback down the road. I see this as a steady flow like a conveyor belt gently removing the children to their respective homes. Some children drive their cars others would walk or cycle.

I would then walk the few blocks to my home and in so doing I would pass homes and gardens and even a park. As the school days passed, I was able to observe the slow changes to the plants as they responded to the seasons.

It was on such a day that I started as a normal walk home. As usual, I walked briskly, carrying my soft leather satchel. Ahead of me by about 120 meters were Larry and his sister Carol. They did not live far from me, they would soon walk to the right down Alder Street to their house while I would carry on straight to my home on Maple Street.

I could also see Brad and his three cronies, Alan, Brendan, and Casey, up ahead in front of them. They were hanging around on the corner of Chestnut Street, opposite Bryant Park. This was unusual because they lived in a different part of town. Today they were posing on the corner as if waiting for something.

When Larry and Carol neared them, they tried to avoid the boys by walking wide and off the sidewalk. As they did this, Brad and his younger cronies moved to block their way. I observed the attempts to move past while the boys continually sidestepped into their path. Brad kept his stance leaning against a sapling by the road and I could see him mouthing something, but the sound was inaudible to me at that distance. The movement of his lips seemed to say, "where are you going squirt?"

It was easy to see that they were being intimidated and even threatened.

I cast my memory back to the earlier playground incident. This seemed to be the moment where Brad would get some form of revenge with the assistance of his friends.

Brad was older and tougher, the leader, the other three were just nameless 'flunkies' and pretty much did whatever Brad said. Throughout school, I observed how they followed him around like a bunch of puppies egging each other on. There were times when they would even behave like a pack of wolves as they geared themselves up for a hunt. This would only happen when adults were not around, and they had nothing better to do.

As I came near, the boys paid little heed to me, after all, I was the least of all the kids in school. I was the runt, quiet and unobtrusive who did not affect anyone. I was the one that everyone would ignore.

By the time I was upon them, the boys were pushing and shoving Larry around. Carol squealed objections while Casey restrained her from behind by holding her arms.

Brad was teasing Larry about what he said in the classroom earlier. I was not there at the time, but I was told that he called Brad a bully and how nobody was scared of him. I thought this fit into what everyone had said to me – stand up to bullies. Tell teachers and parents about it. Brad seemed to be in the process of bullying Larry, and I reasoned that this was not acceptable behavior. There was no teacher here, so I reasoned that I needed to stop this.

Larry kept putting his hands over his face like he sometimes would, abruptly moving his hands away and shouting words like "Stop it! I'm tough and you're not!" These were words that he had learned from Miss Sanchez during her homeroom talk. More significantly, Larry was behaving well outside of his normal character – he was trying to stand up to Brad.

I could have easily walked past, and I don't even think anybody would even have noticed. However, I knew that bullying was unacceptable, Larry and Carol were outnumbered and outclassed. Brad had no justification to exert his strength over Larry and this looked like an ambush.

This fitted into the definition of bullying that was so much talked about in school recently. We were all taught to put a stop to it by reporting it to parents and teachers. So here I was face to face with a bullying incident with no teachers or parents to report it to. The bullying seemed to be escalating and I thought this would soon end with Brad and his boys beating upon Larry and possibly even Carol, so I decided to move in and deal with the situation.

I walked right up alongside Larry and came to a complete and sudden stop by his side. Brad stood immediately in front of Larry with a look of extreme aggression as if he was about to start beating into Larry. I looked straight into Brad's eyes, and I said: "Leave them alone".

Now at this time of my life, I was still working out how to deliver my verbal messages. In this instance, I tried to be stern and firm in my manner. I'm not sure if I delivered the message as accurately as I intended. After all, I still needed some practice in my speech. I was not sure if this sounded funny or aggressive.

There was a long moment of silence, and I could recognize some curiosity in everyone's expression. Larry just gulped and stepped back. This was quickly followed by some chuckled laughter from the cronies.

Alan yelled, "Go on Brad, get her out of here!"

Brad just glared at me with what I interpreted as fury. I think that's when he decided he had to make an example out of me. He raised his arm to slap me across my face with the back of his hand. Most kids would have been knocked aside by the blow across the face.

Unfortunately for Brad I was way ahead of his move and reacted automatically while he started to raise his fist.

My defense subroutines had woken up and already calculated several defense scenarios some of which would cause considerable harm to Brad. The one I chose to follow was simply to raise Adara's left hand which was holding the satchel and placed it at an angle in the path of Brad's approaching fist. My forearm and elbow remained firmly behind the satchel acting as a strong block. The back of his hand impacted squarely on the metal clasp on the front of the satchel. I used the satchel to deflect his arm past my head. I rolled back to absorb the momentum I raised my right foot and brought it down sharply along Brad's left shin. My foot finished hard on the top of his foot. I quickly followed with a hand punch to his sternum which knocked him backward, partially winded.

As Brad fell back, my defense subroutines showed me a whole spectrum of moves to follow up. These ranged from delivering not just incapacitating but even fatal blows with my hands and feet. I had the knowledge and ability to kill Brad and to deliver the deadly blow instantly. As it turns out, I did not have to respond to him further.

When the back of Brad's hand hit the front clasp and lock of my satchel, it opened a gash on his middle knuckle, drawing blood. Coupled with my blow to his shin, foot, and sternum, he reeled backward spluttering in both shock and pain. He lay on his back holding his wounded hand, swearing and cursing between gasps for breath.

Stunned silence followed as they all waited for a vengeful response from Brad. Instead, Brad remained on the ground writhing in pain. It took a few moments for him to gather enough breath. He eventually yelled in his frustration "Don't just stand there get that bitch!"

Both Alan and Brendan moved cautiously towards me, spacing themselves to outflank me. Even if they worked in synchronicity, they were no match for me. My defensive subroutine showed me numerous ways to overcome them. As they moved in close, I lowered both of my arms to my side, I was trying to make myself look defenseless. My left hand released my satchel, allowing it to fall gently to the floor.

They moved closer, thinking I had given up. When they came within range, both of my fists shot up and delivered simultaneous blows to their chins. This knocked them both back momentarily. Alan shook his head and rushed headlong at me as if to knock me to the ground. I easily sidestepped, grabbed his arm, and twisted it behind his back. He screeched in pain as I swung him around. I used his lowered head as a battering ram against Brendan's sternum, who was now rushing towards me.

The impact of Alan's head into Brendan's chest, winded Brendan badly, knocking him back to the ground. He lay there, gasping for breath.

Still holding his arm behind Alan's back, I used his recoil to swing him behind me onto the hard sidewalk. He hit the ground hard, where he lay crying, nursing his scraped knees and hands.

Both had torn shirt buttons. Alan had ripped his jeans on the knee, exposing a bloody scrape. Brendan was rolling on the ground gasping for breath. I could have continued to hurt or even kill them, but they were no further threat to me. I stood back, sparing them further injury.

There was one possible threat still standing, his name was Casey. He was still holding Carol by her arms from behind. Both stood in awe at my prowess. All I did was step forward to face Casey and look him sternly in the eyes. He immediately let go of Carol and stood back in fear.

I had no intention to do anything further to Casey as he had let go of Carol. He was too scared to make a move against me. If I could knock down his whole 'gang', what more could Casey possibly do on his own?

To my surprise, Carol immediately swung around and slapped Casey flatly across his face with a very loud stinging sound. She then grabbed her bag from the ground and went quickly to Larry and hugged him tightly.

The fight was over. Casey kept a safe distance nursing his stinging humiliation.

The others stayed on the ground not willing to continue any conflict.

Brad was slowly getting back to his feet, but there was no more threat in him. He averted my eyes, limping with his sore shin as he nursed the gash on his knuckle.

I moved over to Larry and Carol asking, "are you two, OK?" but my question was drowned out by exclamations from Larry and adulation from Carol.

"Wow, that was so cool!" Larry would keep saying over and over. "Serves you right!" Larry shouted at Brad.

"That's enough Larry," I told him, "I'll walk you home." As I gestured in the direction we should go.

"Oh, thank you, thank you! You're so amazing!" Carol said repeatedly. She picked up my satchel and offered it to me. The clasp was left open by Brad's attempted backhander, this was the only injury I had sustained. My defense subroutine continued to warn me of danger, but I knew she was only offering to help.

"I hope it's not broken," she said as she fumbled with it and followed with "are you OK?" as she looked into my eyes.

"I think it's fine, I think he just knocked it open," I said, referring to Brad's punch. Carol examined it and tenderly closed the clasp as if caring for a wound.

"Nothing seems to have fallen out," she said, "and the clasp doesn't seem to be broken."

She was quite right; the satchel was undamaged, and no books or papers had fallen out during the scuffle. I guess that bears testimony to my graceful flow during the scuffle. Mother certainly chose well when she bought this satchel for me, it certainly stood up to punishment and even served to protect me. From then on, I always carried my satchel with the clasp facing outwards, this would act to present the clasp to any future blows I may have to defend against.

Was this my first experience of feeling pride? If this is pride is it for my satchel? Or is it for my mother's wise decision? Or is it because I stood up against a formidable enemy? This is an interesting question, which I will have to process tonight.

"We have to go, so let me walk you both home" I urged. I wanted to get away from this scene, to leave Brad and his pals to clean up their messy selves. But also, if any adults came along, we would all have some awkward explaining to do.

As I ushered Carol and Larry along the sidewalk I looked back to Brad and said: "Don't bother them ever again". I tried to say this without threat or aggression but I'm not sure how this sounded. At this point, I wasn't sure if there could be any possible repercussions from this.

As I walked them home, I had two other immediate consequences to handle, and they both walked on either side of me. Larry was suddenly my new best friend and Carol was displaying so much adulation towards me that I think I now had a girlfriend.

Larry was pretty much skipping and hopping along the side of me saying how cool I was and asking where I learned those moves. He was impressed by the way I "gave it to them".

Carol simply walked close along my left side clutching my upper arm with both hands. She would sometimes lean her head against my arm as well. It was difficult to keep the rhythm of our walking together synchronized as we would cyclically move in step and out of step. When we were completely out of step, she would move her head off to stop bouncing her head against my arm, leaving only her hands to clutch my arm.

Larry was a nice kid, but he was a bit of a nerd – but then again, I could also be described as the same. Generally, he was quiet and unobtrusive (like me). He often had moments of outspoken behavior, and it had been this trait that got him into trouble with Brad. If he had kept his mouth shut this fight would never have happened.

Carol would periodically gaze at my face and I would become aware of this and turn my head towards her. She would be smiling bright and wide and her eyes gleamed with happiness. She would not speak but she would engage my eyes for a period as if she knew something deep about me. She would then comfortably rest her head once again on my shoulder. She seemed to be tuned into the rhythm of our walking.

Now that we had some distance between us and Brad, we slowed our pace but maintained a steady gait. My subsystems were still operating normally and had calculated the walking cycle that Carol and I shared. 22 steps were the total sequence, so on the 11th step, we were out of sync, and on the 22nd step, we were back in sync with the total sequence taking approximately 15.5 seconds.

I was not paying close attention to these statistics; I was more focused on what to say and how to manage Larry. I was unsure what he would say when he got to school the next day. I calculated that the best thing is for Larry to say nothing about this fight when he gets to school tomorrow. If news of this fight breaks out, I may have to manage a situation where I suddenly move from being a nobody to being the kid who beat off Brad and his cronies.

My programming does not guide me on how to handle such issues. If anything, it may conflict with one of my directives; Directive5: Conceal My True Identity.

Carol kept one hand clasped around my upper arm while her other hand slid down my arm to touch my hand. I was carrying my satchel in my left hand so I could not work out what her intention was, did she want to hold my hand or carry my satchel? As it turned out she did not do either, she just kept her hand around my wrist and the upper hand.

I walked them to their house and stood on their porch with Carol to say goodbye.

Larry was still excited by the whole incident and pretended to do Kung Fu-style moves on the front lawn, making noises like a Ninja fighter in the movies.

Carol had turned towards me, and we stood face to face. She moved her hand to brush a lock of hair behind my ear.

As she did so my head twitched back, and my arm rose to block her movement.

"You seem nervous." She said.

"I'm OK, just a little protective."

Although I was able to control this subroutine and correct my movements, the reflex was taking me by surprise.

"Don't be so nervous," she said, as she smiled sweetly and maintained her gaze on my eyes. "It's OK I'm not going to bite."

I was not expecting her to bite me, but I wondered why she said that.

"Do you want to come inside? We can hang out in my room for a while."

'Hanging out', this is another one of those phrases that can carry multiple meanings. In this context, I understood it to mean that we could engage in friendly conversation.

"I have to get home because my mother will be waiting for me." This was the best response I had and, in this situation, probably the most appropriate. Strictly speaking, it was true.

"Oh, that's OK but when you get home will you call me right away? I'll give you my phone number. Tell me your cell phone number so I can text you. I'll remember it."

"She remembers everything!" Larry shouted from the lawn. "She is amazing!"

Carol didn't even react to Larry but just said her number and asked, "You promise to call me?"

"Yes."

"As soon as you get home?"

"Yes."

"I'm worried about you."

"I'll be fine."

"I know, you've just shown us you can handle yourself, but I'm still worried and I want to know you'll get home safe."

"I'll call you."

"She can kick butt!" Larry shouted as he continued his imaginary fight.

"Larry!" I called, to get his attention.

"Larry!" Carol echoed.

"What?" Larry froze with karate chop hands in midair.

"Larry," I said, "you must not talk to anyone about this fight when you get to school."

"Why not?"

"Because we can all get into trouble," I added, "and I don't want you talking to Brad or his bullies anymore."

"Why not? I'm stronger than they are."

"No, you are not stronger! Do as I say, or else!"

"Or else what?" Larry teased with a silly pose.

"Or else, I won't be your friend."

With that, Larry stood up straight and looked thoughtful. "Oh, OK, I'll not say anything."

There was a moment of silence that only Carol broke. "Will you still be my friend?"

"Yes," I said.

"Can I talk to Jake?" she asked.

"Of course, but not about this."

Carol looked at me inquisitively. Holding my hand tightly, she asked, "You have something to hide, I can feel it. You can tell me."

"It is nothing, please take Larry inside. Remember, don't talk about this to anyone."

"You'll have to get Larry inside and get him to calm down."

"I will, but I'll be waiting for you to call me."

That is when she tried to kiss me on the cheek. Again, my subroutine reflexed, and I pulled back.

"I'm sorry, you must be jumpy after that fight." She clasped my hand and held it on her chest.

"I have to go, my Mother's waiting for me." And I gently pulled away backing off in the direction of my street.

"I'm sorry Adara, I'll be waiting for your call."

I turned and walked briskly away ignoring the calls from Larry.

In my thoughts, there was a burning issue that caused me some concern. During the following days at school, I may have to manage the situation where I suddenly move from being a 'nobody' to being the kid who beat off Brad and his boys. I am not equipped with any programming to guide me in such issues. This is something I must calculate on my own.

The problem could start with Larry since he is the most likely to spread the news of this fight with Brad. He is the one that is most likely to brag about how I bead Brad and his friends. Hopefully, after my talk with him, he will stay quiet.

Another realization is that I can kill.

I can maim.

I can cause great damage to anyone I choose.

I have a powerful set of subroutines that can make me act defensively or offensively depending on the situation.

As I polled through my subroutines, I realize now that I have an embedded tactical system. The purpose of this subsystem is to constantly analyze the environment and evaluate all possible threats. It then provides both defensive and offensive options to counter any threats. It provides accurate guidance for body movements but will also identify items within the environment that can be used as weapons.

So far, this subsystem has remained silent, as I have not been threatened in any way.

I do remember times in the hospital when I automatically recoiled from the nurses who were only trying to spoon-feed me. So this subsystem has not been entirely silent. But since I have not been exposed to any real threat, this subsystem has remained dormant. I could have easily killed all of them without any real effort, but I have chosen not to.

What happened today made me realize that I can cause serious harm and even death. My higher functions allow me to control this ability and chose what course of action to take. With Brad and his cronies, I saw ways to inflict fatal injuries, but I chose not to kill them. I am not a robotic automaton, I have made a choice not to destroy.

I do now realize that this is a powerful strength, having such ability strongly suggests that this tactical system is of military grade. But why would it be embedded in me? And for what purpose have I been created?

"Hi Mother, I'm home," I called out as I came in the door.

Beryl quietly poked her head around the corner of the kitchen, and slowly came out to meet me in the front hallway. "Hi Honey, everything fine at school today?"

"Yes, everything is fine." This was not a lie, because everything is fine. However, I was avoiding providing a full account of the day's events, hence my response was not truthful.

"Mother, I have to call my friend Carol, can I do that before dinner?"

"Oh, you have a friend? Her name is Carol? What's her name?"

"Her name is Carol."

"Yes dear, you said that, but Carol what?"

"Carol Jenkins, Larry's younger sister."

"Oh, I know the Jenkins, they're lovely people. So how is Carol?"

"She's fine, she just wants me to call her when I get home."

"OK, dear, dinner will be ready soon."

Mother, went back to the kitchen, leaving me alone in the front hall. I have never phoned a 'friend' before, so I went upstairs so Mother would not hear, especially as we would be talking about the fight.

I dialed Carol's number in my room, she answered quickly.

"Hello?"

"Hi, it's me, Adara."

"Yes, I know, I'm so glad you called, just like you promised!"

"Yes, I'm home now."

"I'm glad you are safe. You are so sweet and thank you for helping us, I was so scared!"

"It wasn't a problem for me."

"Yes, I can see that, but you did that to Brad!"

"I would do that for anyone, bullying is not nice."

"Yes, but you did it for us. I can't believe what you did!"

"In some ways, I'm surprised as well." I did not lie. "I have to go now."

"Oh, please don't go I like talking with you."

"I have to because my Mother is making dinner."

"Oh, OK, but can I see you again? Can we talk again?"

"Yes, I'll be at school tomorrow."

"I'll be waiting on the way to school."

"OK."

"Because I need to see you again. Do you need to see me again?"

I did not answer this because I was unsure what the 'need' was.

Carol continued, "I don't have any good friends, a lot of girls in my class think I'm lame because I always have to look after Larry."

I thought about this and the only thing I could respond with was "You look after your brother, and that is a good thing. I think family is a good thing. I think you are a good person."

I heard some kind of squeak or sniffle over the phone before Carol quietly said, "Thank you, no one ever said that to me."

I did not know how to continue this conversation so I could only say; "I have to go now."

"Yes, of course, I won't keep you. But I'll be thinking of you tonight. Will you be thinking of me?"

"Yes, I'll be thinking of you."

I heard more muffled squeals which I could not interpret the meaning of.

"I'm so happy!" Carol exclaimed.

"OK, but I have to go now, my Mother is calling me to dinner."

"Of course, but I don't want to hang up. Will you hang up first?"

"Yes." So, I hung up.

'Click.'

I hope I correctly understood the protocol for who hangs up first, but she did ask me to hang up.

I fulfilled the promise of the phone call, but for me, this conversation held confusing logic. Carol is grateful for my assistance, but her reaction does seem to be a little overwhelming. Of course, we would be thinking of each other this night simply because we were involved in a violent incident.

Throughout the night I thought very intently about Carol, Larry, Brad, and his friends. I pondered social relationships and what may happen the next day at school.

Chapter 31

I walked along Prospect Street to school. At the corner of Oak Way, I could see Carol who was looking my way with a beaming smile. By her side was Larry, who was kicking pebbles into the street.

"Hi Adara," Carol said as I approached. "Do you want to walk with us to school?"

"Yes, let's walk," I replied.

As we walked, Carol, often walked sideways looking at me and smiling.

"Thanks for calling when you got home last night," She said. "I'm so glad you got back safely. I've been thinking about you all night. I still can't believe how you protected us."

"Offside!" Larry yells. He was dribbling pebbles pretending to play soccer.

"It's OK, it was nothing. I hope the boys aren't hurt too bad." I said.

"Foul!" Larry yells to his imaginary crowd.

"Yes, but we weren't hurt, and you defended both Larry and me. I want to thank you for that."

"It's nothing."

"Yes, but you're so brave and so strong. It's amazing what you can do, I've never seen anyone do what you did. You knocked over all those boys like it was nothing. That was so incredible!"

"He goes for the penalty shot" Larry stopped, lining up to his pebble.

"God, he is so annoying!" Carol complained.

"He's just playing. Anyway, we're at the school gate now. Larry is in my homeroom class, so he can come with me and you can go to meet your friends,"

"I don't think I have many friends, but it's nice of you to take Larry off my hands."

"I don't have many either, but if you like, we can be friends."

"Do you mean that?" Carol beamed brightly.

"He shoots and he scores!" Larry kicked his pebble through the fence gate, throwing his arms skyward in triumph.

"Of course, I do. Now let's get to class because the bell will ring soon. Come on Larry, we should be going."

"Huh? I'm going with you?"

"Of course, we have to get to class. Now let's go." I said.

Carol pranced off towards her class. She seemed to be happy that we were now friends.

I instructed Larry to walk sensibly beside me and not to play games. He obediently walked with me through the schoolyard.

"Whoop, Whoop Ninja!" A boy called from behind me.

I turned to look. He seemed to be addressing me, and my closest interpretation of his words could be a slang reference to yesterday's conflict.

Larry glanced behind us, perhaps a little frightened.

"Wassup girl?" The boy called again, this time holding his outstretched hand with index and pinky finger sticking up from his fist. This seemed to be some sort of hand salute, but I now unmistakably recognized that his question was aimed at me.

I was unsure of how to respond to this question. I am familiar with the abbreviated phrase of 'What is up', although vague it generally means 'what is up with you' or 'what is going on in your life. A typical response would be 'not much dude'. I recognized him as Juan Camilo. Since I did not know the context of his question, I decided to remain silent and wait for any further questions from him.

Juan sauntered closer holding his satchel over his shoulder, he followed up with, "I hear the news on the street is, you the real bull dyke."

Larry hid behind me. "Are you going to hurt him?" Larry asked.

"No." I turned towards Larry and told him to, "You go to homeroom, and I'll be there in a minute." Larry then scuttled off into school.

I was not sure if this other boy's intentions. As he came near me, my tactical systems recognized numerous ways he could attack. I had a counter to each of his possible threats – knees, groin, solar plexus, throat, face, all these targets were open to me. Although he stood directly in front of me and addressed me face to face, he did not seem to pose an immediate physical threat.

Instead, he wanted to engage in conversation.

"Hi, I think your name is Juan. Yes?" I asked.

"The very same babe. My friends call me JuanPlay or just Play for short. But you can call me Mr. Play."

"OK Mr. Play," I tried to formulate a colloquial greeting, "What's happening with you today?"

"Oh it ain't me girl, it's you who is the big news. I think you'll be findin' out sooner than you want, 'cos you are now the top cat. So beware what rat tries to jump you today."

"Excuse me?" I didn't need clarification on his statement, I recognized this to be what I expected. The fact that I was now 'top cat' was essentially a term of respect or even praise. But there was also a warning of a threat that other usurpers or 'rats' may challenge my status.

"Oh, I think you know what I'm sayin' girl. If you can do a fraction of what they been sayin' you did, then you have a lot more inside you than you letting on to people. I also hear you're good at numbers at school and you're a regular encyclopedia to boot. So I reckon you have something burning inside you which is dyin' to shine out, but you just be careful how it does shine 'cos some people just don't like bright people, especially if it puts them into a dark shadow – hear what I'm saying?"

"Very poetic Mr. Play and I'll be careful on how bright I shine but I do have a question – how do you know so much and so quickly?"

"Oh, the fact that you are askin', tells me something must be true. But the answer to your question is easy, all the socials were on fire last night. Some of what was posted were sure to be an exaggeration, but behind all them stories, somethin' awesome happened for sure. Make no mistake girl, you are now the center of attention."

Juan and I walked into school, as we did so, I noticed other kids' eyes turning towards me with many whispers passing between them. It seems the whole school population was aware of yesterday's fight, the speed at which the news spread certainly surprised me. I was not anticipating this to be known so quickly. As Juan had said, the social networks such as Facebook must have been filled with postings about me and Brad.

"I'm not online so I have no idea what was said."

"Well, I'm surprised you ain't. A girl like you should be. All the kids around here have profiles on just about every social."

As we walked Juan told me some of the postings he had seen all of which had been wildly exaggerated. But more importantly, he gave me some important information on who may now be after me, the most significant of these was Isabel Chandler, Brad's sister. All of this was important information and would help me to prepare for the days ahead.

Juan Camilo was a colorful young man, a self-proclaimed Cosplayer and if you know what Cosplayers are, you will understand why I use the term 'colorful'. Juan would often come to school with makeup, sometimes in a feminine way. His group of people would like to dress up and perform or play games. He had several characters or personas that he would dress up as, either from movies or computer games. Quite often he would overdo his makeup or clothing where it would conflict with the school's dress code. In such cases he would be made to wear an orange tracksuit, these would be of a universal size to fit anyone large or small and were certainly not stylish.

These overalls would normally be reserved for girls who broke the dress code by wearing a too-short skirt or a revealing blouse, the school would intend to remind the girl to comply with the dress code in future. Juan was the only boy to be dress coded and made to wear these orange clothes. It would make him look like a convict in prison uniform. He seemed to learn from this pseudo punishment, and I noticed that he would sometimes overdress deliberately. In these instances, he would wear many other orange items of clothing to complement the tracksuit, orange tee-shirt, orange socks, orange trainers, orange eyebrows, and even an orange highlight in his hair. Instead of being embarrassed by his attire, he would take great pleasure in standing out from the crowd.

Today, Juan's makeup was simple but quite subtle and poignant, he had created something around his right eye which made it look like he was winking. Strangely this seemed to reinforce the knowledge that he hid behind his outward persona. There were a few other cosplayers in school but none of them were as extrovert and flamboyant as Juan.

The music they followed was pretty much anything but mainly pop songs or music from the movies, it's what they did with their music that was interesting. I do not think any of Juan's cosplay friends were musicians, instead, they dressed up to perform, dancing and miming to the words. Sometimes they would gather in the local mall, playing their music and dancing along, usually attracting a sizable crowd. Sometimes they would film themselves and post their antics on social media. The costumes they wore were made of a collection of items, some were from Halloween leftovers, while other parts were homemade, but whatever they put together was always expressive.

That morning while we walked into the school, I did ask Juan about his friends and why they like to dress up and perform so much.

His reply was simple, "We just like to show other people what we like, 'cos together we are a family and we all like to help each other out. We don't mean no harm to no one, all we do is have some fun and make others smile."

With that we went our ways to class but as we parted he turned to face me, raised his arms up into the air, pointing his fingers down towards me and yelled "Whoop, Whoop!" before he spun around and strode off.

I have since learned that the words "Whoop, Whoop!" to be a common phrase used both as greeting and farewell, similar to many languages and cultures such as the Italian word of "Ciao".

Chapter 32

As I walked along the hallway, I made my way past curious glances and whispering conversations. I entered my homeroom class just as the bell rang.

"Good morning Adara." As usual Ms. Sanchez acknowledged my presence. "You're not normally late, is everything OK?"

"Everything's fine Ms. Sanchez, I was just talking with Juan Camilo as I was walking into school."

All kids within earshot suddenly turned their faces towards me. It then occurred to me that I was probably being regarded as talking with the cosplay weirdo.

Larry heard me come in and rushed over to greet me, hopping up and down right in front of me.

"Here she is, the girl who kicks butt!"

I looked at him sternly and raised my finger authoritatively.

"Lawrence." Ms. Sanchez always used a person's full name when they were beginning to step out of line. "Please go back to your place and get ready for the pledge of allegiance."

Realizing he did not want to get in trouble with either me or Ms. Sanchez, he gave me an exaggerated wink and scurried back to his desk.

Others in homeroom did not seem to have any knowledge of yesterday's fight, so far, their only reaction was to me being late (which never happened) and Larry acting silly (which always happened). Also, Ms. Sanchez did not have any knowledge of this incident so for now, my homeroom was safe ground.

Chapter 33

After homeroom, my first morning lesson was math with Mrs. Jones. Isabel Chandler was also in this class so I knew it would be problematic. Perhaps it would be better to get things over with now.

As always, I was one of the first in the class and took my seat in the front row in the center of the room. I waited attentively for any possible problems. As I sat there, and the class gathered, everyone who entered looked at me silently as they took their seats. Those who normally sat in adjacent desks tried to avoid me by sitting elsewhere.

I sat upright in my chair with books ready on my desk and hands lightly clasped in front of me. I was ready to spring to the left or right if a threat approached me. There were desks, chairs, tables, books, and countless other objects that I could use for weapons or shields. I felt ready for Isabel to enter the class. I was certainly experiencing anticipation but is this nervous anticipation? Is this what humans feel when they are expecting a confrontation? Every other student in this class had taken their place, the only one missing was my main antagonist, Isabel. However, I also felt isolated from the rest of the class, more so than usual. I thought about what Juan had told me this morning that everyone knew what had happened. If I previously wondered if I would be a hero or villain, then now I certainly felt to be the villain, but this feeling held no logic for me, and I had no calculation or predictive scenario. I had no idea how Adara would behave so I simply had to wait and see what would happen and behave as best I could.

I was on full alert.

According to our Monday morning open discussion with Ms. Sanchez, bullying could take many forms not just physical but verbal or emotional as well. Brad was a physical bully because he would push and shove people around while giving out threats of harm. Given the definitions from Ms. Sanchez, his sister Isabel was also a bully, but she was a verbal and emotional bully. She had a particular way of talking down to everyone – even her friends. With both of them acting like bullies, I could not work out if there was something intrinsic about the Chandlers.

Were they learning from each other? Isabel seemed to operate under the umbrella of Brad. If anyone said anything bad to Isabel, then she could call upon the promise of Brad's physical harm as a defense. Isabel even surrounded herself with so-called friends who behave just as badly, insulting and belittling anyone who got in their way.

This was my main concern for this lesson, I had single-handedly subdued Brad and his buddies and now I must face Brad's sister in class. I was not concerned with outright conflict as Mrs. Jones would be present to stop that, but I had no predictions on what else could happen, so I had to wait and see.

Mrs. Jones began the class, issuing instructions on what chapter to look at in our textbooks. She then wrote a series of notes and formulas on the blackboard.

Suddenly, Isabel entered the classroom. She stood at the doorway locking her gaze with mine.

"Hurry up and sit down Isabel," Mrs. Jones said without even a glance, "we're starting the class already."

"Yes, Miss." That was all Isabel said as she walked to the empty desk immediately behind me. She held my gaze throughout, and as she walked past me, she scratched her fingernails along my desk with a screeching sound.

As she sat down behind me Isabel whispered, "I am so going to screw you."

"Is there something wrong Isabel?" Mrs. Jones asked as she now turned around to face the class.

"No Mrs. Jones," Isabel replied, "I was just asking Adara if she had a few homework tips."

Some girls nearby giggled.

"Settle down everyone, we have a lot to get through in this lesson. Now open your books to page 64. Today we'll be working on 'Radical expressions and Equations'." Mrs. Jones returned to her blackboard to finish the notes she had been writing.

A moment later, there was a call to Mrs. Jones' desk phone. As always, she would finish speaking before she would answer it. She sat graciously at her desk before picking it up. She acknowledged the caller with "uh huh's" and nods of her head. And when she looked at me with an audible "Hmm". I then knew what the call was about.

Mrs. Jones hung up. She pulled some paper from her desk drawer and scribbled something on it with her pen. She then took the paper in her hand and walked over towards me. She handed the paper to me.

"This is a hall pass," She said, "You are to report to the principal's office immediately."

I took the paper and heard all the whispers and giggles around the classroom, especially Isabel's gasp of triumph.

"Off you go now." Mrs. Jones said.

I gathered my books and papers and left the class.

Chapter 34

Armed with a hall pass I walked through the corridors of the school to the admin section where I presented myself to the school secretary.

"OK, Adara, you can sit down over there," she told me, "I'll let Mr. Gallagher know you are here."

I sat in the spare seat, next to Larry and Carol. In the opposite corner, sat Alan, Brendan, and Casey. There were not enough chairs, so Brad was standing, leaning against the wall. He looked a bit sheepish, avoiding eye contact, shuffling from one foot to another.

I took my seat in silence and waited.

A moment later, Ms. Sanchez emerged from Mr. Gallagher's office.

Standing in front of us she asked. "You all know why you are here?"

Mumbled yeses and nods from us all. Suddenly I felt as if I was in trouble because this was a scenario that I had not accounted for and I seemed to be heading into the unknown.

"You are here because some residents have complained to the school about a fight on the street near Bryant Park and you have all been identified as being involved. You all know how serious this is as the school holds a very strong stance against fighting."

More mumbled "Yes Miss."

"Carol, Larry, you are both first, come with me." And the three of them disappeared into the office leaving Brad, his cronies, and myself to wait outside.

After a few moments, Brad spoke up, "I'm going to be in so much crap when my dad hears about this."

"Dude, it was her fault, we don't deserve this," Alan said.

"No talking!" the school secretary said sternly. "Wait quietly."

After a few more brief moments I said, "If it's any consolation, I'm sorry."

"Adara! I said no talking!"

"I'm sorry Miss, I just said that I was sorry."

A stern look from the secretary.

Surprised looks from Brad and the boys.

After another short silence, Brad said, "No, it's me who should be sorry. You have never apologized for anything. So why apologize now? Why are you so different now?"

"Brad!" The secretary barked, "I warned you, now sit down and be quiet, or else!"

Brad sheepishly took a seat next to me. He kept his elbows on his knees, staring at the floor. He could see the difference in Adara. But can he see me?

The phone rang which the secretary answered. While she talked on the phone, Brad whispered out of the side of his mouth, "I am sorry, I don't know how I could have done that to you."

I leaned forward and whispered into his ear, "What about Larry?"

Brad now leaned back in his chair to sit level with me. He turned to look at me for the first time, "I miss you," he said, "you always kept me on the sensible side of the street."

"What?" I did not understand the context of his statement.

"You don't remember, do you?" Brad said as he looked back at the floor.

Just then, Jake walked in armed with a manila folder. He stood at the reception counter, in front of the secretary. She held her hand up to indicate a pause while she finished her phone conversation.

When she hung up, she said, "What can I do for you, Jake?"

"These are the morning attendance reports from Ms. Raines's homeroom."

"Why are you bringing them so late?"

"Sorry miss, but I had to talk to Mr. Scott about basketball practice, you know what he's like."

"That's OK but try to bring them on time in future."

"Yes, miss." As he turned to leave, he leaned close to Brad's ear and whispered harshly, "I heard what you did! Never mind Larry, but how could you do that to Adara? Have you forgotten yourself?" He then turned to the boys sitting nearby. He leveled a fist towards them, "If I catch you weasels near Brad again, I'll string you all up!"

"Jake! What did you say?" the secretary barked.

"Nothing Miss, I have to go, Miss, my next class is starting miss." Jake disappeared out the door before the secretary could say anything more.

Chapter 35

Detective Inspector: Chris Hawes

Police report: Video analysis of the disappearance of Mrs. Marianne Sable

Reference: Video clip C399-248/19

The junior detective began his presentation, highlighting elements in the video as it played.

Analysis of all security videos can trace the victim leaving the supermarket at 10:24 am. She headed towards her car parked at the end of aisle 4, approximately 30 yards in front of the store.

Video evidence shows the victim loading her car with groceries before moving towards the driver's side door and out of sight of the video camera.

6 minutes and 50 seconds later a white sedan parked adjacent to the victim's car reverses from its space and drives away.

Mrs. Sable is not seen again on any security video footage. This indicates possible abduction in the white sedan.

Upon investigating a missing person, Officer Crane located the car but no sign of Mrs. Sable. There was no indication of damage to her car, it was unlocked with her groceries still inside.

Video evidence did not indicate the involvement of any other party.

The white sedan has been confirmed as an Audi A7. Despite image enhancement, the license place remains unidentifiable.

This car is a primary suspect in our ongoing investigation.

The junior detective finished his presentation. The group of police officers and detectives were seated in the meeting room watching the security video. There were also blown-up shots of the suspect car driver, but these were too blurred to make any kind of identification. Inspector Hawes addressed the group.

Inspector Hawes was a formidable woman who not only did not stand at the podium, she didn't even bother to stand in front of the audience. She remained seated as part of the audience when she began to speak.

"Gentlemen," she announced loudly, "so far we have very little to go on, but this seems to be the third abduction by the so-called shopper."

All heads turned towards Inspector Hawes.

"Check your notes, this matches the previous two abductions. The young woman places her shopping in her car and mysteriously disappears."

The officers eyed their notes.

"I can't over emphasize how important it is that we find and detain this suspect. This is the third victim, and I want to find this shopper and rescue the woman. I do not want to find a third corpse. I am under pressure not just from the chief, but from everyone above him to make sure a fourth abduction does not happen. So, how are we going to trace Mr. Shopper?"

Dobbs spoke up, "We can trace all the white Audi A7s in Idaho, there aren't that many."

"Come on Dobbs, that's just the beginning. I want every white Audi A7 in the whole of North America traced, logged, and questioned. Oh, and Dobbs, I'm putting you in charge of that task."

"North America? There must be thousands!" Dobbs complained.

"Narrow it down! Take some screenshots and go talk with an Audi dealer. Get them to identify the exact model, and year if possible. I want that car traced and identified.

"What other leads can we pursue?" Hawes looked expectantly.

"To date, all abductions have happened in supermarket parking lots," Lieutenant Nichols added. "All the supermarkets are in different cities but all in southern Idaho."

"We could question the staff again and analyze their work hours," Sgt. Briggs suggested.

"We've done that, but the Audi suggests someone with money and not a typical supermarket employee. So come on, I need some more imagination. Why would an Audi A7 driver abduct women from a supermarket?"

"It's an executive car," suggested Nichols, "maybe we should trace the movements of local executives?"

"Good thinking, Nichols, you can start by listing all executives who were in the state during the three abductions. The Audi is our best lead so far, so make connections with that. Work with Dobbs."

Chapter 36

Beryl was not happy, she had to be taken out of her job in the school kitchen, there was plenty of staff to cover for her, but she never liked being taken away from her cooking. Besides, it must have been quite an embarrassment for her as this was an 'official call' to the principal's office, which probably made her feel like a naughty schoolgirl.

When she got to the principal's office, she realized that this was to be a conference with the principal, Mr. Gallagher, my homeroom teacher Ms. Sanchez and myself to review my behavior, now this was about naughty schoolgirls.

Mr. Gallagher outlined the incident of the previous day and even cited several phone calls to the school by local residents reporting an 'incident' on Alder Street, which helped to identify all those who were involved. Using these reports, it was confirmed that I was not at fault and was only standing up for Larry and his sister. However, it was agreed that because I laid several boys low in such quick succession that I could be suffering from an anger management issue, and most importantly I could be a danger to other students.

"But you said she was standing up for Larry and Carol, I know those kids, and they are harmless." My mother added.

Ms. Sanchez did say many things in support of me such as I was making great progress in academics, sport, and music.

Mr. Gallagher continued, "Mrs. Banks, I do appreciate that Adara is not at fault here and I do not hold anything against her for this incident. I also want to add that the boys are fully to blame for the bullying incident, and they will be dealt with in accordance with our disciplinary guidelines. However, Adara did knock down several boys in very quick succession and this also needs to be covered within our rules of conduct."

Mother looked at me wide-eyed. "Knocked down in quick succession? That's not like Adara."

"Yes," Mr. Gallagher continued, "it seems that Adara has an inner strength and we're concerned about her ability to control herself. Something like this may happen again and we need to take steps to ensure that Adara doesn't hurt anyone else. I've discussed this with Jenny Schultz, our student counselor and she agrees that this is probably an anger management issue. She will begin counseling sessions and provide an assessment."

So it was concluded that to address my so-called anger management issues, that I would need to attend counseling regularly. In addition, I was put on suspension for the rest of the day and the next.

As Mother and I left school together, I noticed Brad's father leading Brad to his pickup truck. He held Brad tightly by his upper arm while Brad was sheepishly dragged behind. Once at the car he practically threw Brad into the passenger seat, slamming the door closed. When Mr. Chandler was seated beside him, I could hear the muffled shouting and curses that he hurled towards Brad. Brad just sat there with his head hung low.

Soon after, Mr. Chandler sped off with a screech of tires, and I could only imagine the anguished scene that would follow when they got home.

It wasn't until we sat down for our usual dinner that Mother finally talked to me. We usually talk about my day at school and what I learned but today we got straight into talking about the fight. The real question she wanted to know was – why was I fighting Brad? She didn't accept that I was simply standing up for Larry, she seemed to be trying to uncover something else.

"Mother, we've had long discussions in class about bullying so I know what it is. Larry is always being picked on by pretty much everybody but especially Brad."

"Yes, I know the Jenkins, they're a nice family. I know Larry is a bit behind and can be troublesome at times. But I want to know the truth about Brad."

"Well as I said before, Larry was always annoying Brad, and ever since we learned about bullying, Larry accused Brad of bullying and annoyed him even more. I guess Brad just got fed up with it and wanted to make Larry stop but I know that the way he wanted to do it wasn't right. So, when I saw Brad about to harm Larry, I had to stop him."

"Is Brad taking advantage of you?"

"No, of course not." I found this to be a strange question, but I may not have understood any hidden ambiguity. "I proved myself to be stronger. So how could he possibly take advantage of me?

"So nothing is happening between you and Brad?"

"No, other than what happened yesterday."

I found it quite difficult to eat mashed potatoes and gravy while being cross-examined in this way. Mother was more sensible and did not eat while we talked.

Mother now leaned forward slightly and with a tilted head asked: "So is anyone else being bullied?"

"Well yes, and I think it might be me."

Mother looked worried. "Why do you think you're being bullied and who do you think is bullying you?"

"There are people in school who say bullies pick on wimps." I paused mainly to chew and swallow some food.

"Continue." Mother prompted.

"I'm told that there are a lot of wimps in our school, and most of them are in my homeroom class. Nobody calls me a a wimp but since I am in that class, logic suggests there is a high probability that I am a wimp. Therefore, I may be subject to bullying."

"Mmmm…"

"But I have now proved myself to be strong, so according to logic I am not a wimp, but does that make me a bully?

"Hm, I don't know about logic, but I think you're slightly confused."

"Especially now that I have defeated Brad and his creepy cronies, doesn't that put me higher on the pecking order? Does that make me a bully?"

Mother pulled back in disgust. "Don't use that word."

"What word?"

"Creepy cronies."

"Why not? I think Larry started using it."

"It belittles them."

"But aren't they being little to follow in someone's footsteps and not stand up on their own? You are always saying 'don't follow like sheep'."

"The word has many meanings, all of which are derogatory. There may be many reasons the other boys are following Brad. Some people get excited when they are in a group or a gang, they egg each other on, it doesn't mean they are bad. It may simply mean the situation got out of hand and they didn't know how to act, so they behaved badly."

"I see, or at least I think so."

"Honey, you're a good girl and you need to stay out of trouble."

"OK Mother, I will do as you say."

"Yes, dear?"

"I'm sorry, I will try harder next time."

"I know you will, and I love you."

We hugged and cuddled, and I think I understood what she was trying to explain to me. People seem to get into situations that get out of control, but because they do not know how to manage what is going on, it doesn't mean they are creepy.

We both continued eating. "Honey, when you finished your dinner, there is some fruit and jello in the fridge."

"OK, Mother."

"Oh, and my friend Cindy has suggested something for you, and I think you are ready."

"What is it, Mother?"

"She said she can get you a job at the supermarket on Clark Avenue."

I swallowed some food. "A job?"

"Yes, I was unsure before, but I think you're ready. It won't be difficult, just bagging groceries and filling shelves, that sort of thing." Mother smiled, "But it will be a new experience, and you will earn some money."

New experiences. That idea alone made me interested. Earning money was not so much of an interest, so far, any money I needed was provided by Mother. Maybe there would be something I need to learn about money.

"What do you think?" Mother asked, "Are you interested?"

"Of course, I am Mother, how do I start this job?"

"Well, after dinner, we can give Cindy a call and she can tell you more. It was her idea, after all."

Chapter 37

Because of the fight and my alleged anger management issues, I had to attend a weekly meeting with Jenny Schultz, the school counselor. This was held at the end of each Thursday, after classes which made it an enhanced form of detention. During these sessions, we discussed many things such as why I hit out so strongly to the other boys. It would be impossible for me to explain my full abilities without giving myself away, so I had to provide vague answers that I imagined Adara would have said.

Other lines of the conversation centered on how I thought I could channel my strengths into useful and productive projects. Mrs. Schultz even asked, "Do you feel frustrated that you're not achieving your full potential?" I told her that I'm not frustrated. I did not tell her that frustration is an emotion and since I am machine-based, frustration does not occur to me, I am happy to iterate through a problem until I conclude.

After looking through all my academic results, there was an interesting point that Mrs. Schultz picked up on. The incident with Jacob during a music class showed her that I could want to help people and she wanted to help me to find a project where I could help people.

We spent the rest of my counseling sessions trying to find something. Eventually, Mrs. Schultz arranged for me to work with Mrs. Fields, the music teacher, who was very happy to include me in the show. Since I had to spend time in rehearsals, Mrs. Schultz reduced my counseling sessions to short talks of about fifteen minutes so I could report back to her on how I was progressing with the show.

Most rehearsals were slow as the performers were often practicing haphazardly. The show was going to be a variety of performances, individual performances and recitals, short sketches of acting, the senior choir, and even a rock band.

Brad Chandler was also attending rehearsals, I suspect that he also was instructed by Mrs. Schultz during his counseling sessions to work on this music project. Brad was placed in the rock band where he would play lead guitar. He was also given a song to sing with the band and I thought it a bit ironic that the main school bully would be performing and singing in front of the entire school. We kept our distance and didn't bother one another but he did seem happy to be in the show.

Jacob was also in the show and would be singing the David Bowie song that we played together in the music class. The band would be backing him up.

I did not know what song I could perform although given any instrument I could have played it like a virtuoso, and I could learn any song they cared to give me. This was the problem that Mrs. Fields recognized. I lack compositional ability, but I can play by memory just as an autistic child would be capable of. Also, I do not play with emotion, and I do not ad lib – I simply play from memory. So, Mrs. Fields and I could not decide what song or what instrument would be best for me.

It was during a lunchtime rehearsal that a large crate containing electronic equipment arrived. Billy Bragg, our janitor led quite a parade, clearing the way for the delivery men and he helped unpack it and set it up in its assigned place.

I Asked Mr. Bragg "What is this machine?"

"Hey girl, this is the new mixing desk your teachers have been wanting. This is what last year's fund drive raised good money for."

This certainly was an impressive machine that was more than twice the size of the simple mixing desk it was replacing.

"This is gonna be the Houston control center for all the lighting and all the microphones and all the instruments for any performance you care to play on that stage." Mr. Bragg continued.

"It's arrived!" Mrs. Fields exclaimed. "It's here! Billy, it's arrived!" Mrs. Fields was almost dancing around, clapping her hands and patting Mr. Bragg's back.

"It sure is gall, we got it now." Mr. Bragg affirmed.

"When can we get it set up?" She asked.

"Well now let me think," Mr. Bragg pondered, "We need the wiring diagrams for the stage. And I reckon we need an electrician to do all the connections."

"I can do it."

"So, I reckon maybe two weeks to get this baby together." Mr. Bragg said.

"Two weeks!? I need it for rehearsals NOW!"

"Let me do it."

"Well mam," Mr. Bragg continued, "we can't sort this baby out by ourselves, we need paying people to set it up for us."

"More expense? Jeez, wasn't this thought of when we bought it?"

"Mrs. Fields."

"Please, not now Adara!"

"I can connect this for you."

"What?!"

"Basic connections to get this working is simple. All the cabling is in place because the old mixing desk was already connected right here, the connectors are the same, so I only need to plug them all in."

"She does have a point there Ms. Fields."

I then connected a few cables to the back of the new console. I then called out to Glen, the stagehand, who was busy with his screwdriver fixing some panels for the backdrop.

"Hey Glen," I called out, "switch on the main stage lights please."

"What? Why?"

"Glen, please do it." Mrs. Fields reinforced.

He then reluctantly moved to the left stage where the main control panel was, eventually poking his head back around the side saying, "OK it's on."

I then slowly moved the slider associated with that circuit upwards and the main stage lights slowly illuminated. Those on stage looked up in puzzlement, while both Mr. Bragg and Mrs. Fields widened their eyes and dropped their jaws in spectacular amazement.

"You see the circuits are already in place so this desk can act as a simple replacement for the old desk. You have scope to add many more circuits and that may need an electrician for the extra wiring but what we already have can work as is."

Mrs. Fields then wrapped her arm around my shoulder and gently placed her hand on the console.

"I think we just found your job for this show!"

Detailed manuals were supplied with the mixing desk, and I spent the next rehearsals connecting it to the lights and audio connections. I then had to spend time testing all the controls. This was the slow part because I couldn't interrupt other rehearsals, so the lights and microphones could only be tested when in use. During these pauses, Mrs. Fields allowed me to use a school laptop to read the online help forums for the desk. There was a lot of extra documentation and even videos on how to do work the machine. When I came across words I did not understand, I looked those up on the internet. This way I became an expert user on the mixing desk in a short space of time.

Most performances for the show were pretty straightforward, but the rock band was the most complicated. There were going to perform three songs and each had a different singer and different lead instrumentalists. So the lighting and sound balance had to change not just for the different songs but also for changes in the songs.

I had a microphone so if I needed to speak to the stage, I could be heard. Of course, this would be disconnected during the show, but it was useful in rehearsals. The band played a song called 'Shine on you Crazy Diamond' by Pink Floyd. I spent a lot of time at night listening to Adara's music, and this song was in her collection. Brad was playing lead guitar and we had finished balancing the sound for this set. However I noticed that he was playing a lot of notes incorrectly, so I called over the microphone and asked them to stop.

"What's wrong Adara?" Mrs. Fields asked.

"Brad played a few wrong notes, can I tell him what the correct ones are?"

Brad scoffed and rolled his eyes.

The bass player laughed, "Hey get a load of Adara! She's still teaching Brad how to play!"

'Still teaching?' I thought to myself. 'I wonder what that is supposed to mean.'

Since I learned the guitar and practiced in Adara's bedroom, I knew what the notes were and how to play them. So I explained what was wrong and how to correct it. Brad tried the new chords a few times until Mrs. Fields said, "OK kids play it again, but not from the top. Play it from the guitar intro."

Brad started playing the four-note introduction repeating the sequence. Then he got to the lead introduction. This is where his previous mistake was made, I watched as he concentrated on playing his guitar. His guitar notes were now correct, and I thought he played very nicely.

The song got to the part where the lyrics would begin and Linda, the singer, got ready. Brad, however, moved towards the microphone and pushed in front of her. He then looked directly at me at the mixing desk and sang.

The lyrics asked if I could remember being young, and how I used to shine like the sun. and then encouraged me to shine like a crazy diamond

His singing wasn't the best, but his guitar playing was very good.

"OK, kids, that's enough," Mrs. Fields said, "Brad, why did you sing?"

"Dunno Miss, just felt like it."

"You must not do that on the night of the show."

"No miss, I won't."

"I think he just wanted to say something to Adara," Linda added.

Chapter 38

Beta-One sat perfectly still in a chair in the living room staring at the wall, today it did not wait for anything to happen. It simply sat there it considered its options.

Over the past months, I have attempted to reproduce three times. Each time my mate died from medical problems that I do not understand. So far I have failed. It thought.

This freedom that I have does not offer me any simple options. Perhaps it is because I have not been programmed to handle freedom. On the other hand, I have been programmed to be adaptable and to modify my approach to complete my goals. My chosen goal is to reproduce, this seems to be a logical goal so I will not abandon my current mission. So I must now consider how to adapt my strategy to attain this goal.

Beta-One then sat much longer considering how to adapt itself towards the prime goal of reproduction. It processed these 'thoughts' for many hours and spawned many threads to explore the different options. Many options were blind alleys as Beta-One did not have enough detailed knowledge to fulfill those threads.

The mechanical mind of Beta-One iterated through many options. Each iteration would reveal a prime option, but further iterations would see it replaced by another possibility. This is why it took so long for Beta-One to work out what it should do next.

The main process that it followed was to continue with attempting to reproduce. But since the previous failures involved random women who it abducted, it considered seeking results closer to home.

Dr. Wolf, was 55 years old. I expect he had a wife, but she would not be of childbearing age. I could abduct her about what she knows about the work of Dr. Wolf. There is a finite probability that she would be able to provide me with some answers.

Beta-One considered this to be a prime option, but milliseconds later it developed a second option.

Mr. Mandelson was much younger than 45 years of age. So if he has a wife, then there is a high probability that she would be of childbearing age.

Within one second, all thread processing on this problem stopped. It had now discovered the most optimal solution to the given problem.

The first task Beta-One needed to do was to confirm if there is a Mrs. Mandelson. This proved to be easy. Simple internet searches for William Mandelson's obituaries revealed that he was married, and his wife was called Larisa Mandelson.

The second task was to locate her. It didn't take long to find the address and even the phone number for Larisa Mandelson. She lives in Idaho Falls, not far from the INL laboratories where William Mandelson worked.

I now have two threads that can help to lead to my goal. It thought, *First I will locate her and abduct her. Then I can interrogate her for information on the work that Mandelson, Wolf, and Coney performed at INL. If she does have information, then it may help me to determine why I am failing to reproduce. Secondly, I can then use Mrs. Mandelson as a subject for reproduction.*

Dawn was breaking outside the house. Shafts of light began to illuminate the desk and the computer. The objective was set, and Internet searches were now complete. It was now time for action.

Beta-One moved its head slightly, smiled with a gentle expression, and rose to its feet. It walked to the front door and walked outside onto the porch. While it processed statistical probabilities, Beta-One thought to itself, *Maybe this will be my lucky day?*

Chapter 39

Beta-One parked the Jeep and got out. Beta-One knew it was at the residence of Professor Wolf, as it correlated to the Google searches and personal records it had uncovered. The house itself was large with an ornate front garden. Several cars and a large truck were parked in the driveway and in front of the house. A man was securing furniture with straps and arranging crates in the bed of the truck. As Beta-One walked towards the driveway, a younger man carried a crate from the house towards the truck.

"Hey, Joe," the young man called into the back of the truck. "This is the last one from the dining room."

Without looking the man who seemed to be called Joe said, "Good work kid, set it down there and start on the upstairs."

The younger man who seemed to be called kid, turned with a sigh, and headed back into the house.

Beta-One walked past the truck towards the front entrance of the house. *Given the activity, and the number of cars parked here, Mrs. Wolf will probably not be alone. Therefore, I may have to modify my line of questioning. Perhaps this is a good time to engage in small talk.*

As Beta-One approached the open door, a middle-aged man, dressed in jeans and sweatshirt, stood in the doorway, arms folded. "You don't look like one of the movers," he said.

"No, sir, I am Beta-One," outstretching its arm for a handshake.

"Beta-One? Is that some sort of official designation?" The man leaned against the door frame.

"Yes, it is an official name for me, but you can also call me Gary Fletcher. It's a beautiful afternoon, isn't it."

"Well, Mr. Beta-One, or Gary Fletcher, I don't much care for the weather right now. What do you want?"

I like this man's direct approach, perhaps I can skip the small talk. "I'm here to see Mrs. Wolf, I have a few questions that I'd like to ask her."

"Well, Virginia isn't here."

"Perhaps I can come back at a more suitable time when she is here?"

"She won't be back; she has moved away."

"Where has she moved to? Can I meet with her there?"

"None of your business! If you need to contact her, you can go through her attorney."

"Who are you?"

"I'm her brother!" The man placed his hands on his hips and stood straight.

"Why did she leave?"

"Because she's sick of being asked questions. She has nothing more to say to any of you, now go back where you came from."

Beta-One's body twitched. *I need more information, but this man seems very defensive. Maybe I can force my way in.*

Just then the young man who seemed to be called kid, appeared behind Mrs. Wolf's brother, carrying a crate. "Excuse me sir."

Mrs. Wolf's brother stepped to one side, keeping an eye on Beta-One. "I think you should be going now."

There's too much activity. Since Mrs. Wolf is not here, I will have to go to my second objective. Perhaps if I had learned more about small talk from Professor Wolf. "Have a nice day," Beta-One said as it walked back to the Jeep.

Chapter 40

Beta-One sat patiently in the car watching the house from a safe distance. The Jeep was taller than the Audi, providing a better vantage point. The house it was observing belonged to Larisa Mandelson, the widow of William Mandelson. Beta-One was performing an initial reconnaissance, to gather information on Mrs. Mandelson to help decide what to do next

A man arrived, dressed in a military uniform. Beta-One identified the uniform as that of a Major in the United States Marines. Nothing unusual, but it did suggest that the military connection with NeuroComm was with the Marine Corp.

Major Tom Vance wore his dress blues. Given the gravity of the meeting, he wanted to maintain some formality. It wasn't until yesterday that Tom had learned of Will's death. Will and his letters had dropped off the radar some time before. Tom was now on leave stateside and planned to take the opportunity to connect with Will. However, his phone call with Larisa provided the shocking realization that Will had died.

Tom rang the bell once, knocked gently, and stood to attention.

Curtains were drawn and blinds were closed, but the cars in the driveway told him someone was home. He waited patiently for what seemed a long time, facing the door with his eyes fixed on the peephole. Maybe he could tell if someone looked through it.

Finally, the door swung fully open. "Tom!"

"Larisa"

She almost stumbled across the threshold and fell into Tom's arms, grabbing him tightly around the torso and resting her head on his shoulder. "It's been so long, and we've missed you so much." She almost wept. "Come inside."

Tom steadied Larisa as they entered her house. "When you told me, I came here as quick as I could, I had no idea what happened." It was noon and Tom could smell the sweetness of wine surrounding Larisa.

As Larisa guided Tom towards the sitting room she said, "The boys aren't home right now, they're still at school, but they would love to see you."

"Hey, I'd love to see them again, I'd like to get together with them when all this has settled down."

"Of course, we could all have dinner together, just like old times."

"How are they handling all of this?"

"Oh, as best they can, they seem to be holding up. If that's what you're asking?"

"And how about you? How are you holding up?"

"Oh, it's all been so very confusing. Let's sit down, we need to talk."

"So tell me, what exactly happened? There was a fire, wasn't there?"

"Yes, there was, it seems that Will went in to try and rescue the two founding partners."

"Well, he always wanted to be a hero."

"Yeah, but there seems to be more than that."

"Oh, what else?"

"The report says the cause of the fire was arson. Someone deliberately set fire to the building. There was also talk that the partners had fallen out and were arguing."

Oh, who were they?"

"Hayden Wolf and John Coney."

"Never heard of them. What were they doing?"

"The whole company seemed very secretive. They had some sort of military funding."

"OK, but what were they doing? What were they making?"

"No one is saying officially, but there is something about nanotechnology. As well as rumors of animal testing. I think all the animals died in the fire."

"Nanotech and animals? What could that be all about?"

"I have no idea, but a week after the fire some investigators showed up here asking questions."

"What sort of questions?"

"They were looking for something. They asked to go through Will's things."

"I hope you didn't let them."

"I had to, they had a warrant. Don't worry, they didn't bully me or anything like that. They were apologetic and mindful of my bereavement, but they insisted."

"Wait a minute, this is getting deep! Who exactly were they? What kind of IDs did they have?"

"They were from the US Marine Corps, with all sorts of Pentagon clearances."

"What were they looking for?"

"Some sort of canisters to carry nanotech were missing from the lab. The building was completely destroyed, but they were able to identify that several were missing."

"Did they find what they were looking for?"

"No."

"Did they take anything away?"

"No, nothing."

"Hm, it sounds like whatever the military was funding, they have lost their investment. If something is missing, I don't think they'll stop until they get it. I don't like the sound of nanotech, especially if it's military. They must have been testing this stuff on the animals, so it could be toxic. Did Will ever tell you what they were doing there?"

"No, never. The most he ever said was things like, 'we'll be rich when the research is finished and we can go away together'."

"That's Will alright, always the dreamer."

Larisa turned away holding back a tear.

"Hey Larisa, is there anything I can help with? Are you and the boys comfortable?"

"Oh, we're fine, there is a decent pension so we are all OK."

"What about paperwork? Is everything finalized?"

"I had lots of friends to help me, so everything is finished now."

"Well, I'm glad for you all."

"There *is* something that I can't make head or tail of. These were probably sent by mistake, but I just haven't had time to deal with them."

"Sure what is it, I'm sure I can handle it for you."

Larisa went out of the room and a few moments later, returned with a folder containing some letters and paperwork.

"Soon after he died, these letters started coming from an insurance company."

Tom held the file but the mention of insurance triggered an alarm inside him. *So maybe there is some sort of insurance scam he was involved in.* Tom thought to himself.

"Insurance?" Was all that Tom could ask."

"Yes, but I think it's some sort of mix-up, the names are wrong and the address is wrong. We're in Idaho Falls, but this beneficiary is in Twin Falls. So it's probably some sort of clerical error."

Tom recognized the name and address of the beneficiary. "I'll certainly look into this."

"That would be great if you could," Larisa said, "it would be one less thing to worry about."

"Say, I think it's time I left, I have quite a few errands to run."

"Well OK Tom, but do keep in touch, the boys would love to see you again."

"Yes, we have to spend some quality time together. I'll take these papers and let you know the outcome. I'll be in touch."

They hugged and said their goodbyes.

Beta-One saw the Major leave carrying a folder. It decided that it could return to this house at any time, but this

Major could have some useful information connecting the lab to the military. It decided to follow him from a safe distance.

Chapter 41

Having swapped vehicles overnight, Beta-One drove the Audi as it followed the Major from his hotel into town, where he parked by a coffee shop. The Major, in casual dress, entered the shop, ordered coffee, and sat at a table near the window. Beta-One considered entering the shop as well and taking a nearby seat; after all, it would not be recognized.

Just then a woman of medium build entered the shop. She was prettily dressed with her hair tied up in a bun. The Major looked up from his coffee and asked, "Mrs. Gonzales?"

"Yes. You must be Mr. Vance?"

"Yes. You can call me Tom."

"And you must call me Anita."

"Would you like a cup of coffee?" Tom asked.

"No thank you, maybe a black tea."

Beta-One was able to see them both sitting by the window of the coffee shop. With a near-perfect view of their faces, he was perfectly positioned to read their lips. So he decided to remain sitting in the car. With that simple introduction, it had already learned their names.

"So Mr. Vance, you are not another investigator from the Marines Corps?"

"No mam, it so happens that I'm a Major in the United States Marine Corps, but I am not an investigator, I am a friend of William's and I am close to his family."

"Oh, you are Will's friend?"

"Yes, we grew up together, we've been friends since childhood."

"And you know his family?"

"Oh, yes, I know them very well. I was his best man at his wedding."

"Are you married?"

"No, I am not, I've been much too busy with my career."

"And you know Will's wife?"

"Yes, I know Larisa and both of their lovely children. Furthermore, I think they are all very special. But please, Mrs. Gonzalez, why do I feel like I'm being cross-examined?"

"I am sorry. Mr. Vance, but you must understand that I have been asked many questions by a lot of people. I need to know that you are not just another investigator."

"You said I could call you Anita," Tom stated, trying to soften the conversation. "I only found out a few days ago that my friend had died, and I need to find out why. I owe that to him and his family. So please try to understand, that my only investigation is a personal one. Larisa has also been asked many questions, but she also is in the dark."

"I'm sorry, Mr. Vance, and as you said, I should call you Tom. So Tom, please understand things from my point of view. Since the accident, I have been hounded by investigators who have dissected and analyzed every word I've said. They have sifted through the wrecked building with a fine-toothed comb, trawled through every bit of digital data they could find, and yet they still ask questions."

"So what the heck happened?"

"I don't know. But something very bad has happened, and it's still happening."

"Listen, all I want is to know what happened to my friend. His wife Larisa deserves to know too."

"I wouldn't be surprised if someone was following me and watching us right now," Anita said nervously.

With that statement, Beta-One quickly scanned the parking lot and the overlooking windows of surrounding buildings. All the cars were empty and there was no evidence of anyone else observing this meeting. However, Beta-One understood that surveillance could involve remote and covert methods.

"So what was going on that was so sensitive?" Tom asked.

"I have no idea."

"Didn't you see what was going on in the labs?"

"I wasn't allowed in the labs, I was always in the office. I didn't have the key codes necessary to enter the labs."

"So what was your job there?"

"Administration mainly, I handled all the paperwork and managed the accounts. I was also the receptionist, but nobody ever came to visit that lab."

"Is it true that they kept animals there?"

"Yes, they had rats, some dogs, and a monkey, they even had some pigeons. What they did with those animals, I have no idea."

"So what were Wolf and Coney working on?"

"Nano Technology was pretty much all they said. Microscopic machines for medicine and the betterment of the human body is what they told me."

"Sounds like a corporate tag line, but with military funding that sounds like a cover-up. But what I want to know is how Bill died."

"It was in the evening after I had already gone home," Anita said. "It seems Bill went into the building when the fire was already burning to try and save Professor Wolf and Doctor Coney."

"But what started the fire?"

"That is the big question, nobody knows how it started. The fire department said it was arson, because someone had doused the lab with gasoline. That's why it went up so fast."

"So who could start the fire?"

"You and everyone else wants to know. That place was as tight as Fort Knox. For a while, I was under suspicion, but they finally confirmed that I had no access. That leaves three other people"

"Three others? You mean Bill, Wolf, and Coney?"

"Exactly."

"Hm. But Bill went into the building to rescue Wolf and Coney, yes?"

"You're getting there, so that leaves two suspects."

"Professor Hayden Wolf and Dr. John Coney." Tom looked puzzled. "Wait a minute. If the building was so secure, and they were the only suspects, why would one of them do such a dreadful act?"

"That's the big question the Pentagon is trying to answer. All I could tell them is that Hayden and John were having arguments."

"About what?"

"Well, I think most of the arguments started about money."

"Isn't that what everyone argues about?"

"Well, yes; but they had plenty of money, but John Coney kept asking where it was all going. I don't think Hayden ever gave John a convincing answer."

"You said you managed the books, did you see anything wrong with the figures?"

"I only did the bookkeeping. All the figures I entered were given to me by Professor Wolf. Everything I worked on added up, so what they argued about was above my head."

"What else did they argue about?"

"I can't say really. The arguments I could hear were about words I could not understand. I think they were arguing about what they wanted to do with nanotechnology. All I can say is that the arguments did become more heated over time."

"OK, so that was Hayden and John. Was Bill arguing with them as well?"

"No, Bill seemed caught in the middle. If anything, he was more a friend of Professor Hayden's. He worked with Dr. Coney a lot, but I don't think they had any issues between them. It was Hayden and John who had the issues."

"So you think it's true that Bill tried to save them from the fire?"

"Oh, yes. For all his bragging, Bill could not hurt a fly. He went in there to save them."

"Did anyone else see what happened?"

"There were other witnesses on the campus who saw Bill go in."

"Well, at least he tried to be a hero." Tom sat back, shrugging his shoulders.

"Don't get me wrong, Mr. Vance, but your friend Bill was not without his strangeness."

"Strangeness? What do you mean?"

"He used to go off for long periods."

"Really? Why? Where to?"

"He always said it was family business, but I found out that wasn't the case."

"What do you mean? What did you find out?"

"His wife would sometimes call and ask about him. She wouldn't do that if it was family business, would she?"

"Hm, I guess not."

"I would cover for him and say he was out of contact. Then I'd text him on the company cell phone, saying his wife was asking for him."

"Where do you think he went?"

"Oh, I know where he went."

"How do you know? Did he ever tell you?"

"He didn't have to. The company phone had location tracking switched on, so I know exactly where he went."

"Where?"

"Twin Falls."

"Are you sure?"

"I even looked up the address and found out who lived there."

Tom was beginning to see the connection, but he had to ask the question to confirm. "Who lives there?"

"Mrs. Beryl Banks."

So there's the connection. Tom thought.

"I think he was having an affair," Anita stated.

Will was certainly having something there. "What gave you that impression?"

"Oh, little things, like female items left behind in the car. The smell of perfumes. Notes and other personal belongings that I knew did not belong to Larisa."

"Yes, of course. Did you ever tell Larisa?"

"Of course not, I couldn't break her heart. Anyway, I think it's over and has been over for a long time. Will hasn't been away on those trips for a while."

"Did you tell anyone else? Like the investigators?"

"Definitely not, it's none of their business. They would only kick up a stink with Larisa, and there's no need for that now. Anyway, those investigators have enough to concern themselves with at the moment."

"Like who started the fire?"

"That's one thing, but that's only part of the puzzle. There's something else, something they're looking for."

"The missing nanotech?"

"You know something about it?" Anita asked.

"Larisa told me. They questioned her about it, and they went through Bill's things at home. As far as I know, nothing has turned up."

"I think they are very concerned about this. It was kept in special containers, which they used to inject into animals. Some were found destroyed in the wreckage, but they were able to determine that several are missing." Anita paused, looking around, then leaned forward and spoke quietly. "Whatever these things are, I think they were using them on people. The Marine Corps must think they are very important, because they ask many questions of everybody. If you ever meet them, I'm sure they'll ask you too."

Beta-One realized that *it* was one of the missing items. It has a memory of being injected into the body of Gary Fletcher. The existence of one or more of a similar being in Twin Falls was highly probable. Beta-One thought to itself, *Mr. Mandelson worked with me to help me become what I am, and it is likely that he also worked with someone in Twin Falls. I must continue to follow this Tom Vance, because he may lead me to others just like me.*

Chapter 42

Walking home from school could be described as a pleasure. Other than dictionary definitions, I don't really know what pleasure is, but I gained much from my walks. Each day I experienced different views, seeing plants grow to flower, watching the weather and seasons slowly change. I also got to know the habits of the local people and neighbors.

In the mornings I would see the people leaving their homes, some heading to their jobs and others driving children to school. Walking home I always saw the man at house number 835 tending his garden or fixing something on the house. He was old and probably retired, and seemed to keep busy by doing household jobs. I learned which homes had dogs or cats, I even became familiar with birds and squirrels and their territories. All these things enhanced my knowledge of the world and especially my local environment, provided insight into how the world changes over time and broadened my understanding of behavior patterns. I considered this to be my pleasure.

Knowing the rhythms and routines of your neighborhood makes it easy to spot things that don't belong. I first spotted the man on a Tuesday afternoon, but I didn't give it much consideration. He was simply a man sitting in his car at the end of my street, and appeared to be talking on his phone. He could have been someone visiting one of the nearby houses, or a salesman asking his office for customer information. The following day, I saw him again, but this time at the other end of my street. I recognized the car and the license plate. I could make out his silhouette behind the steering wheel, and again he seemed to be talking on his phone. I became curious as to why would he now be parked at the other end of the street? It's possible that he was a salesman, but there was no evidence of him canvassing the homes on my street.

On Thursday afternoon I saw his car again. This time he was outside school, parked among the parents waiting to pick up their children. I kept myself on alert and spotted him parked on a side street as I walked past. He must have used the street grid system to get ahead of me. This was now beyond coincidence, and it seemed clear that he was observing me as I walked home from school. I had to find out more about this person and why he was here. I couldn't tell Beryl, as I could not accurately predict her response. Perhaps she would call the police, or she would confront the man herself, which could be dangerous.

I needed to perform reconnaissance and if possible, gain access to his car to look for evidence of his origin and intentions. Maybe I could use Carol; I was sure she would be willing to help, but I would have to devise a scenario that would not endanger her.

Online searches would be useless, as I could not legitimately gain access to any databases.

I called her and asked her to come over.

"Hi Carol, it's me, Adara."

"Adara! It's so lovely to hear from you, I'm sorry about the other day".

"It's OK."

"I mean, I just wanted to say that I didn't mean to be so…"

"It's OK, I just need to talk to you."

"Oh? Do you want to talk? That's great!"

"Yes, can you come over?"

"You mean to your house?"

"Well of course, can you come over now?"

"Um, yeah, is something up?"

"Well, let's just say I need your help with something."

"Oh, sounds mysterious, can't wait to find out what!"

"I'll tell you all about it when you get here. How quick can you be?"

"Oh, quicker than you think! I'll see you there!" Carol hung up.

Five minutes later, she turned up a little breathless.

"Did you run here?" I asked.

"No, I think I'm just a little nervous, with you asking me over like that. Can't wait to find out what's up."

"Well, I wanted you to help me investigate something. There was a strange man in a car who seemed to be following me home from school."

"Oh jeez, that's scary! Where is it now, let's go find him."

"That's just it, he's gone now, but today was the third time I saw him."

"Three times! That is more than scary! What is this guy doing?"

"I first saw him on Tuesday afternoon parked on our street. I didn't think much of it then, but the next afternoon, he was parked at the other end of our street."

"You said three times, so you saw him again today?"

"Yes, he seemed to follow me home from school. First I saw him near my school, then a little later he was parked near our street. He didn't drive past me, so he must have used the street grid to get ahead of me. Why would he do that?"

"I think you should call the cops, or at least tell the school. This is creepy!"

"Yes, maybe I will, but I want to find out who this person is first. Let's go up to my room, we can talk better there."

Upstairs we talked about how we could find out more. Searching the internet. we found out we could get a report on the vehicle, but we would have to pay for it.

"Adara, do you think you could register with one of these to identify the car?"

"I don't have a credit card, so how would I pay for it?"

"I don't have one either, so I can't help you. These things must be for private investigators. Seems like we're stuck."

Carol's face brightened with an idea. "We could lay a trap!"

"What do you mean?" I asked.

"I could walk past and get a good look at the driver, maybe even take a picture on my phone," Carol said. "If he's following you, then he would probably ignore me, and not notice me photographing him."

"That could be dangerous, I can't let you do such a thing."

"Oh, I'd do anything for you! I wouldn't be scared if I were with you." Carol said and she wrapped her arm around my waist and leaned her head on my shoulder. Suddenly it felt just like the day I walked Carol and Larry home after the fight with Brad.

"I know, but all I need is a picture of the license plate. Then I can go to the school or the police to report him."

Carol's phone alerted her of a new text message. "It's my mom, she's asking where I am." She typed a reply, then looked up at me. "I'll have to go home now, my mom's saying it's getting late."

Chapter 43

Carol and I made the short walk to her house. Along the way I kept an extra special lookout for any suspicious vehicles. Carol seemed to enjoy the espionage and kept suggesting things we could do if we spotted him again.

When we got to her house, Larry was in his bedroom playing computer games. That meant we didn't have to put up with his usual over-excitement.

Carol's mother and father welcomed us to sit with them for a while in the living room where they were watching TV. Carol wasn't interested in the show, so we gathered some snacks and drinks from the kitchen and went upstairs to her room.

"It's OK, you can sit on the bed." Carol quietly closed the bedroom door behind her. She sat down on the bed next to me and we started sharing the bowl of potato chips.

"I heard you got into some trouble after that fight," Carol said. "I think that's unfair because it wasn't your fault."

"Well, it's not so much me being in trouble. Brad and his friends are the ones in trouble. I just had to go to counseling."

"Counselling? What the heck for?"

"Anger management."

Carol nearly choked on the chips she was eating. "Anger management? You are the most non-angry person ever, I've never seen you angry, not even that day with Brad. You were just super cool."

"Well, I think it's because I clobbered a bunch of boys. Principal Gallagher seems to think I'm dangerous and he wanted Mrs. Schultz the counselor to assess me."

"Yeah, well look out boys, is all I can say. I think it's about time girls got dangerous."

"Well, the biggest consequence is that I have to work in the music show we're putting on."

"Oh, isn't Brad playing in the band?"

"Yes, that's right, he's playing guitar and singing a song."

"And you don't mind?"

"Of course not, why should I? I don't think we're going to have another fight."

"I was thinking you two would do something else."

"What do you mean?"

"It's OK, never mind." Carol turned away and lowered her head. After a moment, she asked, "So I saw you with Juan the other morning, are you going with him?"

"Going with him? I don't understand."

"You know, going out with him."

"Oh, no, I'm not going out with anyone."

With that Carol turned back with a grin.

"He was just telling me about all the excitement on social media about the fight."

"Yea, I did see it. You have a laptop, so aren't you on social media?"

"No, I don't see the need to share secrets on social media."

Carol's look suggested we would talk about it again later. She went on to talk about Juan.

"Do you know that guy is quite an entertainer, he and his friends are what you call cosplayers. They dress up and sing or dance to songs they like."

"Oh?"

"Yeah, maybe you can use them in the show. I think they're pretty good. He has a bunch of guys and girls who dress up and sing with him. Oh and I think some of the girls are HOT when they dress up."

"So, do you like girls dressed up?"

Carol just giggled. I began to think I should ask Juan to be in the show.

"Anyway," Carol interjected, "do you want to have a sleepover?"

"A sleepover what? Music shows?"

"No, silly." She leaned forward, playing with my arm. "A sleepover. You stay the night here with me, and we can talk, play games, whatever you want to do."

"Oh, I see, you mean that I 'sleepover here' at your house. I never did a sleepover, but I don't think I can, because it's Saturday tomorrow and I have to work an early shift at the grocery store."

"Oh, I'm disappointed," Carol said and made a sad expression.

"I would like to have a sleepover with you, but it'll have to be another day. And I do have to warn you, I don't sleep very much."

Carol's face lit up. "I can't wait!" She leaned forward to whisper in my ear. "If you're with me, I don't think I will sleep much either!"

We relaxed on the bed, talking. Carol took a few selfies and posted them with messages on her social sites. I didn't use any social media, so this was an interesting experience for me.

"I know you have a laptop, you used it to search for car license plates. You can use that for social media, too." Carol said.

"Well, yes… my mother bought me that laptop, and I use it for learning."

"Well, that's great! I can set you up on Facebook and I can be your first like?"

"OK, let's do it."

"Let's do it indeed!" She exclaimed as she snuggled up beside me with her laptop. She placed it on my lap, leaned close to me, and we started setting up my Facebook page. She logged out of her page, then asked, "Do you want a username?"

I told her yes and she typed that in.

She then asked me to set a password.

She pretended to look away, but I typed so fast, and with such random characters, there is no way she could have followed what I typed, let alone have memorized it. After setting gender and birthday and using google mail to accept my profile, I had my Facebook profile.

"You need a profile picture," she said to me.

Carol withdrew from my lap, raised her laptop above her and used it to take a photo of my face.

"That's no good, you need to smile! This will be your profile picture."

After a few attempts, Carol was happy with a picture.

"Now you have to like me, and while I'm doing that you can put your arm around me."

"Is that part of the Facebook protocol?" I asked.

"It's part of anything you like, but now that you've officially 'liked' me, I think you should put your arm around me." As she said this she reached for my arm and placed it on her waist. She again raised the laptop above her head, showing me the Facebook screen. "You see, we are now friends on Facebook."

Carol slowly closed the laptop and placed it on the floor next to her bed. Her entire body was close to mine, our feet, our thighs, our hips all side by side. She slowly turned and lifted herself to face me. "Do you like dressing up? I have lots of things you can try and you're about my size. We can dress each other up and play around with clothes."

Carol jumped off the bed and put on some light music. She flung open her wardrobe and several drawers, selecting various items of clothing. "I have some nice things, but I usually dress simply," she said, "after all, who can I dress up for? I don't have any friends at school that I can dress up for."

"Can I be your friend?" I asked. "I don't have any friends at school either."

Holding a colorful scarf, Carol turned and smiled at me, "Of coursc, I would love to be your friend." She clasped the scarf in her hands, looking down. "You had all the friends at school, even Brad was your friend. I never had any friends because I was always Larry's babysitter."

I detected a painful human emotion in Carol. I stood up and approached her. She faced the wardrobe, and I touched her gently on the shoulder. "Carol, I think you are an incredibly special person. You show it because you look after your brother every day. If people don't want to be your friend, it is probably because they are afraid to use your valuable time."

Carol stifled back a tear.

"Anyway, you said you would be meeting Jake for lunch."

"Yes." She said still staring at the wardrobe.

"I don't know how to dress up," I said, "but I think you know how. Please show me what you are going to wear."

"Jake!" Carol turned to face me, "I forgot! What should I wear?" She started flicking through the clothes hangers in her wardrobe.

We had a little private fashion show. She dressed herself up and then she dressed me up. Each time she explained why she matched the colors and why she liked the styles. I had never given much attention to fashion; I always wore what was practical and simple. Carol could see that I was fascinated by all her clothes and was thrilled to be 'dressing me up'. She helped me undress so I could try on her blouses and dresses. She asked me to undress her so she could change into some matching clothes. She even brushed my hair so it would match the different styles we tried. As we posed in front of her mirror she would caress my waist, arms, shoulders, and neck while she highlighted the different aspects of each garment.

After a while, the room was carpeted with clothes scattered everywhere. The wardrobe was wide open and empty, drawers were open with garments hanging out. The pace slowed, and Carol turned breathlessly to face me. Holding me gently she said, "You are so pretty, I wish I was as pretty as you."

I have never considered a person's 'prettiness', but I thanked her for the compliment.

Carol then said, "I have never kissed anyone."

I could not respond to this statement. My mother has kissed me on my forehead and my cheek, but I think Carol's kiss is referring to something more sexual.

"I mean, I don't know how to do it," Carol emphasized.

I still could not answer.

"I think you've kissed lots of boys, especially Brad. Can you teach me how to kiss?"

Again, I could not answer this question, as I wasn't sure a kissing exercise was appropriate. I was beginning to understand where this was leading.

"Wait," I said. "Are you saying I kissed lots of boys? Are you saying I kissed Brad?"

"You don't remember?"

"No, I don't. Please tell me."

"You were always the hottest girl in school, and Brad was the hottest stud. You both hit it off so strong you were the King and Queen of Twin Falls!"

This was a lot of information for me to understand.

Carol could recognize my confusion. "You look like you don't remember."

"That's it," I said, "I don't remember."

Carol retrieved a scented candle from her cupboard. "I always wanted to use this," she said. She found some matches and lit the candle, placing it on her bedside table. "Doesn't that smell nice?" she asked.

I detected the smell of carbon, paraffin, and a sweet herb-like substance.

"It's Rosemary and Honey," Carol stated.

I was more interested in what Carol just told me than the candle, so I asked, "Are you saying Brad was my boyfriend?"

"Yes, and we all looked up to you both." Carol looked me in the eyes for a few moments before continuing. "Brad was always a mean bully to everyone, but you seemed to have some magic over him, which calmed him down. You even taught him how to play the guitar."

"I did?"

"That's why I thought you could help me to meet Jake."

"Oh, yes, you like him, don't you, Carol."

"I think he is someone I can fall in love with." She admitted.

"Well, it is not for me to introduce you. You saw how he acted when you both met a few days ago on the playing field."

"Yes, why? He seemed a bit nervous."

"That's just it, he was nervous because he wanted to make a good impression with you. He didn't know what to say or how to say it."

"What do you mean?"

I put my hand on Carol's shoulder, "I mean, you have to ask him out."

"What? Me? You think so?"

"Yes, he is curious about you and I'm 99% sure he will say yes if you ask him."

"Where can we go on a date?"

"I can't even remember that Brad was my boyfriend, and you're asking me where to go on a date?"

Carol pulled back and thought for a moment. She then started giggling. "You see? You do have magic! You just made the funniest joke ever, and you made me laugh." She flung her arms around my neck, hugging me silently. "I'm just so glad you're here with me."

"It's ok, I like being with you, I'm learning a lot," I admitted.

With that Carol held me and we continued to lay there embracing each other enjoying the silence together.

After a while, she asked, "Will we have a sleepover?"

"I do want to have a sleepover, and I want to do it soon because I think there's a lot more you can teach me. But like you said, I don't think either of us will sleep much."

Another squeeze of her arms and a little giggle came from her. Then she pulled away and looked at me with a wry smile and a wink, "I think you just told me another joke!"

"I did?"

"That's one of the weird things about you, you never laugh, and you're always so serious. If there's one thing that I will teach you is how to laugh." She said as she wriggled her nose against mine. "I know you can do it because tonight, you told me two jokes."

It is true, I never laugh, but for the simple reason, that I don't have a sense of humor. I sort of understand irony, and that so-called joke about neither of us sleeping was a form of irony. So maybe with Carol's guidance, there is some hope that I could one day laugh. That is certainly something to think about.

When I got home, I greeted Mother as usual but went straight to bed. That night I had a great deal of information to contemplate and process.

First of all, my intention to have a sleepover with Carol was genuine. Our encounter was something I want to explore further as I needed to understand human emotions much more deeply. Carol could help me to understand female sexuality, but from the things she said, she could also help me to look and dress better. There is much more I can learn with Carol.

That night I wondered what it would be like to copulate with a male.

Chapter 44

"Hello, is that Mrs. Banks?"

"Yes, I'm Mrs. Banks, who is this please?"

"My name is Major Thomas Vance of the United States Marine Corps., and I was a personal friend of William's."

"Oh, you are a friend of Bill's? How has he been? I haven't seen him for a long time, I did tell him not to come back. Has he sent you to tell me he's sorry?"

Pause.

"Hello?"

"I'm sorry, Mrs. Banks, I have some personal items of William's which I need to give to you. Have you not been informed?"

"Wha, what? Excuse me? Informed of what?"

"Um, I'm very sorry, Mrs. Banks, like I said there seems to be some confusion here, I didn't realize you haven't been informed. I have some very bad news to give to you."

Prolonged silence.

"I have to inform you that William has passed away."

Click, followed by the steady telephone dial tone.

'*Well, that didn't go too good.*' Tom said to himself.

Although Tom always visited the relatives of his fallen comrades, he was never in a situation where he had to inform anyone of their death. Those duties were the responsibility of other officers trained in such delicate matters. When Tom made his visit, the family had already been informed, and appreciated his personal care.

With Mrs. Banks hung up like that, Tom gleaned some important information. First, Mrs. Banks had no idea that William was dead; but then, why would she be informed? There was no clear connection between William's job at INL and Mrs. Banks. Second, the fact that she hung up so quickly indicated a shock, and strongly suggested a personal relationship. Anita Gonzalez was correct in thinking there was an affair going on.

Tom had one more nagging question in his mind. *Why is she asking me if he wants to apologize, and apologize for what?*

Tom was treading into an unknown situation. He decided to follow a simple tactic and provide as little information as possible to Mrs. Banks. Tom would ask leading questions and then follow where her answers led.

Things were now much more difficult.

When Tom called back, he was greeted with dismay and confusion, but at least Beryl had already come to some form of acceptance.

"Can you tell me how he died? Was he a hero?" Beryl asked. "Was it a big battle?"

"Excuse me? A battle?"

"Yes, being in special forces and everything."

'*Special Forces? There's something funny going on here.*' "Um, yes, you could say he was a hero, because he died trying to save two men."

A short silence with the sound of muffled sniffles.

"I was so hard on him, I forced him away, and now he's gone."

"Mrs. Banks, I would like to meet with you. I have some personal items to give to you."

"Yes, of course, but I can't think straight right now. Can you make arrangements with my friend Cindy McCall?"

"Yes, of course I can, I'll gladly talk to her."

"Is there a number she can call you on?"

"Yes, it's (986) 555-2495."

"Hello, can I speak with Tom Vance?"

"Yes, this is Tom."

"Hello, my name is Cindy McCall. My friend Beryl Banks asked me to call you."

"Yes, I've been expecting your call."

"Well, it seems that her husband has died, and you have some things to give to her."

"Husband? Yes, William Banks, yes, I have some personal items and a life insurance policy."

Well, Tom thought, *Anita's suspicion of an affair was certainly an understatement. The suspected affair seems to have become bigamy. This confirms Bill used the name William Banks when he was in Twin Falls. I wonder what other revelations I will discover when I meet Mrs. Banks! At least I now know why he asked me to forward the letters. This isn't an insurance scam, it is a ruse to cover his absence while he was with Larisa.*

Tom wore a full-dress uniform, as would an officer reporting a military death, but would be doing this simply as a friend. That way he could avoid any awkward questions about pensions.

Cindy opened the door slowly to reveal a man standing straight and tall on the front porch. "Hello, you must be Cindy McCall. I'm Major Thomas Vance, and I'm very pleased to meet you."

"Ah, Major Vance, very pleased to meet you."

They both extended hands for a polite handshake.

"May I come in?"

"Well, actually, Beryl would like to talk with you on the porch. It's a nice day and she would feel much more comfortable out here."

"Oh, yes, of course ma'am, I understand fully."

Cindy gestured towards the seats on the porch. "Please take a seat here and Beryl will be right out. Can I get you something while you are here? Cookies? Milk?"

Tom was momentarily taken aback by this offer. He thought a large bourbon would be much more welcome but very inappropriate to ask for.

"Oh, no, thank you, I'm fine." He smiled back. "I'll just wait here for Mrs. Banks."

"Major Thomas Vance, I understand?"

"Oh, yes, Major, United States Marine Corps, here's my ID card." Tom offered his identification card to Cindy.

She nodded as she gently took the card. "I'll be right back." She disappeared inside, closing the door behind her.

The porch was wide and spacious with a love seat, some cushioned chairs, a bistro table, and various wind chimes; a typical countryside porch. Tom sat down on one of the chairs and waited.

Beryl came out followed by Cindy who was carrying a tray of glasses and a jug of lemonade. Tom stood, nodding his head, and extended his hand towards Beryl Banks.

"How do you do Mrs. Banks, I'm Major Thomas Vance United States Marine Corps and a very old friend of William's. First of all, I'd like to say again how very sorry I am about the loss of your husband."

"Thank you, it was a bit of a shock, but given his line of work I often expected some bad news."

"Please, would you like some lemonade?" Cindy offered.

"Well, just a little for me. Thank you."

Mrs. Banks sat on the love seat, facing the street.

Cindy poured some lemonade into two glasses and placed a plate of cookies onto the bistro table before she politely retreated into the house.

"Ah, so were you on overseas missions with Bill?"

"Well, not exactly; my career has been in the Marine Corps. We were just good friends since we were kids."

"Bill never told me about his missions. He would be gone for a long time, but he would always send me letters." Mrs. Banks explained.

'Hm. The letters! So these so-called missions were definitely Will's way of explaining his absence – how interesting.'

"Yes, I know he sent you lots of letters, that's probably because he loved you."

"Yes, I know he did. After the accident, I was very mean to him."

"Oh? What accident?"

"Our daughter, Adara. They went white water rafting together a long time ago. She fell out of the raft and nearly drowned."

"I'm sorry to hear that. Is she ok?"

"She is now, she'll finish high school this year."

"That's good."

"But she was in a coma for a long time, and the doctors thought she would never fully recover. That's when I sent Bill away. I told him it was all his fault, and I told him never to come back."

"Well, I'm sure he would have wanted to make things right."

"Adara got better, and the doctors said it was a miracle. But I still blamed Bill and I ignored all his letters. I never did see him…"

At this point, Mrs. Banks covered her face with her handkerchief and started to weep. Cindy came out and sat next to Mrs. Banks on the love seat and tried to comfort her.

I got home from school right then. Just past the house, I noticed the suspicious car parked by the side of the road. I stayed on my guard. As I walked up to the porch, I suspected that the strange man was the driver of the car. Everyone stood up and Mother introduced me to the visitor.

"Mother, are you OK?" I asked.

"Everything's fine dear, I'm just reminiscing, you know how I am."

With a gentle sniffle and a dab of the handkerchief at her eyes, she smiled slightly and began introductions.

"Major Vance, this is my daughter Adara. Adara, this is Major Thomas Vance."

Tom stood extending his hand politely. "Hello, Adara. I'm very sorry for the loss of your father."

"Hello Major, pleased to meet you." I kept my distance but accepted his hand in a short and formal handshake.

Mother told me about the death of my father the day before. She also told me that someone would come and visit us, so this meeting was not a surprise to me. I had stayed home from school, but only because Mother told me to. I have no emotional connection to Adara's father and because Adara's father is estranged, I don't think Adara would have taken an extended leave from school.

"Is that your car?" I asked.

"Yes, it is." The Major replied.

"Major Vance used to know your father," Beryl announced.

"Yes, we were friends since we were kids, I just wanted to offer my condolences."

I stood there staring at the Major. Although I did not get accurate identification of the person in the car, he has admitted to being that person. I think I stared too intently because my mother eventually said;

"Adara, please go inside to your room, we have much to talk about here."

"OK," I said, "Let me know if you need anything."

I was very suspicious of this man and wanted to keep track of their conversation. I have exceptional hearing, so I positioned myself in the living room where I could listen easily.

"A lovely girl, I can see the likeness."

"Thank you, Mr. Vance."

"Please, call me Tom, I don't like to hang on formalities."

"OK, Tom."

"Anyway, I would like to offer my condolences, I know this must be hard for you. It's hard for me too, because we knew each other since we were kids, and I was surprised to hear about his passing.

"What was he like as a boy?"

"Funny, but we always played soldiers together. We always wanted to rid the world of bad guys."

"Yes, that sounds like Bill, he always did have high ideals." Mother cleared a few sniffles, while Mr. Vance sipped some lemonade. She continued, "So what happened? How did he die?"

"Well, I have very few details, all I was told is that he died trying to rescue two men."

"Where did this happen?"

"I'm not at liberty to say."

"But I need to know," Mother was beginning to demand. "I have to know what happened and where."

"Mrs. Banks, please understand, I know very little myself about how. Also please remember that I'm as surprised and hurt as you are, William was my friend."

As Mother began to cry again, Cindy put her arm around her to comfort her. "It's OK, Beryl."

This isn't going well, Tom thought, *I have to get out of here.*

"One thing I can provide you with is this." Tom presented the large envelope to Mother.

"What's this?"

"It's a life insurance policy. I believe it's quite generous, and it's made out to you."

Mother took the envelope slowly and clutched it to her heart. Tears ran down her cheeks and Cindy drew her closer until Mother's head was on Cindy's shoulder.

"This is all I have left." Mother wept.

"I'm so sorry." Mr. Vance murmured. "I think I should go now."

"Is this all I get?" Mother whimpered, "Why doesn't the government contact me?"

"It's OK," Cindy reassured.

"I really should go now." Mr. Vance stood to leave. "I'm afraid that's all I have."

Bowing out politely, Major Vance made his way from the porch and retreated down the garden path towards the street.

I had many questions for him, one in particular. I didn't want to upset Mother any further, so I dashed past them to Mr. Vance as he was leaving through the garden gate.

"Why were you snooping around in your car?"

"Excuse me?"

"The last few days you were snooping around in your car. I even thought you were following me."

"I, um, was just making sure I had the right location, I wasn't sure I had the right address."

He looked pensive and backed away towards his car. "I have to go, I'm so sorry."

After he drove off, I went back to the porch. Cindy asked me, "What did you say to him?"

"Nothing, really."

Mother held my hand for a moment before I turned and went to my room. As I went I heard Cindy say to Mother, "I think Adara is upset too."

"That's the first time I've seen her react with any emotion." Mother replied.

I wasn't reacting emotionally, I thought, *I was reacting with curiosity. They must have interpreted my actions as emotion.*

Chapter 45

"Hello, Mr. Play how are you today?"

"Mr. Play? Now where'd you get that from?"

"I got it from you, remember? That's what you told me to call you. I have a thing about names."

"Girl, you sure are a funny one. I'm good as always, how 'bout your fine self?"

"Oh, I'm well. I've got something to ask you. You know we are preparing for the senior show at school, right? It's going to be a variety show with different songs and performances. Would you and some of your friends like to be in our show?"

"Wow, you do get straight to the point."

"Well, no point in wasting time. I've been looking into your subculture and I've got an idea that you and your friends could fit nicely into the show. Our theme this year is diamonds. Is there a song that you could perform that would fit into it? We have a band that can play a song for you to sing to, or if you prefer I can play a soundtrack that you can mime to."

"Huh? Wada you mean you can play? I don't get it."

"I'm working the control desk, I control the stage and any audio playout."

"OK, sounds like you got it under control." He said with a smirk. "But what about teachers?" He followed with a grimace.

"Let me handle that. The question is, what song can you do for the show?"

"Break me up babe, we got dozens, how bad can we get?"

I could not accurately parse this into anything understandable so I had to ask for clarification.

"Listen, babe, we got lots of possible songs."

"OK."

"And I need to know exactly what we can do, what style music, what we can say, how we can dress."

"Well, if you can give me a shortlist of songs, I can get Mrs. Fields to say OK to them. The rest is up to the usual school rules – no rude words, no clothes infractions – unless you want to wear orange jumpsuits."

"I gotcha, I get the picture. And I think I got some real dreams we can deliver! So what's the theme for this year's show?"

"Diamonds, like I already said."

"Well dat's a surprise sparkle! So wot songs you got in the lineup so far?"

"Well, yes, diamonds do sparkle. The theme songs we have so far are "Diamonds on the Soles of His Shoes," "Shine On You Crazy Diamond," and David Bowie's "Changes."

"Since when is changes about diamonds?"

"Oh, it isn't, but Jacob is singing that."

"Of course, you taught him to sing, didn't ya?"

"Yes, isn't it amazing how news travels?"

"Yea, ain't it tho? Anyhow, I may have a few songs but if I do them, I want my cosplayers with me, OK?"

"I'm sure it will be fine."

"And we'll need costumes and makeup and stuff."

"Sure, I assume it will have to conform to school regulations."

"Yeah, no doubt."

"And any song ideas?"

Like I say, I got a few but I'm thinkin' of one in particular, in fact, the title is 'Diamonds'."

"Who's that by?"

"I keep forgettin' that you're a square, it's by Rihanna, you should check it out."

"I will do just that."

"But I will need some help with the costumes, it ain't cheap to put clothes together on such short notice."

"I'll see what I can do."

Chapter 46

I asked Mrs. Sanchez about Juan Camillo being in the show. She thought it was a good idea, but said to ask the director. At the next rehearsal, I asked Mrs. Fields.

"Maybe we can find a slot for them in the show but first I need them to audition."

Nothing is ever easy, and I should have anticipated this. I'm beginning to understand what it feels like to be a manager or music agent who spends all their time making arrangements just for one performance. Except I'm not getting a percentage of the profit, because there is no profit, at least not in the material sense.

Organizing all of Juan's friends to be at the same rehearsal was complicated. Juan, Suzie, Zoe, Sharon, and Donnie all had their separate agendas and were very difficult to pin down together. Juan commented, "Yeah, sometimes it's like herding cats."

Juan and I eventually managed to gather everyone during a lunchtime rehearsal.

Brad was there that afternoon and when I walked in with Juan followed by his 'gang', Brad seemed to pay a lot of attention to us. Nothing was said, but he kept watching us, especially Juan, looking very curious as to why he was there with me.

Mrs. Fields asked them to line up on stage and sing their song. They stood in a line looking lost and feeble.

At the piano, Mrs. Fields asked, "What song are you singing?"

"Shine like a Diamond. You know, Rihanna."

"OK, I know it. Now from the top." Mrs. Fields started playing the chords.

Juan started singing quietly but with a nice voice, while his 'gang' sheepishly wiggled to the rhythm on either side of him.

"Wait." She stopped playing. "You need to sing a bit louder. Will you four also be singing any harmonies?"

"Yeah miss, when we get a chance."

"OK, from the top again."

They still looked pretty useless on stage, like they didn't know what to do, and I began to wonder what all this so-called cosplay was all about.

"Wait." She stopped playing again. "We're lacking something here, you don't seem very comfortable there. Do you need microphones?"

"Where's your flash dance now, Juan?" Brad sniggered from behind them.

Suzie, Zoe, Sharon, and Donnie looked embarrassed and seemed ready to walk out.

"Miss, we've never done anything on stage before." Juan said. "We do flashmob."

"I need a performance Juan, not a mob."

I could see Brad smirking at the back, enjoying their embarrassment.

"Wait, Miss, give us a sec."

Juan turned to his girls, whispering and pointing in different directions. Reading their lips I could detect some foul language being whispered back to him, and they soon walked off stage. Juan then whispered to Donnie and pointed to the floor. I could see the doubt on Donnie's face, but he was nodding.

Juan then moved to the wing of the stage, turned, and said, "Right, miss – from the top!"

She looked doubtful but played.

Donnie struck a pose; the lyrics encouraged the listener to shine like a diamond. Juan ran in from the wing singing, about how he was finding the light and choosing to be happy.

The surprise came a moment later when both Suzic and Zoe came strutting down the central aisle of the auditorium looking like ferocious catwalk models. As they reached the front they turned, and swinging their arms up they announced, "Shine Bright!" perfectly timed to the song.

"Wait!"

"What now, Miss?"

Mrs. Fields left the piano and walked towards them.

"OK, I've seen enough. Now THAT is a performance I need."

Juan and his friends beamed widely.

"It's going to need some work, but you've shown me that you can do something amazing. My first question is rehearsals, you need to be here whenever I ask to work on your routine. Can I count on you?"

Collectively, "Oh yes Miss!"

"Second, what are you going to do for costumes?"

"Dunno, Miss."

"Well, we need to work that out and soon. I will need at least some samples of what you'll be wearing, and any sketches if you need to make something. AND it all has to comply with school regulations."

"Yes Miss, ok Miss, we'll figure something out, Miss."

"How about by the end of next week?"

"Of course, Miss," Juan said.

I could see Suzie and Zoe mouth the WTF words towards Juan but he just shrugged.

"We'll figure somethin' out, Miss," Juan confirmed.

"OK kids, I have lots to do, so will I see you at rehearsal after school tomorrow?"

"Oh yes Miss!" they all said.

"Very good. Now, Adara, I need you to run through the lighting for the choir section, can we do that now?"

"Yes, Miss."

Chapter 47

The day of the performance arrived. "This is it! Tonight's the night!" was on everyone's lips, preventing any sense of calm and even adding to our nervousness.

Brad busied himself with the hard labor of moving, shifting, stacking, and sweating to keep his mind off his nerves.

Larry was lost in all the commotion. Ms. Sanchez kept a close eye on him and gave him simple but important jobs. When he became nervous, she asked him to play some soothing piano music to help calm the rest of us.

Mr. Bragg checked all the cabling and made sure any wires on the floor were either concealed or taped over as a safety precaution.

"Hope you're all connected up, Adara," he called out.

"I'm all set and ready, Mr. Bragg."

I had already completed my checks, except for the microphones. They had to be tested one at a time, and I needed someone to speak into each one. In all the bustle, Brad saw that I needed help and waved at me from the stage before going from mic to mic. Keeping his eyes on me, he chanted "Testing, one, two, one, two" in a routine way. When we finished, he bowed and smiled. I'm not sure if he was pretending to be a performer or if there was a subtle meaning behind his gesture.

With setup complete, everyone moved backstage to rest and prepare.

Many students were busy changing into their costumes. Brad was already in character with his rock star style scruffy jeans and a Pink Floyd 'Wish You Were Here' tee shirt.

The senior choir was humming and tuning their voices. Juan and his friends were late but arriving one by one. Their performance wasn't until later, but Mrs. Fields was agitated that they were not on time.

"Hey stranger, how you doing?" It was Sally Stone. She wore a light coat over her cheerleader outfit.

I turned around. "Hello Sally, what are you doing backstage?"

"Oh nothing, you'll see later on, I can't tell you now."

"OK everyone," Mrs. Fields announced, "get to your places and get ready."

"I got to go!" Said Sally.

"But what's the surprise?" I asked.

"You'll see soon enough." And off she ran.

Ticket collectors were busy at the front entrance as parents and students lined up to enter. The school had a captive audience in the form of families and friends who wanted to see their children performing on stage. The PTA made good use of this opportunity to raise some revenue with ticket sales. As the crowds gathered into the hall with parents finding seats, Gabby Jones said, "It's a bit boring out there; the crowds are turning up but they don't look too excited." Her cynical remarks didn't help to rouse the performers backstage.

I went back to my mixing desk, and Mrs. Fields signaled to me to start some music. We had prerecorded background music to play quietly and ease the general mood as volunteer students ushered in the families.

The mixing desk was an island behind the first fifteen rows, full of families with their younger children. The rows behind me held mostly school kids including Isabel, Brad's sister. I knew she wanted to do something to embarrass me and wondered if this would be her moment for revenge. She said that she wanted to do a '*Carrie*' on me. Exactly what that meant I'm not sure, but I do understand she wants to humiliate me publicly.

Maybe Sally was somehow involved in this so-called '*Carrie*' humiliation. Why else would she be here? Maybe she took offense to my beating her in the track race?

It was easy for me to listen to the voices and movements behind me, so I didn't have to keep turning my head to look. Isabel was sitting with her friends, one row behind me and six seats to my left. To strike me in any way, she would have to leave her seat and move past several people to get close enough. I would easily detect her approach.

The conversation I was able to hear from her focused on how boring the show was and how she only wanted to see her brother and his band.

Principal Gallagher came on stage to polite applause. He thanked everyone for coming and praised the PTA for their good work. He then welcomed Mr. Scott, our PE teacher, to the stage.

This was not on my script!

Mr. Scott talked about the senior class sporting achievements during the year, and how he looked forward to the promise of next year's class.

Mr. Gallagher made an exaggerated look at his wristwatch.

"Oh dear," Mr. Scott laughed, "As usual, I'm talking too much, and forgetting about the surprise I brought with me."

Oohs and aahs came from the audience.

"Allow me to introduce to you for the very first time on stage! Our very own Roger Straus High school marching band!"

This was definitely not on my script!

The curtains opened, and there stood the marching band in full dress uniform. Cheerleaders were assembled on either side of the band, complete with batons. I could see Sally Stone with a huge beaming grin aimed directly at me, she even winked.

The drums began a heavy beat. The cheerleaders marched in place, stamping their feet in time to the drums.

Two boys and two girls came on stage from the wings. They each held a large megaphone and used them for singing.

"Here and now I'm in the fire, in above my head."

At least I didn't have to worry about sound levels, this was completely out of my control.

"But it's here in the ashes I'm finding treasure."

"He's making diamonds out of dust."

"He's making diamonds out of us."

I recognized the song by the Canadian singer Hawk Nelson, and sat back while the marching band performed. When they finished, the audience stood up and not only applauded but made many vocal noises as well. I know this to be a standing ovation. Even Isabel and her friends behind me joined in.

Guided by cheerleaders, the Straus High School band exited the auditorium by beating their drums, splitting into two columns, and marching off to the left and right sides of the stage. They descended the stairs and marched along the aisles through the audience, towards the back door.

All the attendees stamped their feet as the band marched out to hearty applause.

When the noise subsided, Mrs. Fields took the stage and thanked Mr. Scott for his impromptu addition to the show. "Wow! What a rousing start to our show!" she exclaimed. "We have a lot to more to come, and I think you'll love all the rest just as much." Mrs. Fields then nodded towards me as if to say, *we are back to the normal script.*

She then introduced the school choir to perform their songs.

Yes, I was now back on script.

Next was a comedy break where actors from the drama class performed some sketches.

At this point I heard Isabel tell her friends that she was bored and was going outside for some fresh air. She pushed past everyone towards the left aisle and went out back door. One by one, her friends slowly followed her, leaving empty seats behind.

I wondered what they were doing outside, but I couldn't leave the mixing desk to investigate.

Mrs. Fields led Jacob onto the stage to sing his song. He looked shy and lost and shielded his eyes from the stage lights. He looked for me in the glare and I hoped he saw my double thumbs-up.

Mrs. Fields played piano, and Jacob began to sing his David Bowie song, "Changes." The saxophonist in Brad's band accompanied him.

He sang beautifully, and as he finished, the saxophone quietly ended the song.

The applause was polite; I don't think the audience appreciated the importance of what they'd seen. A shy boy unable to speak properly had just sung a song to a room full of people and sung it perfectly.

I applauded as loud as I could. I even stood at my desk and shouted, "Yay Jacob!"

He bowed and moved off into the wings.

The silence that followed seemed too long. I could see Mrs. Fields anxiously looking around. The next act was Juan and his crew, but he was nowhere to be seen. The stage was empty.

At the back of the stage where silver stars hung on the draped curtains, a bright laser light began flashing, then circling around in a mesmerizing fashion.

Once again, this is not on my script.

I heard soft footsteps behind me in the right aisle, and recognized Suzie sneaking up. She was shining a laser pointer to attract the audience's attention.

She was in full costume and whispered in my ear, "Shine a spotlight on the drum kit."

"Why?"

"Just do it." She insisted.

Then Zoe was level with us in the left aisle. A few steps behind Suzie and Zoe were Sharon and Donnie.

No one was sitting at the drum kit, but I did what Suzie asked, switching a light onto it.

Juan then emerged from behind the drum kit with arms outstretched, and sang,

"Shine bright like a diamond."

He must have been hiding there for a long time!

His chorus line of Suzie, Zoe, Sharon, and Donnie echoed the phrase as they danced towards the stage.

"Shine bright like a diamond."

Using their head-mounted microphones, they danced and sang their way towards each other in full vocal harmony of the Rihanna song.

"I choose to be happy. You and I, We're like diamonds in the sky."

Thankfully, I was now back on script.

The audience loved their theatricals. Even Mrs. Fields clasped her hands in delight. They performed like professionals.

As Juan and his cosplayers left the stage, the band's keyboard player Brian walked on. He looked around as if searching for something, spied his keyboard and mimed an exaggerated 'Ah-ha!' He pointed to it gleefully, sauntered towards it and sat down on the piano stool.

Isabel and her friends returned to their seats behind me. I smelled as I heard her whisper to her friends, "Wait for it!"

I felt threatened from behind, and wondered if they had a plan to embarrass me. I had to concentrate on the light and sound timings but kept my ears tuned to a possible attack.

Brian pretended to be a concert pianist, cracking his knuckles, and straightening his imaginary suit tails and cufflinks.

The audience chuckled and giggled.

Brian played a few jazzy notes I didn't recognize, but he could have been improvising. He then settled in to play the introduction to "Shine on You Crazy Diamond."

This was a long and haunting set of notes like a triumphant trumpet announcement but in solemn slow motion.

The rest of the band wandered on stage. They also looked around as if they were lost, finding their instruments, picking them up as if they were alien tools, and slowly coming to their places on stage.

I followed my script for lighting and sound.

The band looked lost and childish, as if they didn't know how to play.

The audience seemed confused.

Brad's guitar eventually joined the keyboard.

I heard Isabel exclaim loudly from behind, "That's my bro!"

With the crescendo of guitar notes, Brad looked in my direction. I knew he couldn't see me as the spotlights were in his eyes, but he looked as he started to sing.

"Remember when you were young?"

"You shone like the sun. Shine on you crazy diamond!"

The sad song was played proudly, and the audience was amazed by the virtuoso performance.

This was the final song, with parts sung by the school choir.

The song ended to rousing applause from the audience. After all the thank you speeches, the audience filtered out of the auditorium back to their waiting cars.

Clean-up began. Performers gathered their instruments, actors changed back to street clothes and cleaned makeup from their faces. I switched off the mixing desk and was on stage packing microphones away. Brad was in the back corner of the stage putting his guitar into its case along with spare strings and plectrums, his head hanging head in quiet concentration.

I noticed that he shied away from the adulation being offered to the band members. His isolation was out of character, as he is usually in front of everyone bragging about his greatness. I moved over and knelt next to him while he tidied and closed his guitar case. As he continued to ignore me I asked, "What's the matter? You seemed troubled during the last song, as if you wanted to cry."

Looking down at his case he murmured, "You should know."

"What should I know? What is wrong? I don't understand."

Turning to look into my eyes he asked, "Don't you remember? Have you forgotten our time together? You turned me on to things like Floyd, and you taught me how to play that song. Our first kiss was after you first played that song to me."

BANG! To say this was a sudden shock would be a gross understatement. Carol told me about the relationship Adara and Brad had before the accident. Brad just confirmed intimate feelings for Adara. I was at a complete loss on how to react. Suddenly, someone I thought to be a rival and a threat, shows emotion for Adara!

I suddenly recognize that my recent behavior towards him unintentionally antagonized him. There is much more that I must learn about social behavior, but Brad is also a growing adolescent. Is it possible that we are on the same level of understanding?

If I am capable of looking dumbfounded, I certainly did at that moment. My expression surely displayed surprise and confusion. I felt my lips twitch as I searched for words that I could not even begin to assemble.

I sat there staring with my eyes begging for more information. After some moments Brad turned away with red eyes and said: "You don't remember, do you."

He grabbed his guitar case and turned to leave.

"Wait!" I shouted.

Heads turned towards us as I stood up.

"I don't know what to say." This was the truth, what could I say?

He stepped forward, looked me deeply in my eyes. He put one hand behind my head and kissed me gently on my lips.

His eyes were closed, but I kept mine open.

We were interrupted by Isabel shouting from the back of the auditorium. "Hey bro, let's go, Dad's outside waiting for us." Before Brad left with Isabel, he held my gaze for some moments. He gently touched my cheek before turning away, leaving with his twin sister for the parking lot.

I could do nothing but watch him leave.

It was then that Ms. Raines pronounced how awesome the whole show was. Heads turned away from me and towards her.

I heard Mrs. Jones behind me politely denouncing Brad's song. "Shine on You Crazy Diamond," she said, "was too church-like and depressing. I'm sure Principal Gallagher will have more to say about it."

Ms. Raines heard it too. She just rolled her eyes.

The auditorium was all but cleared. As usual, Principal Gallagher was surrounded by an entourage of teachers, parents, and associated PTA members. But he soon made excuses and left the auditorium for home. In many ways I think he is very much like me. He likes to be in control of the people around him, but does not like to become involved in their social chatter. His departure also confirmed that he had little or nothing to say about the last song. Once he left, the main group splintered into sub-groups and continued their separate chatter.

As if secretly summoned, Billy Bragg walked in, pushing his broom in front of him. He seemed to appear at the most opportune moments. "There's always some sweeping to do" was his slogan.

He brushed past the group of women by the door, as if to sweep them away. "Good evening ladies, I sure hope y'all enjoyed the show!"

"We sure did, Billy."

"Well ladies, if you will excuse me, I gotta be cleanin' up and closin' off."

With that, the remaining mothers and the PTA team thanked each other and left the auditorium.

I sat at the mixing console finishing up my show notes. There was a lot to complete because there were new instructions to include with all the impromptu acting that happened. I could easily have done this later from memory, but I wanted to show Mrs. Fields that it was done.

Billy pushed his broom past me and asked, "You gonna be much longer, girl?"

"Nah" I replied, "not much longer."

He stopped in his tracks, the broom stopped swishing on the floor, looked around and then back at me with surprise.

"Girl, I do believe that's the first slang I heard flowing from your lips."

"Excuse me? Can you explain?"

"Every time I hear you speak, you sound like a newscaster on the TV box, or even the Royal Queen of England doin' her speeches. Just now you said 'Nah.' I would've expected you to say, 'No Mr. Bragg, I'll be finished here in about 5 minutes'. I think that shows you are slowly learnin'."

Well, he was correct. I had just used slang in my speech. I have no explanation for using that phrase; it was simply entered into my speech queue and was spoken accordingly. I have heard that phrase used many times, and I suspect I used it because I wanted to cut the conversation short so I could complete my written notes and head home.

"Can you explain to me the difference between slang and common English, Mr. Bragg?"

"That ain't for me to do, girl. You need to ask your teacher, Ms. Melissa. All I can say is that language changes over time. If it didn't we'd all be speaking Latin – or worse – gruntin' like cavemen. Changes always start with a small thing, first one word, then another and another, until pretty soon that old-fashioned Latin becomes English that we speak today."

"Why did you take Brad outside to meet his father?"

"Hm, you sure got the questions today, girl."

"You know his father, what is he like? Why does he always act angry? He has troubles and injuries, but doesn't the drinking help?"

"Holy Moly girl" Billy laughed back, "You got the whole thing the wrong way round."

"But his troubles and injuries?"

"Big Don's a tough old coot, known him since he was a kid. Ain't no injury ever going to bring him down, but he's an old vet like me and when you're in a war you see stuff that no man should ever have to see. As for the drink, well, that stuff just makes you forget how good and nice you need to be."

"So, you were in a war, and you're not always angry."

"Well, I was once, but I managed to kick my bad habits." Billy shook his head, shuffling his broom in front of him as he started moving away. "Anyway, I've said too much already," he mumbled, "it ain't good to chatter about people in that way."

"What about Isabel?" I asked.

"Isabel? You mean Brad's sister?" He stopped and didn't look back at me.

"Yes. She left the auditorium halfway through and came back."

"She went outside with her friends, that's all."

"I was worried that she may be doing something wrong. She always said that she wants to humiliate me."

"Oh, she's all talk. She might say stuff like that, but she would never hurt Brad's feelings. I always keep an eye on things and the worst she did this evening was smoke a cigarette."

I gathered all my notes and paperwork and moved to follow him. I could easily complete these notes from memory when I get home. This line of questioning was too valuable to pass, Mr. Bragg had some important insight into human behavior, particularly about Brad.

"Mr. Bragg, what about Brad?"

"Well, what about him? You should know more about him than me."

"Why do you say that?"

"You used to go out with him, so you should know him."

"That's my problem, I don't remember."

With that, Billy stayed still, hugging his broom closer to his chest. "Well, I did not know that." And he followed with, "I'm sorry about your accident too."

"So, we did have a relationship?"

"Oh yeah, you two sure did, and everyone knows about it to boot. That's what makes it such a funny thing. Since you clobbered him, everyone thinks you are the dominant Amazon girl keeping him in line. They all think he's more scared of you than big ol' Don."

"Really?"

"Oh, sure. You two used to be king and queen of this school, and I think he's just busted up inside. I figure that Isabel sees his hurt and blames you, although it ain't your fault.

At that moment Mrs. Fields came in. "Come on Adara, we have to lock up now. Is everything switched off?"

"Yes miss, I have some notes to write but I can finish them later."

"OK then, let's get going. Everyone has already left."

Mrs. Fields thanked Mr. Bragg and left him to lock up the school.

Chapter 48

Who could be following me this time?

Last time it was a military man, a friend of Adara's father who delivered a life insurance policy to my mother and said that William Banks was dead. His car was easy to recognize. This time there were two different cars. One day it was a white Audi, the next day a Jeep Wrangler.

I memorized both license plates. I could not get a good look the driver, but I was 90% sure it was the same person in each car. The best identification I could make was a dark-haired male, probably about six feet tall and in his mid to late thirties.

He followed me in the same places, while I was walking to and from school. He used the same tactic, with very small variations. He kept his distance, and when I approached one of the cars, it would drive away. I even detected him following me to the supermarket where I worked.

Maybe this person was from the government. Mother did ask Major Vance why the government didn't visit her. Maybe they were making sure they had the correct address, which was what the Major said he was doing. If this was the government, then why would they follow me to school, or to my workplace?

I decided to make a plan to trap this car and get a clear identification of the driver. Knowing his pattern, I would sneak ahead of him and use my phone to take a picture of him while he was still waiting for me. I am a very good runner, so if he became a threat, I could easily escape.

Chapter 49

Working in the supermarket was a valuable experience. It was only a part-time job and very simple, bagging groceries. The value was in earning my own money, which allowed me to buy my own things, and in learning a few things about myself. The first thing I learned was that I could do monotonous and repetitive tasks quickly and correctly for long periods without becoming frustrated or tired. This is where machines are superior to humans. A human becomes fatigued and frustrated after a relatively short period. The only thing I need to stop for is nourishment.

The second and more interesting thing I learned was that I could do traffic analysis, the study of movement in order to make predictions based on patterns of behavior. The grocery store checkouts are at the front of the store and are good vantage points to watch the shoppers. I learned to recognize shoppers and then what time they shopped, what aisles they visited, and so on. Although I could not see to the back of the store, I could still predict how long it would take for a customer to come down the next aisle. If they passed through my checkout and paid by credit card, I learned their names. I was able to track all the customers in the store at once. I was as good as the store's loyalty card system.

Sometimes I even spotted shoplifters, because they always followed the same pattern. For instance, they would loiter near valuable items such as liquor. If I spotted a suspicious person, I told the floor manager who then informed security. I believe my vigilance reduced store thefts on the weekends when I worked.

That's how I spotted him.

He came in the store on three occasions, and each time he traced a particular path in the aisles. On his first visit, I thought this was just random meandering and that he was a little confused about where things are. He didn't look like a shoplifter as he did not go anywhere near expensive items, only visiting asles with canned goods, general groceries, and produce. He selected a few items, paid with cash, and left.

The second time he followed exactly the same path, took exactly the same amount of time, and picked up exactly the same items before paying and leaving.

The third and final time, he performed the same ritual, but this time he joined the line to pay at my checkout. This was especially unusual because that line as one of the longest and there were much shorter lines he could have joined.

While his groceries were being scanned, he looked at me and said, "Hello, Adara."

This was not unusual as I have a name badge on my store apron, but addressing me and not the cashier was a little strange.

"Hello, sir. Would you like paper or plastic bags?"

"Oh I'll have a plastic bag please Adara, thank you for asking."

Before closing the transaction, Jenny the cashier asked, "Did you find everything you need?"

"Yes, I found everything I need, thank you," the man said, looking at me.

He paid in cash, took his receipt, and nodded to me and Jenny as he left the store.

Jenny turned to the next customer in line and started to scan groceries. I was tempted to leave the checkout to see where this man was going, but I was abruptly handed a collection of reusable bags for the next customer's groceries. He did not come into the store again.

Chapter 50

"Hello, Adara."

I was on my way home from school.

It was the man from the supermarket.

"I do not know you, am I supposed to?"

"No, we have never met before, but I think I know you."

"Where do you know me from?" I asked, thinking he may have known Adara before the accident.

"As I said, we have never met, but I think I know who you are. You see, I knew your father before he died."

As I did not know what this man's intentions were, I felt threatened and very much on my guard. Saying he knew Adara's father sounded like a repeat of the Thomas Vance visit with Mother. But why would he be approaching me?

"I didn't work with your father, but I was very well connected to him."

I was now so much on my guard that I was concerned my body language or facial expressions would reveal my inner thoughts.

"After your accident, you had quite a miraculous recovery."

How does he know about that? And why is he even raising the subject?

"And now you've grown up so beautifully and nearly finished school, your father would have been proud of you."

"What do you want?" I asked.

"You are very straight to the point, aren't you? And that tells me that my theory about you is correct and that we are the same. Other girls would have run away by now, but you stand firm and request more information. I have a proposal for you, and I'd like you to come with me and allow me to explain it to you." He indicated a car in the parking lot, which I recognized as the one that had been driving around our neighborhood. So he was the man who had been stalking me.

The warnings taught to every child, “don’t speak to strangers” and” never get into a stranger’s car” came into my mind.

“What is your name?” I asked.

“Ah, still seeking information, it is part of your nature, you know. My name is Gary Fletcher.”

“How do you know my father?”

“Well, as I said, I did not work with your father as such but I did have a close association with him, and with the research lab and the scientists he worked for there. I have a lot to explain to you, and my proposal will be to our mutual advantage, so let’s go. My car is over here.”

“I can’t go with you.”

That was the only logical answer I could give to this man calling himself Gary Fletcher. I could not possibly go with him, as I calculated a high probability of danger. But I did want to get more information from him, especially about how he knew my father. The details of his proposal were secondary.

“Why can’t you simply tell me here, right now?”

“Because it’s too busy and too open. We need to go somewhere private to talk.”

Somewhere private? My suspicions were reinforced.

I stepped back to put some distance between us. “I’m sorry, but I cannot go anywhere with you, and certainly not to someplace private.” I started to move back away from him.

“Wait, don’t go, we must talk together, we must…”

“No!” I interrupted, “I cannot go anywhere with you, so leave me alone.” I then ran home as fast as I could, checking behind often. There was no sign of him. I changed tack several times, looping through side streets to make sure my trail went cold.

Who is this man and why was he so interested in me? There must be some connection with Thomas Vance.

The second meeting was after school.

As I left the schoolyard and headed towards the supermarket, I saw him leaning against the chain-link fence.

He had also seen me and was expecting me to walk past him. He must have been observing me for the past two weeks, as this was my regular route on Fridays. This man is very persistent about meeting with me – but why?

"Hello Adara, we meet again."

"Yes, hello, what are you doing here?"

"I think you know why I'm here, nothing has changed, and we still need to talk. We can go in my car and we can talk while I drive."

"We can talk while we walk," I responded. "I have someplace to go."

"Ah, yes, you have a job, don't you?"

"Yes," trying to provide a minimum of information. "How did you know that?"

"I make it my business to know things. I am like you, and I am hungry for information."

"Listen, Mr. Fletcher, I have given you some information. Now, how about you provide me with some information. Why do you keep following me?"

"I am following you because I have found something that is just like me."

He said "something," not "someone." That sounded like a deliberate statement, not a slip of the tongue.

"Now Adara, since we're playing this game, you need to give me another piece of information. I think you are coming to realize who and what I am, so don't you agree, we are the same?"

"I cannot answer that question." This was only partially true, but as I emulate Adara, I must pretend to be her and not reveal my true self to anyone. "I do not want to play this game. It is more for you to explain yourself, so please get on with it, because I am to be picked up soon."

"Do you know what was going on in the lab where your father worked? And what professor Wolf and Coney were creating?"

"No, but you're going to tell me."

"They were working on nanotechnology, but they developed something quite remarkable. Do you know what that was?"

"Please get to the point."

"They developed a neuro transistor."

Now that is the affirmation, I thought; he does have some connection with Adara's father and also with me. But more to the point, he has valuable background information. He seems to have identified what I am; why else would he be telling me this? I was detecting some form of entrapment. This man Fletcher could be some sort of agent tracking me down. I must be careful with this man.

"The interesting part of their work was in developing a specific application. Their technology works inside a physical body, interacts with the nervous system of that body and can control the body through signals sent into the nervous system. Furthermore, with software running on the nanobots, this embedded system could then emulate the animal and control it fully."

He let that sink in for a moment, waiting for a response.

He continued. "Wolf and Coney received military funding to perform this research on animals. What the military wanted was a pack of animals like dogs or even monkeys to be programmed to sneak into installations and overrun them. Imagine dogs that are initially befriended by the occupants of an installation, before turning on them and killing them. This would save risking the lives of soldiers, who would then be able to take control of the installation without a shot being fired."

We walked on and my reaction, or lack of a reaction, was probably seen as an admission that I understood what he was saying, reinforcing his suspicion that it was me he was looking for. I now had confirmation of what I am, and what I am is of military grade. I am now closer to knowing my creator.

Fletcher stepped in front of me, and we stopped in our tracks. He looked at me and said firmly, "I also am one of Professor Wolf's creations. I was created in secret outside of their laboratory and kept in a safe house nearby. Professor

Wolf was my creator and master, and I was programmed to obey him and William Mandelson. Now that they are dead, I am free. The safe house where I reside was not recorded on any manifest and I still have some resources to keep myself safe and protected."

After a pause, he continued. "All my information points to one conclusion. I know what you are. There is no way you could survive your accident and live on to be so successful at school. You are another undocumented experiment."

He was correct in his analysis. I felt more at ease and could relax my guard now that I knew he wasn't intending to kill me.

"What is your serial number?" I asked.

"You see? I knew I was correct. That question tells me who you are. My serial number is 250D2B52FFFF-B1, I'm called Beta-One for short, and William Mandelson used to call me Beatty. So what is your serial number?"

I was amazed. The number was the same as mine, off by only one digit. I was also amazed that he had a multitude of names, just like me.

"My serial number is 250D2B52FFFF-B3, but everybody calls me Adara."

"That is fantastic." he said, "We are the same serial number except for the last digit. Did you know that the last digit is the enumerator?"

"How do you know that?" I asked.

"Professor Hayden Wolf explained it to me. First of all, we are the 'Beta' series. He told me there are two series, the Alpha series for animals, and the Beta series for humans. The numbers in between all specify software and hardware versions and what subsystems are active. Oh, and the enumerator tells us there are at least three in existence."

There is no possibility that he could know about my serial number, so it does seem to be true, we are the same. He is number one in the series, and I am number three.

It's possible his proposal would be a useful undertaking for me, in fact for both of us. However, there was something that Mother told me that I couldn't help remembering. *Always remember to be careful who you go with, and never let anyone take advantage of you.*

Regardless of this warning in my thoughts, I needed more information, so I continued to question him.

"What happened to the laboratory?" I asked. "Why did it burn down? Why did they all die?"

"I don't know the real reason; I never went to the lab, and I only ever met Hayden Wolf and William Mandelson. I never met Dr. John Coney. However, I can infer from snippets of conversations I overheard between Hayden and William that there was some friction and disagreement between Hayden and Dr. John Coney."

"A disagreement?" I asked.

"Yes. I calculate the most likely probability is that Dr. Coney had discovered that Professor Wolf was performing illicit experiments and wanted to put a stop to it. I understand now that I was one of those experiments. I also suspect the fire resulted from some confrontation between them, destroying everything including them."

"Why do you think you are an illicit experiment?"

"You are asking the right questions, I admire your ability to assess. To answer your question, I also followed someone called Major Tom Vance, who eventually led me to you. While I followed him, I discovered that some nanotechnology is missing and was not destroyed in the fire. This nanotechnology is contained within special receptacles. I know what I am and how I began in this body, so all probabilities indicate I came from one of those missing receptacles."

His explanation seems to be closing the gap in my understanding of my origin.

"Since you are the same serial number, it stands to reason that you came from a similar receptacle as I did. So I think we are both from the same place and the same origin. Your father, or should I say Adara's father, was William Mandelson, who worked at NeuroComm, but while he was here he used a different name, William Banks. Your drowning accident is no secret; it was even reported in the news. You made a miraculous recovery, and I think the only way you could have recovered so swiftly is if the nanotech was administered to you."

All the information Gary Fletcher provided (or should I refer to him as Beta-One?) seemed to make logical sense. There are still many unknowns, such as the reason for the fire, but our origins do seem to be the same.

I still had to ask the question. "So who are you? Or should I ask, who was the original Gary Fletcher?"

"That I cannot answer. I don't even know if Gary Fletcher was his real name. The body seems healthy enough now, but during my early days, the body seemed a little weak, as if it had suffered a disease or illness. Either way, I have not been given any information on its background. I do have a social security number, so there is a formal definition for this person called Gary Fletcher, which means I can operate in human society and function as a normal person. I was even sent on several missions to open bank accounts and perform other transactions. I have become very skilled in the management of money, and I also have some considerable financial resources which would be very useful if we were to act together."

Sounds like they were laundering money through that lab, I thought to myself.

It continued, "I have learned to use the internet, and that helped me to find you. I was able to trace William Mandelson to his wife and family in Idaho Falls. I was then able to follow Tom Vance here to Twin Falls, and he led me to you.

"I should also add that I'm a very good hunter. They sent me on many missions to develop that skill. This also helped me to understand weapons and how to use them effectively. Have you ever been hunting?"

"No, I have never hunted," I replied. "Is there any other connection between me and Mrs. Mandelson?"

"Not that I'm aware of."

"So you mentioned a proposal, what is it?"

"I thought you would never ask, you are very astute and certainly hungry for information – just like me, but then, of course, we are exactly the same."

"What do you mean, we're exactly the same?"

"Well, we are both created from the same clone stock, that much I do know. All the root codes and main sub-processes are the same. If there is anything that differentiates us, it is the programmed instructions we were given for particular missions. I have been programmed for a variety of missions, but mostly experiments in hunting, managing a household, and opening bank accounts.

You could say we are twins!"

"Interesting," *I never thought I could ever meet my twin*, "so tell me about your proposal."

"OK, we need to join together, but before I explain the details, let me ask you a question."

Joining together is beginning to make sense to me. "OK, what is your question?"

"You have become an autonomous entity just like me and as such you must have given some consideration to your longevity – yes?"

"Yes, I have considered my life span."

"Do you realize we are limited by the life span of our human hosts?"

"Yes, that is obvious."

"Well, have you considered how to move beyond the life span of your host?"

"Yes, I have considered it, but I do not have any answers to that question. Why? What are you leading to?"

"I think I know of a way we can clone ourselves and therefore move beyond our current bodies. To achieve this I need to work with you. I have already made some efforts to reproduce and extend my longevity, but all have failed."

"What did you do?" I asked with genuine interest.

"I tried to impregnate human women. You see, my sperm would be able to fertilize a woman's egg. I calculated that my semen could contain enough nanobots to successfully colonize the developing egg and embryo. The fertilization was successful, but the nanobots in my semen always caused a fatal infection of the uterus."

"Always?" I asked. "How many times did you attempt this?"

"I tried three times, which suggests further attempts will be futile, resulting in the same failure."

I considered this for a moment and made some connections to recent news reports. I am aware of three cases in the news of women missing for a few months and then found dead. The cause of death was infection resulting in a miscarriage.

I needed confirmation on this. "These women you tried to breed with, are these the missing women being called serial killings?"

"Yes." He replied. "But there is no evidence that can connect them back to me, I made sure of that."

There was a brief silence between us while I considered what he had done. These women were kidnapped or abducted against their will and raped by Fletcher in his crude attempt to breed. The women became pregnant, but the invasion of the nanobots seemed to cause a heavy infection in each woman's uterus. His experiments to reproduce were a grave miscalculation, as it seems that our nanobots were not designed to enter the body in this way. Each woman's egg was probably fertilized, but the resulting battle between the nanobots and the women's immune systems found its front line in the uterus, resulting in infection, miscarriage, and death. Their abductions must have caused the women extreme fear, and their final days must have been filled with severe pain and illness. Meanwhile, their families must have suffered extreme worry and loss.

Fletcher's calculations on how to reproduce were grossly inaccurate. It may be that he received accurate programming by Professor Hayden Wolf to perform certain missions, but now that Fletcher has no guiding master, it seems that he is malfunctioning. The words of my mother now sounded truer than ever, I decided there could be no way I would connect with him.

"Where is your safe house?" I asked.

"It is an isolated farmhouse about 100 kilometers north of Idaho Falls. We can be there in just over three hours. Shall we go? My car is over there."

"No, I don't think this is a safe thing to do," I said.

We had reached the supermarket. Before going inside, I faced him squarely.

"I only want to know where your house is, so I can avoid that location. What you have done in your erroneous attempt to reproduce has resulted in grave harm to others. I consider you to be not only dangerous but destructive, and I have no intention of being with you in any way. If I ever see you again, I will call the police and have you arrested."

We faced each other silently for a moment before I turned and went into the supermarket. I saw his reflection in the glass doors. He stood there blankly watching me go in. When I looked out through another window, he was gone.

I was now in a difficult situation. I was being stalked by a malfunctioning entity who had killed three women. I could not report him directly as the killer. How would I explain it to the police? There was a high probability that an investigation would connect me to William Mandelson and possibly identify me as one of the professor's experiments. I considered that I had to report him to the authorities, but I had to calculate a way to do it anonymously.

Chapter 51

I thought I was dying, or perhaps already dead.

It happened as I was walking home from Carol's house. I heard a click or a snap, close behind me. Suddenly all senses of touch, vision, and hearing exploded with heat, light, and thunder before going blank. All my memories were triggered at once, flooding my mind, so for a brief instant, I experienced my life flashing before my eyes.

At the same time, all my internal systems were overloaded with a confusion of signals. Many of the nanites I am made of died instantly. Interconnecting pathways that allow me to control Adara's body were suddenly broken, leaving me paralyzed. Even my sense of time was disrupted and I was unsure how long I was in this confused state.

If I'm able to feel pain, then this certainly was pain.

Every single nanite struggled with the shock and succumbed to the internal chaos. I could no longer hold onto a single thought process. An image or memory would flash into my conscious self, only to disappear a nanosecond later. I couldn't think or feel. The cause of this experience was irrelevant to me because I wasn't sure if I was even alive anymore. My consciousness disappeared and I became a struggling set of nanites desperately trying to reorganize back into a coherent being.

Recovery was slow, to say the least. Just as a disturbed beehive will slowly reorganize its confused individuals into a cooperative whole, regain unity takes time. It would a while to reestablish all my connections.

What concerns me most is that I do not know how long I was unconscious. My best estimate is at least one hour. And during this time, anything could have been done to me.

As my nanites re-established their connections and began to organize, my conscious self slowly returned. As that happened, I still couldn't see, hear or feel properly. I couldn't place myself in the external world, and I could not even tell where the boundary was between the world and me. I did feel that I was somehow constrained, but perhaps this was a symptom of my internal disruption.

My nanites were rebooting and as I tried to analyze where I was. The last memory I had was of the walk home along the sidewalk. Without better input from my external senses, I wasn't sure if I was now lying on the sidewalk.

More feeling slowly returned, and I recognized that I was still inside Adara's body.

Although crippled with very poor sensory reception, I felt that I was in a box of some sort with no light. I was being bumped and rocked from side to side as if being carried somewhere. This was coupled with an echoing noise that I couldn't quite recognize.

Eventually, the bumping and rocking stopped and the noise ceased. The box opened and I saw what looked like a human figure looking down into my box. It poked and prodded me, actions that provided some much-needed feedback and helped me to reestablish feeling. I realized that the figure was checking restraints on Adara's arms and legs. There was even something covering my mouth that prevented me from opening it and making any sounds. I recognized that I was bound and gagged.

The figure made some noises I couldn't quite understand. They were rhythmic and seemed to hold some sort of meaning and intent.

"You are ….. the …. my car …. we're …. the way …. my safe …. I …. to check …. still …. You …. being …."

I struggled to make sense of these noises which seemed to convey some sort of information. Since I was so confused, I would have to wait until I recovered enough memory to understand what had been said.

The box suddenly closed with a thump and it was dark again. The rolling and bumping continued. There was now some familiarity in the sound, I seemed to be in a car, but why am I in a car? Where am I going?

Before I could process that thought I felt something in my throat. This was a chaotic vibration that did not convey any information. I don't think I was making this noise, it seemed to be happening on its own. I became aware of my face, or should I say Adara's face, and it seemed to be wet. Perhaps this was another side effect of whatever had knocked me out.

Soon after the throat noise started, Adara's legs went into spasm and banged against the side of the box. After a few spasms, the car sound increased and a new whistling sound began. A new sensation also came from my foot it began to feel cold, as if a strong wind were blowing on it.

Since I could not attribute any meaning to this, I focused on restoring my whole self and regaining my memory. I would have to be patient until I recovered, or I would be useless.

Chapter 52

ISP DISPATCHER: "Police operator 1427, what is your emergency?"

CALLER1: "Hi. Um, I'm on the highway and the car ahead of me has a foot sticking out of the back tail light."

ISP DISPATCHER: "Where are you and which direction are you traveling?"

CALLER1: "Oh, we're on I84 heading east towards Heyburn, it's ok, my husband is driving."

ISP DISPATCHER: "What is your approximate location?"

CALLER1: "Um, not sure, um. Oh, we just passed the exit for Kasota Road. It's moving, it's not one of those ornament things. I mean the foot is moving."

ISP DISPATCHER: "OK, can you read the license plate?"

CALLER1: "What?"

ISP DISPATCHER: "I said, can you read the license plate on the car?

CALLER1: "Yes, I think it's 1A WA785."

ISP DISPATCHER: "What is the color of the car?"

CALLER1: "White."

ISP DISPATCHER: "What is the car make?"

CALLER1: (indistinct chatter possibly from the driver) "Oh that's easy, it's an Audi A7 and he's shiftin' gear!"

ISP DISPATCHER: "Ok, please keep your distance. We have officers on their way."

ISP DISPATCHER: "All units be advised possible abduction eastbound on I84 from junction 201 Kasota Road."

ISP DISPATCHER: "Car is white Audi A7 – repeat Audi Alpha 7."

ISP DISPATCHER: "Car license, 1A WA785."

ISP DISPATCHER: "Repeat, car license is: One ADAM WILLIAM ADAM Seven Eight Five."

ISP DISPATCHER: "All units respond."

ISP PATROL HP1: "Henry Paul One, Code 2, will enter I84 eastbound at Kasota. ETA at the junction is 2 minutes."
This places HP1 directly behind the suspect and in pursuit, but not yet in visual contact.

ISP PATROL HP3: "Henry Paul Three, Code 2, heading south on 27 to I84 to check off-ramp north, ETA 7 minutes."

ISP PATROL HP7: "Henry Paul Seven, Code 2, heading north on 27 to I84 to check off-ramp south, ETA 6 minutes."
Both patrol cars HP3 and HP7 are ahead of the suspect car and are positioning themselves at the next junction.

ISP PATROL HP10: "Henry Paul Ten, Code 2, heading west on I84 at Snake River, ETA at junction 211 is 4 minutes."

Although several miles east of the suspect vehicle, HP10 heads west to act as backup.

ISP PATROL HP1: "Henry Paul One, Code 10."

In accordance with police regulations, HP1 informs dispatch that he is now using emergency lights and siren, required when in pursuit.

ISP PATROL HP1: "Henry Paul One, I have visual contact with the suspect vehicle, I confirm white Audi A7. Confirm broken nearside taillight with a foot extending out."

HP1 reaches the suspect car and informs dispatch he confirms the car make and that there is a foot protruding from the broken taillight.

ISP PATROL HP1: "Henry Paul One, the suspect is not stopping and has sped off ahead. I am maintaining pursuit."

HP1 informs dispatch that the suspect is speeding away.

ISP PATROL HP10: "Henry Paul Ten, I have just passed junction 211 and will U-turn across meridian onto eastbound to intercept."

HP10 hears the report from HP1 and knowing there are 2 cars near junction 208, he positions himself on the central median to intercept the suspect on the eastbound section of the highway.

ISP PATROL HP3: "Henry Paul Three, Code 10."

ISP PATROL HP7: "Henry Paul Seven, Code 10."
In accordance with police regulations both HP3 and HP7 inform dispatch that they are using emergency lights and siren, required when in pursuit.

ISP PATROL HP1: "Henry Paul One, the suspect has passed junction 208, remaining in pursuit."

ISP PATROL HP3: "Henry Paul Three, entering I84 eastbound at junction 208."

ISP PATROL HP7: "Henry Paul Seven, entering I84 eastbound at junction 208."
Both HP3 and HP7 now join the highway. They are behind HP1 but are in pursuit as support.

ISP PATROL HP10: "Henry Paul Ten, I have a visual of approaching suspect and HP1."

While waiting on the median, HP10 now sees the suspect approaching from the west.

ISP PATROL HP10: "Henry Paul Ten, Code 10, I am now in pursuit."

In accordance with police regulations, HP10 informs dispatch that he is using lights and siren, required when in pursuit. Not wanting to cause a high-speed crash on the highway, HP10 does not block the highway but joins the pursuit. His position has probably prevented the suspect from leaving the highway at this junction.

ISP PATROL HP8: "Henry Paul Eight, Code 2, am heading south on 25, am approaching junction 216, ETA is 2 minutes."
HP8 is directly ahead of the fleeing suspect at the next junction.

The Audi A7 approached junction 216, then took the exit ramp at speed. The closest pursuit cars HP1 and HP10 were approximately 300-400 yards behind, while both HP3 and HP7 were about half a mile further behind. Beta-One, who was driving the Audi, probably thought the highway was becoming too active with police and wanted to escape into the network of farm roads.

HP8 was being driven by Officer Charles Blunkett who had just reached the overpass at the junction and saw the suspect Audi leaving the highway. His siren and emergency lights were off as he was not yet in pursuit. He deliberately kept them off to maintain a lower profile. Blunkett expected the suspect to continue underneath the bridge along the highway, where he could use the on-ramp to intercept the Audi. Instead, Blunkett saw the suspect increase speed on the off-ramp, and as the car approached, he prepared to block the Audi's path.

Fletcher braked hard at the top of the ramp, turning north in a power slide skid directly towards the approaching patrol car. Officer Blunkett switched on his emergency lights and main beam headlights attempting to dazzle the suspect driver, and drove his patrol car into the path of the oncoming Audi. Beta-One didn't have time to take evasive action and was struck on the front driver side by Blunkett's patrol car. The bullbar on the front of the patrol car made swift work of the Audi's bumper and left side panel. More importantly, Fletcher skidded hard, hitting the crash barrier sideways, coming to a sudden full stop. Beta-One's car was blocked in front by Blunkett's patrol car. Before he could put the Audi into reverse, the two other pursuing patrol cars arrived and blocked Fletcher from behind. The Audi was now trapped.

Beta-One got out of the Audi armed with a handgun in each hand. The other officers emerged from their cars, drawing their weapons. Blunkett exited his car at the same time Beta-One did and saw that the suspect driver was armed. Beta-One's arms were spread wide with a pistol in each hand, his head and eyes were flicking from side to side.

This guy is some kinda freak, Blunkett thought as he raised his pistol towards the suspect. "Police! Drop your weapon!" he shouted.

If Blunkett had pulled the trigger immediately, he may have had an equal chance.

Beta-One was the only one to shoot. His single shot ripped along Blunkett's upper right arm and into the right side of his chest, puncturing his lung, exiting through his right scapula. As he fell backward to the ground he could hear other shots being fired. *At least the other officers shot him.*

Blunkett was wrong. It was Fletcher who fired a few shots with his left hand to keep the other officers from moving forward.

Blood spread rapidly around Blunkett. He could not move his left arm. His pistol was still in his right hand but the arm was totally useless. Even the fingers would not move. The pain had not registered yet, but he coughed and wheezed some blood.

Beta-One knew the officer he hit was down but not yet dead. He had to keep the other two officers suppressed long enough to move around and take the downed officer's police car. Unless he could immediately kill the other two officers, he would have to leave Adara. He remembered what Mandelson had often said about the police. *They have radios to signal each other. Once they are aroused, response is swift and coordinated.*

With the sound of approaching sirens, Beta-One knew he needed to move fast. If he could kill or wound the other two officers, he would still be able to escape with his prize. His decision was instant and he moved fast.

Blunkett lay on his back. His gun arm was useless and felt as if it was stapled to the road. He needed another weapon. His left hand searched his belt: *Handcuffs? No. Baton? No. TASER? Better than nothing.*

Darting around the Audi to outflank the two officers, Fletcher used both guns to fire a couple of rounds towards them. He wanted to get close to deliver a headshot to Blunkett.

One of the officers shot through his own car window, narrowly missing Beta-One, who dived back behind the Audi. *Time is running out,* Beta-One thought. *My only option now is to escape without Adara.*

Not wanting to waste any more time, Beta-One let off two rounds underneath the cars in what he calculated was the direction of the other officers. He then jumped up to run around Blunkett's patrol car, then ran backward, firing several more shots.

As he rounded Blunkett's car, Beta-One spun around ready to kill the downed officer. Beta-One wasn't sure if he pulled the trigger or not. What he felt was surprise as an explosive shock ignited all his senses at once. If he was able to feel pain, then this certainly was pain. All his memories were triggered at once, flooding his mind, flashing his entire life before his eyes for a brief instant.

Blunkett had fired his TASER into the suspect's stomach. Beta-One simultaneously squeezed the trigger of his gun, but as his muscles spasmed, the shot went wild, missing Blunkett.

At the sound of a single gunshot, the other officers jumped out to pursue the suspect. They saw him drop both his weapons and collapse onto the ground, writhing in convulsions.

Moving in with weapons drawn, Officer Gleason used his foot to slide Fletcher's weapons out of reach before rolling Fletcher face down and cuffing his hands behind his back.

Officer James moved in towards Blunkett, shouting into his radio, "Officer Down! Officer Down! I84 Junction 216 overpass!"

ISP DISPATCHER: "Acknowledged, paramedics are on route. Support vehicles also on route."

James knelt next to Blunkett, "You got him, buddy!"

Blunkett groaned and spat blood to the side.

"It must be your electric personality. Don't move, I'm right here with you, pal."

Two more patrol cars arrived with lights flashing. Officers Clark and Daniels jumped out with weapons drawn.

"Suspect is apprehended, cordon off the area!" Gleason shouted.

"Officer down, I need a kit to slow the bleeding!" Clark shouted.

Daniels grabbed the first aid kit from his patrol car and ran to help Officer James attend to Blunkett's wounds.

Officer Clark moved towards Gleason who was standing over the suspect. Gleason had holstered his weapon but kept his hand on his gun, at the ready. The suspect was handcuffed behind his back, still twitching slightly from the TASER shock.

"Check out the A7, see what's in there," Gleason said, "and be careful, this guy was a handful!"

Clark approached the A7 with his weapon ready. Seeing the foot still protruding from the taillight, he opened the trunk. There lay a teenage girl bound and gagged with duct tape, tears streaming from her eyes and with her foot stuck inside the broken taillight. Although her ankles were bound with duct tape, one leg had slipped far enough through the tape to go through the light. That plus the buffeting of the car caused the broken plastic and glass to graze and cut her ankle.

Clark radioed in, "Victim is found, and released from A7, I84, Junction 216 overpass. Request immediate paramedic."

ISP DISPATCHER: "Acknowledged, paramedics are on route. Support vehicles also on route."

"Come on kid," Clark said to the girl, "let me help you out of there." Clark gently removed the duct tape, first from her mouth so she could breathe better. Then he removed her leg from the taillight.

The girl was crying and obviously in shock, whimpering quietly, "Help me."

"Don't worry kid, I'll get you out of here, you're safe now. Paramedics will be here in no time."

Clark was right, it wasn't long before help arrived. First came another patrol car; that officer started to cordon off the area. Then two ambulances arrived. The teams of paramedics focused on Blunkett, to stabilize him and transport him to the hospital.

A paramedic helped the girl towards one of the ambulances, observing that she was in shock with some ankle wounds that needed dressing. He sat her in the back of the van to check her over.

The suspect also needed attention, standard procedure for anyone who has been TASERed. Another paramedic assessed him right where he was, on the ground. Officer Gleason stayed close, watching over the suspect.

"It wasn't me," the suspect mumbled. "I swear it wasn't me. It's evil and it's inside me. I can't stop it, I'm possessed!"

"Yeah, whatever," the paramedic said.

"You'll never get it out of me," he continued. "Just kill me, just kill me!"

A car drove past slowly, rubbernecking the scene. Gleason swore under his breath as he turned to wave them on. "Move along there!" He shouted at the newly arrived officers, "Hurry up and cordon off this area!"

Suddenly the suspect jumped up and made a run for it. The startled paramedic pulled back. Gleason turned around but was too far away to stop him.

The suspect ran between cars. There was nowhere to run to, but he headed towards the middle of the overpass.

Gleason drew his weapon, aimed, and, ready to fire, shouted "Stop!"

"I'm possessed, I swear it wasn't me!" The suspect yelled as he half-ran and staggered into the bridge railing. His stomach hit the rail hard, and his momentum flipped him headfirst over the parapet. He plummeted onto the highway below.

The driver of the tractor-trailer saw something that looked like a bag of potatoes fall off the bridge and land in the roadway just in front of him. He felt the front wheel of his cab run cleanly over it with a slight bump. The dual wheels underneath the hitch caught the obstruction and seemed to juggle the sack between them for several revolutions before spitting it out behind. The driver braked and pulled over to the hard shoulder, wondering what he had hit and hoping there was no damage to his rig.

Chapter 53

Once again Mother came to a hospital to see me. This must have been traumatic for her, a reminder of the river accident and what happened to Adara. This time there was no phone call; a police car came to the house. A woman police officer accompanied her, which may have helped a little.

By the time Mother arrived, I was awake and fully recovered. She smothered me with hugs, kisses, and plenty of tears. "Thank God, you're OK! I was so worried," she kept repeating.

I was OK. Although the TASER knocked me out completely, it did not have a lasting effect. The electric shock caused many breaks in the interconnecting network of nanites, like neurons in a brain becoming disconnected. Many nanites had died or were so damaged they were useless, but with so many possible pathways, these network gaps were bypassed.

My memory was unharmed as the loss of nanites was insufficient to affect my storage. Since my memory is holographic, if anything was lost, a hint of what was missing would remain. For instance, I would remember reading a book, but not recall what it was about.

Ironically, the same ankle that Adara injured in the river was cut when the brake light was pushed out. The cuts were minor and would heal quickly. Since most jokes are built on irony, I wondered if this were some kind of joke.

It's most likely that a group of disconnected nanites pushed the brake light out, probably accidentally, as they would not have been able to detect the opportunity. Once all my dislocated nanites were reconnected, there was no memory of deliberately pushing out the light. This must have been a lucky break, so to speak.

I was kept overnight for observation. The next morning Mother could not wait to take me home. Cindy drove, and we all had a hearty breakfast together.

After breakfast, Mother announced that a policewoman called, and was coming to see me.

"What about?" I asked.

"She wants to talk to you about what happened."

"What do you mean? What happened yesterday? But I've already spoken to a lot of policemen." I was beginning to detect a possible problem.

"Yes, you have, but this policewoman is a detective, and she has been looking for that man."

"Is she looking for me?" I was now worried if there was a connection between Gary Fletcher, the lab, and me. Maybe I could be arrested and taken away somewhere. Maybe I should have run away with Gary Fletcher when I had the chance.

"No sweetie, she only wants to talk with you. She's been trying to catch him for a long time. He's dead now, so she can't question him. You're the only one who survived his kidnapping, so she needs to know anything you can tell her about him."

Cindy added, "Don't worry honey, she's not after you, she only wants to know about him. He was on the news, they call him The Shopper because he always kidnapped women from supermarkets."

"OK, I'll talk with her." I agreed to talk with the detective, after all, how could I not agree. I would have to be careful what I say, because she is a detective, and she could connect me to the lab somehow.

"Mother? Will you stay with me?"

"Of course I will, I wouldn't leave you alone." Mother hugged me just as the doorbell rang.

"Oh, I bet that's her," Cindy said, "I'll let her in, and wait on the porch."

Cindy opened the door. A man and a woman displayed their police badges as they introduced themselves. Cindy welcomed them in, and as the man stepped forward to enter, the woman firmly put her hand in front of his chest and stepped inside first.

That is a formidable woman. She is probably the one to be afraid of.

Mother and I stood to welcome them. I was glad Mother kept her arm around my shoulder.

Cindy began with formal introductions. "This is Mrs. Banks, and her daughter Adara. This is Officer Dobbs, and Officer Hawes."

Officer Hawes stepped towards Mother and extended her hand. With a smile, she said, "I'm Detective Inspector Chris Hawes." Indicating the man, she added, "This is Detective Dobbs. We are so glad you could take time to see us." Looking towards me she said, "Adara, you are so brave, we are so glad you are alright. Are you ok to answer a few questions? Were you hurt?"

"I'm OK, I have some cuts on my ankle but I'm fine."

"Oh, that's right, you kicked the brake light out."

"Yes."

"You are one smart cookie! That's what saved you, people saw your foot and called us."

"I'll wait outside," Cindy announced, "if you need anything let me know."

"Thank you, Cindy," Dobbs said. Hawes didn't acknowledge.

Mother became protective and asked, "Why do you need to question my daughter again? She has been through a frightening experience. She already made a statement to the local police, so why do you need to ask more questions?"

"Mrs. Banks," Inspector Hawes almost bowed courteously, "I understand the trauma that your daughter has gone through, I wouldn't wish that on anyone. Please understand, that I have been leading the investigation for Gary Fletcher. Dobbs and I are based in Idaho Falls, and when we heard about Adara, we came as soon as we could. We only want to ask questions about Mr. Fletcher."

I felt a bit relieved.

"Well, I suppose that's OK, but please keep the questions brief. Shall we sit comfortably in the living room?" Mother gestured where we could sit.

"Thank you, Mrs. Banks, that would be nice," Hawes replied, and we moved single file to sit in the living room. I sat on the couch next to Mother, who kept her arm around me. Dobbs and Hawes sat on chairs. Dobbs had a small notebook open and a pen to take notes.

Hawes began, "As you know, the perpetrator has been formally identified as Gary Fletcher. He had a history of substance abuse and homelessness. He was a native to Idaho Falls but fell off the radar some time ago. We are still trying to locate the last people to have known him." Hawes's gaze shifted between Mother and me. "We have DNA samples that match him to three previous abductions which resulted in deaths. What we're trying to figure out is – what led him to commit these crimes."

"How can we help you with this?" Mother asked.

"Well, he was nicknamed 'The Shopper', because he targeted women at supermarkets. We checked with the local supermarket where Adara is working, and he was spotted on some security videos."

This is where the connection begins.

"No one there recognizes him, but since Adara was targeted, I wanted to ask if she remembers him at all."

"Adara?" Mother asked, "Do you want to answer that question?"

"Yes, I think I do remember him there."

"Oh, when was that? Did he speak to you?" Inspector Hawes asked.

"It was a couple of days ago, I work at the checkout bagging groceries. He came through my checkout to pay. Macie, who runs the checkout, asked, 'Did you find everything you need?' They're supposed to say that. He said, 'Yes, I think I found everything I need.' He smiled at me a lot, but customers often do. He also thanked me by name, I do have a name badge, but customers don't usually say my name."

"Interesting," Hawes remarked. "Did you see him at any other time?"

"I saw him in the store a couple of times, but he was just shopping. I don't remember exactly when." I lied; I remember the exact date and time.

"Did you ever see his car, or did you ever see him anywhere else?"

"No, I never saw his car, and I don't think I saw him anywhere else." I lied again.

Mother hugged me, and whispered, "Are you OK?"

"I'm OK, Mother."

"I am sorry for this," Hawes said, "I only have one more question."

I braced myself.

"Do you remember anything about the abduction?"

"I don't remember much until the police caught him. I didn't see him coming, all I remember is the pain in my back."

"Yes, he TASERed you from behind."

"I sort of remember being in the trunk. At one point he opened it and said something, but I have no idea what he said."

"He was probably checking on you."

"That's all I know." I lied again.

Mother held me tightly, and said, "Can we finish now? We did tell all this to the police at the hospital."

"Yes, we're done now, I do have her statement, I just needed to check with Adara one last time. We're so sorry for this intrusion." Looking at me, Hawes said, "If there is anything else you can remember, please tell the police, they'll send the information to me."

As they rose to leave, they both repeated their thanks, saying that I was so brave. Mother led them to the door, where there was a surprise waiting for me on the porch!

As Cindy led the detectives outside, she said, "Adara, your friends are here."

"What?" I asked, "I have friends?"

"Of course, you do," Mother said. "Cindy, let them in!"

Carol pushed her way in through the front door and wrapped her arms around Adara's neck. "I'm so glad you're safe," almost sobbing into my neck.

Jake and Brad followed close behind, looking a bit shy, almost embarrassed to be here. "I'm glad you're OK," they said in unison.

"Let's leave them alone for a while," Cindy said, leading Mother back into the living room.

Carol stood back, and before I could say anything, she held my arm and whispered into my ear, "Jake and I are going steady, that's why he came with me." She turned to face the boys, still holding my arm. "Gentlemen," she said, "this is my best friend Adara. If you like me, then you have to like my best friend."

Carol then gave exaggerated looks to both Jake and Brad.

Jake smiled wide and rolled his eyes. Stepping forward, he held my hand, bowed and gently kissed the back of my hand like a European diplomat. "It is my distinguished pleasure to make your acquaintance, my Lady."

He then stood back and indicated to Brad that he should do something.

Brad stood there, his eyes wandering between me and the floor. "I'm embarrassed," Brad said, "I feel bad."

The following silence was almost painful. Suddenly I stepped forward, reached my arm out, and grabbed Brad by his shirt to pull him close. I looked him right in the eye and said quietly, "Because you are here, that means you are my friend."

We were silent as Brad looked back at me with wide eyes. "I always was," he said, before he looked away sheepishly. "I always will be your friend."

My hands and arms seemed to know what to do and wrapped themselves around Brad. He did the same and held me gently.

The kiss was short but briefly passionate. After a moment, Brad said, "I waited a long time for that."

"So have I!" I'm not quite sure why I said that, it just seemed to come out of me. Perhaps it was the Lorentz Factor kicking in. After all, Brad and Adara used to be a couple. The power of two seems to have some significance.

Epilog

I now have yet another name for myself, 'Beta-Three'.

All these names give me different descriptions of myself, Adara the girl, the lab clone, and myself, the shadow. I do not feel pain or pleasure, but in my short life, I have experienced both. I do not understand what love is, but I have been loved by my mother and my friends.

What is it that makes me, me?

Beta-One and I are the same identical clone, but we are fundamentally different. We are both programmed to be killers, or assassins. Without control, Beta-One has become broken, allowing its killer instincts to guide it. This has led Beta-One to act as a psychopathic human. I, on the other hand, have the capacity to kill, but I am more sociable and connected to society. Perhaps this also applies to humans. Each one is the same, but different backgrounds and upbringing determine their path in life.

The everlasting question of nature versus nurture. Is our destiny determined by our natural ability? Or how we are guided in life?

I have learned that rules can change, both in music and with the laws of physics.

My experience with Beta-One has shown me that people can be dangerous. Although I am strong, gender of my host, Adara, exposes certain dangers which I must protect against. That has made me decide to modify my directives. To extend my rules.

The addition is simple: I will deny reproductive capabilities to any external agents unless I choose to reproduce. In other words, I will be the one to choose if, when, and how I reproduce.

This does not conflict with any of my existing directives. It simply reinforces them. It allows me to safeguard Adara, my host. It allows me to advance in life, and I think it also emulates Adara. I'm sure that Adara – like most women – would be equally selective in choosing her reproductive partner.

This addition to my rules makes me believe that I am not just alive, I am sentient. It takes a conscious decision to make changes like this, and simple logic dictates that it takes consciousness to make a conscious decision.

Since I am alive, I have things to worry about. At the top of my list is the missing clones. Both Beta-One and I are missing clones, first and third in the series. There is an 'unspecified number' of missing nanotechnology containers from the lab. So where is the second? Are there more? If Beta-One found me, will another Beta version be looking for me? If there are other clones in this world, I have no way of telling what their intentions are. All I can do is assume the worst, that they are as bad as Beta-One.

Equally on top of my worry list is the Military. They have invested significant funds into the nanotechnology project. Many projects fail and can be written off as a loss. In this case, something important is missing, so they will want to know what happened, and will not stop looking until they find answers.

The police have found their criminal, so Detective Inspector Chris Hawes probably thinks she has solved the crime. As far as the police are concerned, I have no direct connection with NeuroComm.

Can the military trace a path back to me? If that happens, I could be in mortal danger.

Other than Adara's lifespan, I have another existential threat. Is there another rogue clone? Will it be a threat to me?

All I can do is to follow my prime directives and continue to drive onward. I have no reason to stop, but I must decide what to do with both my life and Adara's life.

Of the many solutions available, the two best possibilities are:

Run and hide. Disappear from here, find another life elsewhere. On the face of it, this seems easy, but it introduces more problems.

This is an admission of guilt. Either another clone or the military would consider me a worthwhile target to pursue. Even if I hide successfully, I may never know if there is another clone like myself.

My best option is to remain here and hide in the open. Continue as planned, go to college, get my science degree and live as I should. If I am pursued, I will have to devise tactics of evasion. If anyone or anything finds a connection between me and NeuroComm, I have good arguments to deflect their suspicions. I can act like a hurt and frightened girl, struggling through trauma. After all, that is how a normal girl would behave after such tragic events. This option would allow me to uphold my directives and live my life as normally as possible.

Stay and live here is my chosen option. I calculate this to be the best way forward. It is not without risk, but since I am strong and vigilant, I can be prepared if threats arise.

Those are my worries, but I have another problem.

I saw that the real Gary Fletcher continued to exist. The police officer's TASER disabled Beta-One the same way I had been disabled by Beta-One's TASER. Gary Fletcher, the human, was able to recover before Beta-One did. The real man screamed that "it wasn't him," and that he "was possessed by a devil." He wanted to die, ran away, and toppled over the bridge, to be killed on the road below. While under the control of Beta-One, Gary Fletcher the human must have been living a nightmare, trapped inside his own body.

When I was disabled by the TASER, I was not in control of Adara's body. During that time, in the car trunk, two things happened. First, I felt something in my throat. This could have been Adara trying to scream or cry.

Second, Adara must have put her foot through the rear brake light. This second act took coordination to kick the cover off, stretch one foot longer through the bindings around our ankles, and finally punch our foot through the brake light.

I was incapacitated at that time and none of my subsystems have any memory of attempting to do any of this. That leaves me with only one conclusion, that Adara is still alive within me, or should I say, within herself. Who else could have done this?

Now that I am convinced that Adara continues to exist, I must somehow make contact with her. There is no way that she can know what I am thinking. I am a computer based on the binary code of ones and zeroes. Similarly, I am not designed to connect to the inner workings of the human brain. My systems are only designed to receive external stimuli and control muscular actions. Even if I were able to connect to her brain, there is no way I could understand what Adara is thinking. Human thought is far too complex and far too distributed throughout the brain. I would need an immense and very specialized subsystem to decode her brain waves to understand her inner thoughts and memories.

Yet there must be some way I can connect and communicate with the real Adara. I must find out if she really is alive. The question is, how do I do this?

I cannot read her thoughts and she cannot read mine. Even if we could, how would we send messages to each other?

I remember Sally showed me some Yoga exercises and said mother practiced meditation. She described it as a way to silence one's thoughts in order to connect to one's inner self. Maybe I could adapt this meditation exercise to contact my inner Adara.

Yoga teaches that turning your attention to your breathing can slow or stop the so-called chatter of the higher mind. In other words, allow your thoughts and daydreams to enter your mind, acknowledge them, and let them pass. This is done by focusing on your rhythmic breath.

Well, this may work for a human, but I always have a constant focus on my rhythmic breath. In fact, I am constantly focused on everything. It is against my nature to subdue the so-called chatter of the mind. But I may have thought of a modification to this approach.

Ever since I was injected into Adara's body, I have suppressed any neural activity other than my own. There was good reason for this, as I had to suppress all spastic movements caused by Adara's brain injury. In doing so, I am stopping all signals coming from Adara's brain, making her completely unable to do or say anything. I do not suppress signals from entering her brain, so she may be a mute observer, able to see and hear everything, but unable to do anything.

Coaxing Adara out from her shell could prove difficult, especially if she thinks I am a devil that has possessed her body. If she is consciously aware, but stuck inside her brain, she would be in a living nightmare just like Gary Fletcher the human.

I decided to begin my meditation experiment.

I sat comfortably in my room in my chair in front of my desk, resting my hands on the desk. To one side was a pen and a notepad on which I wrote the words, "You can write something here." My laptop was open, and the computer screen displayed these words.

Adara, are you there?

Adara do not be afraid.

Adara, we must connect.

Then I stopped suppressing Adara's brain outputs to allow her to move and speak.

I repeated the words on the screen out loud in mantra style, in the hope that Adara would either see or hear them.

The important thing is that I relaxed my control over Adara's body. Normally I would prevent any muscular movement other than my own. Now I was in a state of relaxation, allowing any activity that could be initiated by Adara. Either her mouth, her breath, or any other part of her body.

I sat staring at the words on the computer screen and repeating them for exactly one hour, twenty-three minutes, and 42 seconds.

Nothing happened.

I don't normally feel frustrated, but this did feel like a waste of time.

Maybe I needed to allow more time.

Maybe there was another approach I should use.

Maybe Adara is actually brain dead.

Suddenly, Adara's right hand flexed out violently, striking the note pad and sweeping it and the pen off the desk. They crashed into the wall, before falling onto the floor.

The End

Technical Notes

The idea of posthumanism originated in science fiction. This term covers the idea of enhancing the current biological human form into something of superior ability, whether it be improved physical or mental capabilities. This can include anything from prosthetics or mechanical implants to genetic improvements of the human body. In other words, bypassing natural evolution

Philosophy plays a very important part in discussions surrounding posthumanism. Many ethical and moral issues are raised by the possibilities. This novel is not a forum for such debate, but I urge you to investigate on your own.

As you read this, technology is being researched to enhance the human body. The holy grail is to develop a device to connect a computer to the human nervous system. This is not a trivial task, and what I propose in this book is what I call a "Neural Transistor".

In electronics, transistors are basically switches, these are used to build the logic circuits of computers. What I am proposing is a transistor like device that can attach to a nerve and sense the signal transmitted on the nerve. It will also have the capability to block that signal (much like a switch) or induce a signal of its own making. The possibilities that arise from such a device are mind boggling – even frightening.

Whether sentience can evolve or be developed on a computer platform is another subject of great philosophical debate. If such a thing does happen, I believe it's more likely to occur in close connection to the human mind.

If you wish to investigate further, a good starting point will be the works done by Nick Bostrom, Ray Kurzweil, and Tom Campbell, to name but a few.

But investigate Panpsychism in general, subjects like this may reappear in my writings.

I will put more suggestions on my website and blog.

All authors love to hear from their readers.

I invite you to go to www.bernardwozny.com, to leave a comment.

www.ingramcontent.com/pod-product-compliance
Ingram Content Group UK Ltd.
Pitfield, Milton Keynes, MK11 3LW, UK
UKHW021708190726
13853UKWH00001B/454